A TIME TO LOSE

A TIME TO LOSE

REPRESENTING KANSAS IN
BROWN V. BOARD OF EDUCATION

Paul E. Wilson

 University Press of Kansas

Published by the University Press of Kansas (Lawrence, Kansas 66049), which was
organized by the Kansas Board of Regents and is operated and funded by Emporia
State University, Fort Hays State University, Kansas State University, Pittsburg
State University, the University of Kansas, and Wichita State University

Library of Congress Cataloging-in-Publication Data

Wilson, Paul E.
    A time to lose : representing Kansas in Brown v. Board of
  Education / Paul E. Wilson.
      p. cm.
    Includes bibliographical references and index.
    ISBN 0-7006-0709-9 (cloth : alk. paper)
    1. Segregation in education—Law and legislation—United States.
  2. Brown, Oliver, 1918- —Trials, litigation, etc. 3. Topeka
  (Kan.). Board of Education—Trials, litigation, etc. I. Title.
  KF4155.W545 1995
  344.73'0798—dc20
  [347.304798]   94-41098

British Library Cataloguing in Publication Data is available.

Printed in the United States of America

10 9 8 7 6 5 4 3 2 1

For
Harriet and our children,
who believe I was on the wrong side.
May this book mitigate their decades of embarrassment.

To every thing there is a season, and a
    time to every purpose under
    heaven:
A time to be born, and a time to die; a
    time to plant, and a time to pluck
    up that which is planted;
A time to kill, and a time to heal; a
    time to break down, and a time to
    build up;
A time to weep, and a time to laugh; a
    time to mourn, and a time to
    dance;
A time to cast away stones together; a
    time to embrace, and a time to
    refrain from embracing;
A time to get, a time to lose; a time to
    keep, and a time to cast away;
A time to rend, and a time to sew; a
    time to keep silence, and a time to
    speak;
A time to love, and a time to hate; a
    time of war, and a time of peace.

Ecclesiastes 3:1–8

Contents

Illustrations

Preface

Friends and others who are interested have urged me to record my personal recollections of *Brown v. Board of Education of Topeka*. Their encouragement, along with the continuing public interest in the case and my growing awareness of my own mortality, have provided the motivation for this task.

I write with three objectives. First, I want to tell the story of the Kansas case of *Brown v. Board of Education* from the perspective of a Kansas lawyer who was an actual participant. Second, relying on my personal experience, I seek to develop and illustrate the evolution of the attitudes of many white Kansans toward race and interracial relationships in the twentieth century. Third, in the context of *Brown* and from the vantage point of more than fifty years as a member of the bar, I shall express some of my views of the lawyer's role in the judicial resolution of social conflict.

With these objectives in mind, I have attempted to relate and record as faithfully as I can my present understanding of the events of the *Brown* case in their historical and political setting. Other districts and other states were involved in the school segregation cases but my concern has been limited mainly to the case from Kansas that supplied the title by which the Supreme Court's consolidated opinion is usually cited. Although the account is based largely on my own experience and memory, wherever possible I have refreshed and verified my recollection by reference to external sources. I have tried to be candid. To evaluate the quality of my assertions and interpretations may require an understanding of my personal values and where I came from. Hence, I have thought occasional autobiographical digressions to be proper. Since my overriding purpose has been the presentation of a forthright and lucid account of my personal recollection of happenings long past, I have deviated from the accepted standards of traditional scholarship. If I have transgressed, I ask indulgence.

This presentation has been a solo endeavor, but along the way I have been helped by others to whom I am particularly grateful. Although I am no longer a teaching member of the faculty of the University of Kansas School of Law, the dean continues to provide an office for my use; the active faculty and staff tolerate my presence; and I have free access to the school's extensive library. In the early stages of the project I had the assistance of Ms. Genine Normore, then a third-year law student, who was compensated from research funds made available to me by Dean Robert Jerry. I have drawn upon the resources of other components of the University library system, particularly the Kansas Collection in the Spencer Research Library and the microfilm section of the Watson Library. Staff members of the Archives Office of the Center for Historical Research of the Kansas State Historical Society at Topeka and the Dwight D. Eisenhower Library at Abilene have cheerfully assisted me in locating and retrieving relevant materials in their files.

The insights of Mrs. Berdyne Scott whose late husband, John Scott, was one of the Topeka attorneys for the plaintiffs, have helped me to understand the black perspective of Topeka and its schools at mid-twentieth century.

For their help in obtaining photographs for use in the book and for their other valuable suggestions, I am especially indebted to Nancy Sherbert of the Kansas State Historical Society; Cheryl Henderson of the Brown Foundation for Educational Equity, Excellence and Research; Deborah Dandridge of the Kansas Collection, Spencer Research Library, the University of Kansas; Cathy Eason of the library staff of the United States Court of Appeals for the Tenth Circuit; Steve Aase and Frans Jansen of the Office of the Curator, Supreme Court of the United States; Randy Hearrell, Esq., of the Kansas Judicial Council; and Gerald L. Goodell, Esq., son of the late Lester M. Goodell. For the interest and courtesy of each I am grateful.

If, in spite of this assistance, I have erred, the responsibility is mine.

Introduction

This is the story of a lawsuit and of a country lawyer's unsought, unplanned, and unearned brush with history. The story reached its climax at high noon on Monday, May 17, 1954, in the Supreme Court Chamber in Washington, D.C. On that occasion the Court opened its session by announcing its decision in *Brown v. Board of Education of Topeka* et al.[1] As an obscure assistant attorney general of the state of Kansas I had a not very important role in the *Brown* case. I was one of the losers. What follows is in the nature of a memoir. After four decades I am attempting to recall and to record what I observed, what I thought, what I felt, what I did, and what I said during the preparation for and presentation of the argument.

It is common knowledge that *Brown v. Board of Education of Topeka* is the case that ended legally sanctioned racial segregation in the public schools of this country. It may not be equally well known that *Brown* was not one case but four, or perhaps five. Four of the cases, including *Brown*, attacked state segregation laws as denials of equal protection guaranteed by the Fourteenth Amendment. The fifth case originated in the District of Columbia and claimed that public school segregation in the federal district violated the due process clause of the Fifth Amendment. The basic issue in each was the constitutionality of laws sanctioning segregated schools. All were assigned to-gether for argument and decision.

Hence, *Brown v. Board of Education* has both a specific and a ge-neric meaning. Specifically, it is the name of a lawsuit that originated in the United States District Court for the District of Kansas, one in which I participated at the appellate stage. Generically, *Brown* refers to a principle of constitutional law that redefines and establishes new boundaries of constitutional concepts of equal protection and due process of law. Heard by the Supreme Court in sequence in the Octo-ber 1952 and the October 1953 terms were cases from Kansas,[2] South Carolina,[3] Virginia,[4] and Delaware,[5] as well as the District of Colum-bia.[6] Each case had originated in a different court, had been tried and decided on its own facts, and had attacked the law of the jurisdiction in which it arose. The cases were separately docketed in the Supreme Court, and each appeal proceeded to argument on its own record. Because all involved the same basic question—the question of the constitutionality of racial segregation in public education—the state cases were collectively disposed of in a single opinion. Its title was *Brown v. Board of Education of Topeka, Kansas* only because the Topeka case occupied the first position on the Supreme Court's docket. Had one of the other cases reached the Court first, the opinion and the principle for which it stands might have been styled *Briggs v. Elliott* or *Davis v. County School Board of Prince Edward County* or *Gebhart v. Belton*. Since the District of Columbia appeal was focused upon Fifth Amendment due process instead of Fourteenth Amendment equal protection, a separate opinion was filed in that case.

I propose generally to limit my account to the Kansas lawsuit, *Brown v. Board of Education of Topeka, Kansas*, Case No. T–316 in the United States District Court for the District of Kansas and Case No. 8 in the October 1952 term of the Supreme Court of the United States. I believe that this story is worth a separate telling, and I have no knowledge, other than that shown by Court records and other writ-ings, that enables me to discuss competently what may have oc-curred in the cases from the other jurisdictions with which Kansas was aligned before the Supreme Court.

From many standpoints *Brown* may be the most important deci-sion rendered by the Supreme Court during the twentieth century. It repudiated a policy in public education that had been accepted from the beginning of the public school system, and it gave new dimensions to the constitutional concepts of equal protection and due process of law. It enlarged the definition of basic justice in intracommunity relations in a multiracial society, and in so doing it withdrew the law's sanction from values that had become firmly embedded in our culture.

In a system of jurisprudence that assigns a preeminent role to precedent, the significance of a judicial opinion may, in part, be measured by its impact on subsequent decisions. *Brown* has been cited by appellate courts in literally thousands of federal and state cases, and its contribution to legal scholarship has been equally impressive. Dozens of books currently in print examine *Brown* and its implications for American public education and the civil rights of minorities. Since 1952, articles and symposia exploring *Brown* and its progeny have abounded and continue to abound in law reviews and other scholarly publications. Citations to *Brown* in published articles, comments, and notes are aggregated in thousands. The opinion in *Brown*, usually with comments, is included in every constitutional law case book and is considered in every constitutional law treatise currently in use in American law schools. For at least thirty-five years, every law student has had the opportunity to think about and become familiar with the case.

In view of this abundance of judicial and scholarly attention, this plethora of literature, is further writing on *Brown* necessary? Will it add to our understanding of the case and its significance to America? An honest answer to these questions is "I don't know." Why, then, in this late season have I chosen further to burden the literature of *Brown*? Perhaps it is a matter of subliminal vanity. But there are other articulate reasons that I can and do offer by way of justification.

First, *Brown v. Board of Education of Topeka* (the Kansas case) merits a separate examination because it was different from the others with which it was docketed. Only the Kansas case portrays the ambivalence and misgivings of state officials reluctant but required to defend a position supported by history, tradition, and the known standards of the law yet contrary to personal conviction and inconsistent with a people's self-created image of itself. Only in Topeka were school officials unwilling to defend a policy of racial segregation that they and their predecessors had practiced for nearly a century. In his book, *Simple Justice*,[7] Richard Kluger examines each of the five cases in depth. Published in 1975, Kluger's book is based on extensive interviews and the examinations of both published and unpublished documentary sources. It traces the entire story of public school segregation from its remote legal and cultural roots to its repudiation by the Supreme Court, and two full chapters plus other references deal specifically with the Kansas case. I commend Mr. Kluger's account of *Brown*. I write as a Kansan who shared in the Kansas ambivalence, a state official who experienced the intellectual discomfort of reconciling personal conviction with official duty; a lawyer who lived with the case day after day, week after week; an advocate of a cause doomed from the outset. In so doing I hope to add a dimension to accounts of the case not present up to now.

Second, among the jurisdictions before the Supreme Court, Kansas had a unique history with respect to the status and rights of its black citizens. Only Kansas was admitted to the Union under a constitution that prohibited slavery. That constitution was a product of seven years of struggle during which the overriding issues were whether black slavery would be permitted in Kansas and, indeed, whether black persons would be permitted to reside in the state. In that struggle the advocates of freedom won. The extent of their victory has been the subject of more than a century of litigation in which *Brown* was an important milestone.

Third, the Kansas statute under attack in *Brown* permitted but did not require racial segregation in the public elementary schools in twelve cities with 15,000 or more inhabitants, designated by law as "Cities of the First Class." Determinations as to the maintenance of separate schools were made by boards of education in cities covered by the statute. Thus, the law was intended to permit the implementation of local policies most consistent with local customs and attitudes. In each of the other jurisdictions before the Court, segregated schools were mandatory and pervasive.

Fourth, in one respect, *Brown* may have been the most important of the several cases before the Supreme Court. Segregated public schools had been justified by the doctrine of *Plessy v. Ferguson*,[8] decided by the Supreme Court in 1896. According to that opinion, if the public facilities provided to citizens of all races were equal, the mere fact of separation did not offend the Fourteenth Amendment clause that forbids a state to make or enforce any law that would deny to any person within its jurisdiction the equal protection of the laws. The *Plessy* case involved racial separation in public transportation, but in deciding the 1927 case of *Gong Lum v. Rice*[9] the Supreme Court recognized that the separate-but-equal principle applied in public education. Equality, not separation, was the critical issue in the pre-*Brown* equal protection cases. In the Kansas case, the facilities provided in the racially segregated schools were found to be of equal quality. In each of the other states before the Court, the public school facilities were not only separate but unequal. The facilities provided to black students were inferior to those available to members of other races. Thus, *Brown* was the only case that presented directly to the Court the issue of the validity of the separate-but-equal doctrine.

Fifth, one other reason for this effort is a desire to add equilibrium to the literature of *Brown*. Most of the writing about the case has been done by scholars who shared the viewpoint of the plaintiffs and whose writing has seemed to be in the nature of a celebration of the opinion. Little has been heard from those who sat on my side of the table. A current investigator may inquire how a responsible public official could possibly argue for any result other than the one reached in the opinion of the Court. That inquirer is reminded that the events and facts which produced *Brown* occurred more than forty years ago and that the collective conscience of the people and their attitudes toward social problems have undergone a dramatic evolution and growth since that time. Hence, I shall attempt to portray *Brown* in the context of its time, not according to standards and understandings that exist today. The position of the state of Kansas in the *Brown* case was not a frivolous one. It was justified by legal precedent, by history, and by values that were then accepted and approved in our culture. It reflected a view of federal-state relationships that had prevailed throughout the history of constitutional government in the United States. Kansas was entitled to have its position explained and understood, even though history and good conscience may have demonstrated it to be fallacious.

Finally, I relate these things because I may be the only one who is left to tell, firsthand, the story of the losers. None of the others have been heard. During the arguments on the merits, in 1952 and 1953, six lawyers spoke to the Supreme Court on behalf of the four states and the District of Columbia, and urged their legal right, wisely or unwisely, morally or immorally, to separate races for the purpose of public education. Those lawyers represented a wide spectrum of professional ability and accomplishment. At one end of the spectrum was John W. Davis of New York, former congressman, former solicitor general of the United States, former ambassador to the Court of St. James, former president of the American Bar Association, former presidential nominee, and senior partner in one of the great Wall Street law firms. Mr. Davis appeared for the state of South Carolina at the invitation of Jimmy Byrnes, then governor of that state and Mr. Davis's longtime friend. Mr. Davis may have been the greatest constitutional lawyer of this century. His argument in the segregation cases was his 140th before the Supreme Court, a number that in the history of the Court had been exceeded only by Daniel Webster and by Walter Jones, a District of Columbia prosecutor in the very early life of the Court.[10] I stood at the other end of the spectrum. I was a former county attorney of Osage County, Kansas, and an assistant attorney general of the state of Kansas. My professional activity had been limited largely to county and district courts of Kansas. I had never argued before any appellate court. Appearing elsewhere in the spectrum were two state attorneys general, the senior partner in one of Virginia's most distinguished law firms, and an experienced appellate lawyer from the staff of the Corporation Counsel of the District of Columbia. Among the members of this distinguished group, I now enjoy one distinction. I am the only one still living. According to the actuarial tables, I can reasonably expect not more than eight years before my inevitable encounter with the grim reaper. Hence, if the story of the losers is to be told, the time for its telling is at hand, and I, by reason of longevity, am to be the teller.

There may be another reason why I undertake this commentary on *Brown*. It relates to my understanding of the lawyer's role in the resolution of disputes. The law that permitted school segregation in Kansas cities was controversial. Its defense was not approved by all Kansans. Many were, and are, disposed to identify the lawyer personally with the posture of his client. Stated differently, some have apparently believed that the position that I took in the *Brown* arguments brands me as a defender of racism and bigotry. I have often been identified as the lawyer on the "wrong" side of *Brown*. My more charitable friends suggest that while I defended the constitutionality of the Kansas law permitting segregation, my heart was not in it. I protest both identifications. First, in a serious lawsuit, neither side is right or wrong. *Brown* raised a legitimate issue with profound constitutional, social, and political implications. The Court could make a sound determination of the issue only after it had been fully informed concerning the positions of the contending parties. The task of the lawyer is to inform the court of the views of his client as honestly as he can. In so doing he performs a service to the court and all parties before it. He is neither right nor wrong. Second, more than fifty years ago I gave my allegiance to the law. As I understood it, the oath that I then took imposed upon me the duty to present my clients' views and positions to the court as fully and candidly as I can. I did that in the *Brown* case. If the assertion that my "heart was not in it" means that the quality of my effort was diluted by personal predilections, the statement is unjust. As a human being, endowed with the capacity to make value judgments, I find that any scheme that classifies people on the basis of race or color and withholds from one class benefits that are enjoyed by others is morally indefensible. As a lawyer, I spoke in defense of a law that permitted such a result. As I saw it, my duty was to uphold the law. Whether the policy reflected by the law was morally, socially, or politically correct was the business of others.

I have two further comments by way of caveat. My first is that any views that I may express are my own. I have not read, nor can I expect to read, all that others have said and written about *Brown*. My thoughts and assertions may be neither profound nor mature. However, they are mine, and they are honest. My second caveat is this: the facts that I report are based largely upon my memory. I did not keep a diary. More than forty years have passed since I first stood before the Supreme Court to speak about *Brown v. Board of Education*. During that time the sun has risen more than 15,000 times, and I have become an old man. The memories of old men are sometimes tinged with romance. They remember things not as they were, but as they might have been or ought to have been. Here, I appear as a witness, testifying as to things that happened a long time ago. I am mindful of the witness's obligation to tell the truth, the whole truth and nothing but the truth. But I am also an old man.

1

1951

In September 1950, Linda Brown, an eight-year-old African-American child who lived in Topeka, Kansas, was ready to begin the third grade. Her first years of education had been spent at Monroe, an all-black school located about twenty-one blocks from the Brown home. In a modest neighborhood, the Monroe school building had been constructed in 1926. It was of brick in the Italian Renaissance style, well-cared for and maintained. According to a witness called by the *Brown* plaintiffs it was "a credit to the community" where it was located.[1] The Brown's home was in a racially mixed neighborhood. The children of white and other nonblack families of the neighborhood attended Sumner School about seven blocks from the Brown residence. Named for abolitionist leader Charles Sumner, the first school on the Sumner site was initially for blacks only, but in 1885 it was designated for white students. The current building at Sumner was built in 1935. It was constructed of light-colored brick with a good deal of ornamentation. The testimony of the expert witness was that the Sumner classrooms were more spacious and the facilities more ample and in keeping with a good school situation.[2] The academic programs at Monroe and Sumner were comparable.

Bus transportation was provided for Linda and other Monroe

Sumner Elementary School *(top),* the white neighborhood school where
Linda Brown was denied permission to enroll. Monroe Elementary School
(bottom), the all-black school attended by Linda Brown twenty-one blocks
from her home. Both structures have been designated National Historic
Landmarks by the Department of the Interior. (Courtesy of the Kansas State
Historical Society)

students along a designated route. Linda boarded the bus at a pick-
up station about seven blocks from her home. There was no shelter
for waiting passengers, and to reach the pick-up station Linda and
other black students had to walk through a railroad switchyard and
cross Kansas Avenue, Topeka's main commercial street, where the
motor traffic was heavy. No such hazards were encountered by students walking to Sumner.

As the 1950–1951 school term was about to begin Oliver Brown,

Linda's father, was concerned about his daughter's safety and comfort, the inconvenience of her daily trip to and from Monroe School, and the quality of the educational opportunity afforded her by the Topeka school district. On the day appointed for enrollment he led Linda to Sumner, the neighborhood school, and requested that she be admitted. The request was denied solely because the child was black and the rules of the board of education limited attendance at Sumner School to white, or approximately white, children. Linda continued to attend Monroe, but the events of that September morning commenced a series of happenings from which Linda Brown emerged as a celebrity and a folk heroine of the civil rights movement.

PRELUDE—THE NAACP DESIGN

Shortly after the *Brown* decision, a writer for the *St. Louis Post Dispatch* entitled an editorial "Why Kansas?" Pointing out that Kansas was the spiritual godchild of New England and that the Puritan tradition was still manifest in its laws, the writer inquired why Kansas stood beside the former slave states of South Carolina, Virginia, and Delaware and the District of Columbia, where slavery had been practiced with the sanction of law, to defend what the writer believed to be a vestige of slavery. Further, the writer wondered whether the state officials who purported to represent the people of Kansas had ever asked the people about their views. The writer's inquiry deserves a thoughtful response.

As I was not a participant in the *Brown* case at its early stages, I was not privy to the planning, preparation, and presentation of the case of either party. The facts that I relate concerning the early proceedings are drawn from public records, press reports, and the after-the-fact oral and written statements of some who were there. The inferences are my own.

Brown v. Board of Education of Topeka was not an isolated episode in American judicial history. It was part of, and with its companion cases, the culmination of a planned strategy of the National Association for the Advancement of Colored People (NAACP) to strike down racial discrimination in America. Sixteen years before the decision in *Brown* a trend toward that result was begun in a case from Missouri.[3]

Missouri's only tax-supported law school was located at the state university at Columbia, which did not admit black students. Lloyd Gaines, an African-American, sued to compel his admission to the university's school of law. Missouri law then authorized the state to pay tuition for black Missourians attending universities in adjacent states to study subjects not available to them at Lincoln University, the state's segregated institution of higher learning. There was no law curriculum at Lincoln. Gaines, denied admission to the law school at the University of Missouri, could have attended the state university law schools in Kansas, Nebraska, Iowa, or Illinois with tuition paid by Missouri. This, said the Supreme Court, is not good enough to satisfy the equal protection requirement of the Constitution. While affirming the separate-but-equal principle, the Court wrote: "The admissibility of laws separating the races in the enjoyment of the privileges afforded by the state rests wholly upon the equality of the privileges which the laws give to the separated groups within the State."[4] To place upon black students the burden of leaving the state to attend law school was constitutionally impermissible.

In 1939 the NAACP set up a separate corporation to secure and provide financial support for the legal programs of the association. Named the Legal Defense and Educational Fund, often abbreviated to Legal Defense Fund, this agency became the litigation arm of the NAACP.[5] The fund's director was Thurgood Marshall, who had already achieved stature as a civil rights lawyer. Lawyers on the staff later included Robert Carter and Jack Greenberg, who, with local counsel, tried *Brown v. Board of Education* in the Kansas federal court.

After *Gaines*, ten years elapsed before the Supreme Court again entertained an important problem of discrimination in tax-supported education. Ada Sipuel, a black woman, was denied admission to the University of Oklahoma Law School on account of her race and for the further reason that the state of Oklahoma expected soon to provide a law school for black students with facilities equal to those of the university. Before the Supreme Court of the United States it was contended that to require Sipuel, on the authority of *Gaines*, to wait for and attend the proposed segregated school violated the equal treatment guarantee. Holding that Oklahoma must provide Sipuel with a legal education in "conformity with the equal protection clause of the Fourteenth Amendment, and must provide it for her at the same time it provides such education for members of any other group," the Court remanded the case to the Oklahoma courts for implementation.[6] The state court's mandate to the regents was that they must forthwith (1) provide a separate and equal law school for Sipuel to attend; or (2) admit Sipuel to the University of Oklahoma School of Law; or (3) admit no students to the law school at the university. In an apparent effort to comply with the first alternative the board of regents secured and roped off space in the state capitol designated as a "law school for Ada Sipuel and all others similarly situated" and designated three teachers from the university law school to provide instruction. After a finding by the Oklahoma trial court that the law school set up for Ada Sipuel was equal to the school for whites at the university and an appeal to the supreme court of the state, Oklahoma yielded, and Ms. Sipuel was admitted to the University of Oklahoma School of Law. Because the issue was not raised earlier, there was no U.S. Supreme Court determination of whether segregation per se was a denial of equality.[7]

At the time that Ada Sipuel was contending with the Oklahoma board of regents, in the neighboring state of Texas, Heman Sweatt, a young, black mail carrier who aspired to be a lawyer, was similarly engaged. The law of Texas restricted admissions to the state university to white students. Sweatt's application to enroll in the law school was denied. He was offered admission to a separate law school newly established by the state for black students. He refused and sued to compel his admission to the university. The law school at the University of Texas was a distinguished one. The quality of its facilities, its library, its faculty, students, and alumni placed it among the country's ranking programs of legal education. The separate law school for blacks was established after the Sweatt litigation began. Not yet accredited, its stature as a law school was in no way comparable to that of the university school of law. Sweatt's claim of denial of equal opportunity was rejected in the state courts of Texas. His appeal brought the issue before the Supreme Court of the United States.[8]

While *Sweatt* was still undetermined the action shifted back to Oklahoma. George McLaurin, a black teacher and a citizen of Oklahoma, wished to study for the degree of Doctor of Education. As required by statute, his application for admission to the state university was denied solely because of his race. A federal district court held that the state had a constitutional duty to provide him with the education he sought if it provided that education for applicants from any other group. Following this decision, the legislature amended the statute to permit the admission of blacks to university programs not offered at the Negro schools of the state but provided that such admissions should be "upon a segregated basis." McLaurin was enrolled as a doctoral candidate but was assigned to a seat in a section of the classroom surrounded by a rail and marked "reserved for colored." Although the rail and sign were later removed, he was required to sit in a row specified for colored students and at a special table in both the library and cafeteria. McLaurin's motion to modify the conditions was denied by a three-judge federal district court, and he took an appeal to the Supreme Court.[9]

The *Sweatt* and *McLaurin* cases were argued on consecutive days in April 1950. Both appellants contended that the action of their respective states denied them equal protection of the laws. Both cases were decided on June 5, 1950. Each reversed the decision of the court below. Both were unanimous. In *Sweatt* the court emphasized the disparities between the University of Texas School of Law and the new school established by the state for blacks and the denial of the black law students' opportunity to be associated with racial groups with whom they would deal as members of the bar. In *McLaurin* the court found that the restrictions placed upon the student impaired and inhibited his ability to study, to engage in discussions and exchange views with other students and, in general, to prepare for his profession. Both opinions appeared to enlarge the concept of equal opportunity to include elements that are not tangible, that cannot be measured in terms of physical equipment, square feet of classroom space, and teacher-student ratios. Significant in the court's determination of inequality were disparities in law school reputation and prestige, denial of opportunity to interact with members of other ethnic groups, and the constraints inherent in treatment different from that of other participants in the same academic programs.

In none of the higher education cases did the Supreme Court find that the mere fact of separation according to race constituted a denial of equal opportunity. In each case there was a difference in facilities or treatment on which the court chose to base its finding.

Gaines, Sipuel, Sweatt, and *McLaurin* arose in different states and involved different parties and different facts, but it was clear that each was a skirmish in the broad NAACP attack upon racial segregation in all state-supported education and that each had a relationship to the others. The NAACP developed the strategy and coordinated and provided leadership and counsel in local cases. Legal Defense Fund attorneys argued and were on the briefs in each case. A week after the *Sweatt* and *McLaurin* opinions were handed down planning was begun for an offensive designed to end segregation in public education at every level. After much discussion involving civil rights lawyers, constitutional law professors, social scientists, board members of the NAACP, and staff members of the Legal Defense Fund a strategy was agreed upon: a series of lawsuits in selected jurisdictions where disparities and discrimination in secondary and elementary education were believed to exist.[10]

TARGET: PUBLIC EDUCATION

The jurisdictions whose school systems were selected to be the NAACP's initial objectives were Delaware, Kansas, South Carolina, Virginia, and the District of Columbia. Whether by design or chance, each involved public school segregation practiced in a factual, historical, and legal situation distinct from the others. South Carolina was representative of the Deep South, and segregation was required in all its elementary and secondary schools. Virginia was in the upper tier of the states in the former Confederacy; its laws required segregation on all levels, but the case brought to the Supreme Court involved only high school students. Delaware, a former slave state, had not seceded from the Union, but historically its law had required segregation in all its public schools. Kansas was unique. After a bitter struggle it had entered the Union as a free state and was an active participant in Union military operations during the Civil War. Its law did not require segregation in any of its schools but permitted local officials in a few communities of the state to establish and maintain racially separated schools for the elementary grades only. In each state case there was claim of a denial of equal protection of the laws as guaranteed by the Fourteenth Amendment. The Fourteenth Amendment applies only to states; since the District of Columbia is not a state, a different line of attack had to be pursued there. The D.C. plaintiffs argued that the due process clause of the Fifth Amendment was broad enough to preclude racial segregation in schools subject to its limitations. When the Delaware appeal, the last to reach the court, was docketed, the basis was laid for an inclusive challenge to all racial segregation in America's public schools.[11]

Although the impact of the Supreme Court's decision was less dramatic in Kansas than in other jurisdictions and post-*Brown* commentators and media productions have focused on other states, the Kansas case was an important component of the litigation. It presented facts and issues that were unique, and it was a necessary party to the final settlement of the broad social issue. Topeka provided an appropriate launching site for an attack on the Kansas segregation law. It was the state capital, a university town, the home of many of the state's business and professional leaders, and had a history of commitment to cultural concerns. In Topeka a resurgent branch of the NAACP under the leadership of activists McKinley Burnett and Lucinda Todd and others was being heard to protest Topeka's segregated schools. When their protests were dismissed by Topeka school officials, the local group provided an important base of support for the NAACP offensive in Kansas.

In 1951 there were twenty-two public elementary schools in Topeka. Four, including Monroe, were designated for black students only, and the remaining eighteen were almost—but not quite—lily-white. Hispanics, Asians, and American Indians also attended the white schools. Within the district, subdistrict or neighborhood boundaries were established with a white school located in each neighborhood. White students were required to attend the schools in the neighborhoods where they lived. The four black schools were located in or near areas where black populations were concentrated. Black students were permitted to attend any one of the four schools established for them, the choice being made by the students or their parents.[12] Some black students lived in mixed neighborhoods in other sections of the city, and their homes were considerable distances from the schools they attended. Linda Brown was one of those students. Hence, bus transportation to and from school was furnished to black students without cost to their parents. No transportation was supplied for white children.[13] There was no other material difference in facilities and treatment of students in the segregated schools.

THE STAGE IS SET

The first Topekans were New Englanders. As I have perused their diaries and other writings, I have concluded that many were highly literate people with a keen sense of the importance of learning. Although they lived in an atmosphere of controversy with the threat of violence ever present, they were able to assign a high priority to education. Before the town was three months old private schools for young children had been started. In September 1855 the first community school was established. The early schools were supported by voluntary subscriptions and assessments against town shareholders. It was not until 1862 that the first tax for school purposes was levied, and public funds first became available for school purposes in July 1863—nine years after the arrival of the first settlers.

In 1865, a small, frame building in a downtown location was rented as a school for black children. When white children needed these quarters, blacks were moved to the attic.[14] From that date until 1953 Topeka adhered to a policy of limited racial separation in its public schools.

The first Topeka schools were governed by the Topeka Association, a group of citizens who were shareholders in the town company. Upon the organization of Shawnee County and the creation of the office of county superintendent of schools, the Topeka schools became part of the county system. Legislation passed in 1867 removed the schools from administrative jurisdiction of the county and subjected them to control by the city. In that year the first school election was held, and a four-member board, consisting of president, secretary, treasurer, and superintendent, was chosen. From this modest beginning the Topeka Board of Education of the mid-twentieth century evolved, in response to population growth, changes in the community's political and social structure, and new methods and theories of education.

In 1951 the structure and powers of the Topeka Board of Education, the method of selecting its members, and their qualification and tenure were provided by statute.[15] Six board members were elected at large for four-year terms. At the city election held in April of each odd-numbered year three members were chosen for terms commencing the first Monday in August following their election. Board elections were nonpartisan, and board members served without pay. Service on the board was regarded as significant public service, and members enjoyed a considerable amount of prestige. According to the terms of the statute, the board possessed the "usual powers of public corporations" to exercise "sole control over the public schools and school property," including the power to maintain separate schools for the education of white and colored children in the elementary schools only.[16] Among the board's other enumerated powers was the election of a superintendent of schools who would have charge of the schools of the city, subject to the rules, regulations and orders of the board.

The Topeka Board of Education named as a defendant in the *Brown* case consisted of five men and one woman: Marlin S. Casey, usually called Mike, was an attorney engaged in civil practice; Charles Bennett, Kenneth B. Hobbs, Kelsey H. Petro, and A.H. Saville represented the business and entrepreneurial segment of the community; Mrs. David Neiswanger was identified as a housewife but was a well-known social and civic leader. All were recognized as people of competence and integrity. All were apparently successful in their personal endeavors. A review of their personal and public records would lead to the conclusion that it was a blue-ribbon board. Yet it was hardly representative of the population served by the public school system. All of its members were white. All were prosperous. None wore blue or unstarched collars. All lived on the "right" side of town.

In cases involving plural plaintiffs or defendants the title of the case often names the first of the several parties and refers to the other parties as et al. In *Brown* the phrase "et al." included Dr. Kenneth McFarland, superintendent of Topeka schools, and Frank Wilson, principal of Sumner Elementary School. Dr. McFarland was the most visible leader in the system. He was also the most controversial. A native of southern Kansas, an area where antiblack feeling lingered, he had earned degrees at Kansas State Teachers College at Pittsburg, at Columbia University, and at Stanford. In 1942, still in his mid-thirties, Dr. McFarland became superintendent of schools in Topeka. His fifteen years of prior experience in Kansas public education included seven years as the head of the Coffeyville, Kansas, school system, which had segregated schools. Dr. McFarland was a strong and active administrator who unified control of the school system in his office and assumed full responsibility for implementing the policies of the board of education. Politically, McFarland was conservative, as were most of his Topeka contemporaries. With extraordinary skill as a public speaker, he spent a considerable amount of time on the lecture circuit and was sometimes spoken of as a possible Republican candidate for governor.

Topeka's black population was divided in its attitude toward the issue of public school segregation. Black teachers were apprehensive that integration might threaten their jobs. Other members of the black middle class were not dissatisfied with their positions in the community and felt no urge to disturb the status quo. After World War II new black leaders appeared in Topeka. Many were veterans and had performed military service of the same kind and quality as other participants in the war. They were unwilling to accept a diluted kind of citizenship in their own community. Under new leadership the local chapter of the NAACP reorganized and became a more effective force. Pressures were exerted to integrate places of public recreation and entertainment. Attention began to focus on the elementary schools that remained segregated throughout the city. Why? was a recurring question.

From the perspective of the emerging black leaders, Kenneth McFarland and Harrison Caldwell, his black director of Negro education, were the principal obstacles to integration. Both were said to be arrogant and insensitive. McFarland apparently sincerely believed that Topeka was not ready for integrated schools. Caldwell was claimed to favor keeping the grade schools racially separate in order to retain his position of power. Although racial separation did not extend to high schools and junior high schools, segregation on these levels continued in most nonclassroom activities. Blacks did not participate in mainline student government, athletics, social activities, and events, nor did they mingle with white students in the cafeteria, the playgrounds, the library, and other places where students assembled. This separateness was claimed to have been encouraged by school administrators. Rightly or wrongly, McFarland bore the brunt of black resentment for Topeka's segregated schools. It was claimed that he dominated the board and that its policies were unduly influenced by the views of its chief administrative officer.

Oliver Brown's lawsuit was filed on February 28, 1951. April 3, 1951, was election day in Topeka. Board of education members Hobbs, Petro, and Saville were candidates for reelection. The incumbent slate faced spirited opposition, most of its ire being focused on the superintendent. Proponents of the opposing candidates argued that members of the sitting board were mere puppets, with McFarland pulling the strings. It was also contended that McFarland's lecture schedule impinged on his performance for the school district. A preelection inspection of the board's financial audits by the *Daily Capital* disclosed that the district's fiscal practices did not conform with the letter of the law and the repeated recommendations of their independent auditors. Although the incumbent candidates had the support of teachers and others working in the school system, all were defeated for reelection. Elected to succeed them were M.C. Oberhelman, a bank president, Jacob Dickinson, an attorney, and Dr. Harold E. Conrad, a professor of political science and history at Washburn University. All were white, male, prosperous, and lived on the right side of town. So far as I can determine from contemporary news stories as well as from my own recollection, racial segregation in the elementary schools was not an overt issue in the campaign. At the same time, a vote against the incumbent candidates was regarded as a vote against McFarland and his administration. It is therefore a safe assumption that the antisegregationists joined in the effort that unseated the incumbents. Moreover, both Conrad and Dickinson were known in the community as political liberals, and it was commonly and correctly believed that their presence on the board would strengthen the integrationists' hand.

The newly elected members would take office on the first Monday in August. Two days after the election the superintendent submitted his resignation, to take effect on August 1. In his letter of resignation McFarland stated, "Our tie to the Topeka school system is founded principally on the exceptionally high quality of the citizens who constitute the present board of education."[17] He also paid tribute to the loyalty and devotion of the teachers in the system. McFarland was succeeded by Dr. Wendell R. Godwin, a political moderate, who had been superintendent of schools at Hutchinson. I cannot say whether the defeat of the incumbent board members and the departure of Dr. McFarland had an impact on the board's later decision not to contest the *Brown* appeal. The facts are simply that when the decision in Case No. T–316 was announced, half the members of the defendant board and the defendant superintendent of schools were no longer associated with the public schools of Topeka. If the election had come out differently and had Dr. McFarland remained at his post, this might have been a different story, but I am persuaded that the ending would have been the same.

THE BROWN ROLE

If the Brown family had stood alone in its challenge to and rebuff by Topeka school officials, would they have had the will and the wealth to carry the issue to the federal courts and to press for a final determination? The question need not be answered. The Browns were not alone and unsupported. Other black families in the district had had like experiences and were similarly aggrieved. For many months the local NAACP had protested Topeka's segregated schools and had sought through negotiation to bring an end to the board's historical policy. Their protests had produced no affirmative response. Through the local branch the NAACP headquarters in New York was kept informed of goings-on in Topeka, and when in late summer 1950 it was advised that the local group was ready for litigation to test the validity of the Kansas law and the Topeka practice, the resources and expertise of the Legal Defense Fund became available.

The Topeka case was not the NAACP's first venture in Kansas. The organization had participated in 1949 in the Johnson County segregation case of *Webb v. School District*.[18] NAACP staff attorney Franklin H. Williams had assisted Topeka attorney Elisha Scott in the argument before the Supreme Court of Kansas, and Thurgood Marshall's name appeared on the plaintiff's brief. With the decision to make Topeka an initial target in the massive attack on public school segregation, the September morning encounter between Oliver Brown, a concerned parent, and Frank Wilson, a dutiful school principal, became a cause celebre.

The only persons eligible to challenge the Kansas law permitting school segregation and the policy of the Topeka Board of Education requiring it were those who could claim injury resulting from their enforcement—black students denied access to neighborhood schools because of their color. Thus, the first task of the challengers was to identify and recruit black families who had experienced such rejection and could claim resulting denial of constitutional rights. The late Charles S. Scott of Topeka was a member of the NAACP and one of the attorneys who helped prepare the case. Twenty years later Mr. Scott was interviewed about the case by Dr. James C. Duram and Mr. Robert Bunting of Wichita State University. When queried concerning the initiation of the case, Mr. Scott's reply suggests that the Browns and other black plaintiffs were cooperators rather than instigators in bringing the action. In part, Mr. Scott said:

> The NAACP would go and solicit families or parents of children and explain the thrust of the NAACP and would they consent to

being used as plaintiffs, as guinea pigs, as we refer to them quite frequently.

Rev. Brown was a minister of the AME church, St. Mark AME Church in Topeka, and he had the young lady, Linda, who lived in a very strategic neighborhood just approximately two or three blocks from an all white school. We felt that she would serve our purpose perfectly, along with others that had lived in a similar situation. And so we—when I say we I'm referring to the committee that we had at that time—we solicited and gained the consent from these parents to use their names as well as the children in the test law suit.[19]

When the complaint in Case No. T–316 was filed its title contained the names of thirteen Topeka parents who sued on their own behalf and as representatives of their twenty children, who were also appearing as plaintiffs. All were black. All of the children were public school students who had been denied access to their neighborhood schools on account of their color. Because the aggrieved students were minors and without legal capacity to sue, each was represented by his or her parent.

The order in which the names of the several plaintiffs appear in the title to the case provokes a collateral inquiry. The first-named plaintiff is Oliver Brown, appearing for his daughter, Linda Carol Brown. Brown's name is followed by those of Mrs. Richard Lawton, Mrs. Sadie Emmanuel, and ten other parents who sue on behalf of their respective children, all of whom are named in the title to the complaint. Mrs. Darlene Brown is the ninth-named plaintiff.

Although the question has no relation to the merits of the case, the curious observer may inquire why the limelight of history has centered upon the Browns while twelve other Topeka families with nineteen children and dozens of other similarly situated parties in Delaware, South Carolina, Virginia, and the District of Columbia have been forgotten. I am sure it is due to no intent or design of Oliver Brown or his daughter. The answer to the question "why the Browns" comes in four steps, three of which are obvious and the fourth more obscure. First, "Brown" is the only name specifically mentioned in the abbreviated caption of the official report of the Supreme Court's opinion.[20] Other plaintiffs are included in the "et al." catchall. Second, of the four school-segregation cases decided in the Supreme Court's

The Reverend Oliver L. Brown and daughter, Linda Carol Brown

Mrs. Richard Lawton and daughters, Victoria Jean Lawton and Carol Kay Lawton

Mrs. Lucinda Todd and daughter, Nancy Jane Todd

Mrs. Andrew Henderson and daughter, Vicki Ann Henderson, and son, Donald Andrew Henderson

The Kansas plaintiffs in *Brown v. Board of Education*. (Courtesy of the Brown Foundation, Topeka, and the Kansas Collection, Spencer Research Library, University of Kansas)

Mrs. Vivian Scales and daughter, Ruth Ann Scales

Mrs. Lena Carper and daughter, Katherine Louise Carper

Mrs. Shirley Hodison and son, Charles Hodison

Mrs. Marguerite Emmerson and sons, Claude Arthur Emmerson and George Robert Emmerson

Not pictured: Mrs. Sadie Emmanuel, James Meldon Emmanuel, Mrs. Iona Richardson, Ronald Douglas Richardson, Mrs. Alma Lewis, Theron Lewis, Arthur Lewis, Martha Jean Lewis, Frances Lewis, Darlene Brown, Saudria Dorstella Brown, Mrs. Shirla Fleming, Duane Dean Fleming, and Silas Hardrick Fleming.

consolidated opinion of May 17, 1954, the *Brown* case was the first to have been entered on the Supreme Court's docket; hence, the inclusive opinion bore its caption. Third, Oliver Brown's name appears first in the array of plaintiffs in the caption of the district court case.[21] Fourth, the reason why Oliver Brown was named first is unclear and speculative.

I first assumed that the plaintiffs names had been arranged alphabetically. One need only to look at the record to know the error in that assumption. The second- through fifth-named parents, Lawton, Emmanuel, Todd, and Richardson, are hardly ordered alphabetically. Moreover, in an alphabetical scheme, Darlene Brown, ninth on the list of parents, would probably have preceded Oliver. Some have thought that Oliver Brown was the first plaintiff recruited in the NAACP solicitation. Thus, he was given top billing. Richard Kluger, who interviewed many who participated in the planning stage, seems to conclude that Brown was selected as the leadoff plaintiff because of his personal characteristics. He was a young family man—modest, nice looking, steadily employed, a union member, an assistant pastor of his church—who enjoyed the respect of both his black and white associates. He was not an active NAACP member and was known to be nonmilitant. His was a good name to be associated with an effort that might produce controversy and anger.[22] Members of the Brown family believe that there may have been an element of sexism in Oliver Brown's assignment to first place on the list of plaintiffs. He was the only male parent appearing for his child. All others were moms. In a long-ago conversation, Charles Scott told me that there was no rational explanation for the order in which the plaintiff's names appeared on the caption. They were entered randomly by the secretary who typed the complaint, and it was a matter of chance that Oliver Brown appeared first on the list.

Although chance and history have cast the Browns as the most visible players in Topeka's school segregation drama, the presence and contributions of others must be recognized. Thirteen parents and twenty children joined to invoke the jurisdiction of the court. All were similarly aggrieved. All sought the same relief. Before the court they were equals—all plaintiffs. Other Topekans not mentioned in the record had important roles. For initiating and pursuing the protest against Topeka's segregated schools much credit must be given to the local branch of the NAACP and its leaders, among whom the names of McKinley Burnett and Lucinda Todd often appear. For molding the protest into justiciable form, the commitment and talents of attorneys John and Charles Scott and Charles Bledsoe were indispensable. It does not diminish the Brown role to suggest that the victory often attributed to Oliver and Linda Brown was the successful climax to the vision and strivings of many Topekans.

WHY KANSAS?

In 1951 there were twenty-two American jurisdictions whose laws either permitted or required racial segregation in their public schools. Five became targets of the NAACP offensive. Why was Kansas one of these states? Clearly there were other states where racial discrimination was more widespread and egregious. Why then were not NAACP resources directed against those states? In this context the question, Why? arouses two lines of inquiry.

The first question is why the NAACP selected Kansas as one of its targets. Here the answer has already been suggested: Kansas was different. Set apart by its antislavery origins, its admission as a free state, the permissive character and limited application of its law, and the substantial equality of school facilities made Kansas special and restricted debate to issues that could have been avoided in the other cases. A further reason for the selection of Kansas, with less academic but perhaps more pragmatic significance, was suggested to me many years later by Judge Constance Baker Motley, who was a staff attorney for the Legal Defense Fund in 1951. Judge Motley recalled that it was felt that Kansas, with its unique history and relatively small black population, would offer less resistance to a lawsuit to end segregation than states where patterns of discrimination were broader and more firmly entrenched.[23] Later events were to validate that judgment.

A more basic and more difficult problem is implicit in the question, Why Kansas? Why was Kansas, with its unique history and relatively small black population, a place where racially segregated schools existed in 1951? Why was Kansas vulnerable to an NAACP attack? The answers to these questions require recognition of a historic ambivalence that has characterized the attitudes of white Kansans toward members of other races.

Kansans cherish the history of their state. They are proud of their

New England heritage. They recall with satisfaction the long and bloody fight to exclude slavery, the antislavery triumph, and the emergence of Kansas as a free state. They look upon their state as a place of equality, toleration, and understanding.

Other facts of Kansas history are less often spoken of but equally real. Most of the early Kansas immigrants were not New England idealists but middle western farmers, artisans, and tradesmen. Although opposed to slavery, their first objective was economic rather than political. Most came from states where some form of racial discrimination existed. They came bearing the attitudes and bias that they knew. A majority of the antislavery partisans would have excluded all blacks from Kansas. The constitution that prohibited slavery withheld voting rights from black citizens. The first state legislature, dominated by antislavery members, empowered all local school officials to establish racially segregated schools. Later legislatures limited the power to those districts where blacks were most likely to be found.

In Kansas communities, by virtue of policy or local custom, blacks were effectively excluded from the mainstream of community life. Living in isolated neighborhoods, their access to places of public accommodation, entertainment, and recreation was limited or denied. Separation in social, fraternal, patriotic, and religious organizations has been the rule. Kansans are heirs to a tradition of freedom; as we recognize this proud tradition we must acknowledge that Kansans, like most other Americans, are also heirs to a tradition of racism. I here use the word "racism" to describe an assumption that one race, usually one's own, is superior to others. The result of such an assumption in a multiracial democracy traditionally has been that the race that produces the most votes elects leaders who seek to protect the values of the majority against dilution by exposure to the values of others and to protect members of the majority from annoyances that may arise from association with people whose color, manner of speaking, and cultural patterns are different from their own. Historically, the majority of Kansans have been white, Anglo-Saxon, and Protestant. Their repudiation of black slavery was not tantamount to an acceptance of black equality. Hence, during the first century of statehood, few nonblack Kansans were disturbed by a policy of racial segregation in public education.

Why Kansas? Why not Kansas?

2

The Historical Context

It is usually assumed that the exclusion of persons of African descent from the mainstream of American life is the consequence of black slavery. Although the isolation of blacks would have existed in modern America regardless of prior black servitude, the two, slavery and discrimination, have a common basis which, stated poetically, is man's inhumanity to man. The existence of a significant black population in America is the result of the importation of blacks to be employed as slaves. Moreover, the political implications of slavery were of paramount concern at the beginning of Kansas. Hence, slavery is the reference point from which any history of race relations in Kansas must begin.

During the first seven decades of our national existence the issue of slavery and its extension, containment, or abolition was the overriding political, economic, and moral concern of Americans. To the states lying in the southeastern quadrant of the contemporary United States, the existence of slavery was vital. It was argued and believed that the prosperity of the plantation economy, which provided the economic basis for southern culture, required the availability of slave labor. The North, by contrast, was mainly a region of cities, factories, and small farms in which the employment of slaves was not economically feasible. In this environment moral and political considerations assumed more important roles. The quality and extent of righteousness appear to vary inversely with their cost. Although their antislavery attitudes differed in intensity, northerners were generally opposed to the spread of slavery and in favor of its eventual extinction.

Although policies relating to slavery and the status of slaves were determined by state law, because of the interstate aspects of the slave trade and the mobility of slave property, the slave states looked to Congress for assistance in protecting the interests of slaveholders. Since Congress controlled the admission of new states, an effective proslavery voice in the admission process was necessary to assure the continuation of a numerical balance of power. A principal weapon in the proslavery arsenal was a sympathetic United States Senate. Whereas the states of the North had much larger populations, each state, regardless of population, was entitled to two senators. By maintaining a balance of representation in the United States Senate, the South was able to prevent federal legislation that might be prejudicial to the "peculiar" institution of slavery. By mid-nineteenth century the protective equilibrium was being threatened.

At the beginning of 1850 the Senate was composed of sixty members representing thirty states. In fifteen states slavery was prohibited by law[1] while in an equal number it was authorized and practiced.[2] Before the end of the year California had been admitted to the Union as the sixteenth free state.[3] The territories of Minnesota and Oregon were being groomed for statehood. Because of their locations and restrictions imposed by Congress on the territories from which they would be created,[4] it seemed likely that both would become free states. To maintain the historic but tenuous balance of power the South looked to the West and Southwest.

Two new territories—New Mexico[5] and Utah[6]—were organized in 1850 from lands ceded by Mexico after the Mexican War. The Organic Act of each territory neither sanctioned nor prohibited slavery during the territorial period and provided that the issue should be determined by the state constitution when statehood was conferred.

Between the Rocky Mountains and the settled frontier whose western boundary, in part, lay along the Missouri River was a vast unorganized region officially described as Indian Country but commonly spoken of as the Nebraska Territory. It was here that the proslavery South saw its best opportunity for expansion. In part the territory shared a common boundary with the slave state of Missouri. It was not far from the slave states of Arkansas, Kentucky, and Tennessee. Also, it was believed that of all the lands of the trans-Missouri region, those lying immediately west of Missouri were most amenable to the development of a slave-based agrarian economy. But there were obstacles. Soil and climatic conditions in the northern and western parts of the Indian country seemed hardly favorable to plantation agriculture. Also, slavery had been forever prohibited in the territory by the act of Congress that had admitted Missouri to statehood.[7] The Congress and the president did not find the problems insurmountable.

The legislation commonly referred to as the Kansas-Nebraska Bill[8] addressed both issues. First, the southern part of the territory— that most suitable for slavery—was detached and organized as the separate Territory of Kansas. Second, those parts of the Missouri Compromise of 1820 that prohibited slavery in the lands from which the territories were organized were repealed. Instead, it was provided that both Kansas and Nebraska, when ready for statehood, were to be admitted with or without slavery as their state constitutions should provide. Subject only to federal constitutional and statutory limitations, state constitutions are the creations of the residents of the proposed states. At the beginning, Kansas Territory was virtually without population. The legal status of slavery would be determined by the majority of those who settled in the territory before adoption of a state constitution. Thus, the migration of a sufficient number of their own partisans to control the electorate became the objective of each of the competing interests.

The most visible proponents and supporters of the free-state migration to Kansas were found in New England, where opinion ran not only to containment of slavery but to its abolition. In contrast slaveholders from Missouri, who felt most threatened by the prospect of an adjacent free state of Kansas, assumed leadership in the proslavery migration. Proximity and friendly national and territorial administrations gave the initial advantage to the advocates of slavery; however, the antislavery migration was more sustained, and the free-state settlers more durable. By 1857 the proslavery power had begun to wane, and a free-state majority was emerging. Kansas seemed destined to join the Union under a constitution that prohibited slavery.

Although the political, moral, and emotional issues of slavery reflected the divergent values of New England and the Plantation South, neither region was a major contributor to the actual settlement of Kansas. Most of the immigrants to the new territory came from the middle Atlantic and middle western states where the subject of slavery was less volatile. The federal census of 1860 fixed the territory's total population at 107,206. The same census listed a total of 4,208 settlers from the six New England states. The census of 1870 disclosed a similar distribution. By that time the total population of the state was 364,399, of which 10,025 were New Englanders.[9] The years prior to 1870 were critical ones in the formation of the government and policies of the state of Kansas. An analysis of the sources of population of the new state suggests that most of the settlers may have been motivated less by the politics of slavery than by the desire for homes and economic advantage. Land, not idealism, was the lure that brought settlers to Kansas.

THE RACE ISSUE

Although the views of the earliest Kansans diverged sharply on the issue of slavery, there was nearly complete agreement on the superiority of the white race. Most accepted the exclusion of persons of African descent from some of the benefits enjoyed by white citizens. Seven states, none of which were parts of New England or the Confederacy, supplied more than half the Kansas immigrants prior to 1870. Two, Missouri and Kentucky, were slave states, whereas five prohibited slavery. All remained loyal to the Union during the Civil War. In each of these seven, whether slave or free, there was a history of racial discrimination. The attitudes of the early Kansans were the products of the history and culture of nineteenth-century America. The superiority of the white race was an almost pervasive tenet of that culture.

The Free State party of Kansas was organized at Big Springs on September 5–6, 1855. The convention recorded its opposition to slavery and its demand that Kansas be admitted as a free state. It also adopted a resolution declaring "that the best interests of Kansas require a population of free white men, and that, in the organization, we are in favor of stringent laws excluding all Negroes, bond or free, from the territory."[10]

During the period 1855–1859, Kansas's admission to the Union was sought under four proposed constitutions. The first, drafted at Topeka in late 1855, proposed the admission of Kansas as a free state. Although approved in a territorial election, it was rejected by Congress. In the same election a proposal to exclude free Negroes from the state was approved by a three-fourths majority. A constitution drafted at Lecompton, the territorial capital, and sent to Congress in early 1858 was a proslavery document. It was approved by the Congress and the president but eventually rejected by the voters of the territory. A third proposed constitution was drafted in Leavenworth in 1858. With provisions prohibiting slavery, it was essentially a political maneuver designed to frustrate Kansas's admission under the Lecompton constitution. It was not pursued when it became apparent that the Lecompton constitution would fail.[11]

The record of events after the failure of the Lecompton constitution suggests that the demise of the proslavery movement had little impact on the issues of political and social equality of the races. A fourth and final Kansas constitutional convention assembled at Wyandotte on July 5, 1859. Of the fifty-two delegates, eleven had formerly lived in New England. Four were from slave states. Four were of foreign origin. The remaining thirty-one members were from the middle states of Ohio (fourteen delegates), Indiana (seven), Pennsylvania (six), and New York (four).

At the beginning it was clear that the convention would produce a proposed constitution prohibiting slavery, but as the convention progressed, it was equally clear that the legal status of Kansans of African descent remained disputed and uncertain. Early in the convention and throughout its sessions the issue of prohibiting settlement by Negroes in the prospective state was raised and debated. Although not adopted, the proposal to exclude mustered substantial support.[12] A provision to confer the right to vote in public elections upon white, male citizens was adopted.[13] This language, which purported to limit suffrage to whites, remained in the state constitution until 1917, although it had long been inoperative by reason of the Fifteenth Amendment to the Constitution of the United States.[14] Service in the militia was limited to able-bodied white males.[15]

Perhaps the most spirited debates of the convention were those focused upon the education of black children. The range of views expressed included (1) exclusion of blacks and mulattoes from public educational institutions and facilities on all levels from the elementary grades through the university; (2) separate schools for black students, with appropriate allocations of state school funds for the support of black and white schools respectively; and (3) the mandated admission of all eligible students to the common schools of the state, without regard to race or ethnic origins.[16] Although the place of the Negro student in public education provoked sharp disagreement and excited debate, the issue was finally resolved by avoiding it. The education article, as adopted, provided only that the legislature should establish a uniform system of public schools and schools of higher grade.[17] Decisions as to admission policies and racial separation were left to the legislature and the people. The debates reveal no evidence of an intent to limit or preclude the establishment of separate schools for black students if the legislature and the local school officials deemed it proper. Indeed, an analysis of the reported proceedings leads to a contrary conclusion.

On January 29, 1861, Kansas was admitted as the thirty-fourth state in the American Union. Its constitution assured freedom from slavery to black persons within its jurisdiction. It denied them the right to participate in the political life of the state. The constitution was silent and the people ambivalent with respect to the black person's right to public education.

BLACK EDUCATION IN KANSAS TERRITORY

The concept of a uniform system of public schools, supported by state and local taxation, had begun to emerge before Kansas appeared in American history. An earlier view that education is for the private benefit of individuals and should be paid for by those who are benefited was yielding to recognition that informed citizens are necessary components of a democracy and that to foster and maintain the common schools is a basic responsibility of government. In the Act to Organize the Territory of Kansas, Congress reserved land from the public domain "for the purpose of being applied to schools." The lands so reserved, two out of each thirty-six square miles, provided the first increment of public financial support for education in Kansas. The reservation was repeated among the conditions imposed on the state by the act admitting Kansas to the Union.[18]

Although the merits of a uniform system of public schools were seldom disputed, public education did not enjoy a high priority in the turbulent politics of territorial Kansas. Those responsible for implementing the Act of Congress were preoccupied with more mundane issues of freedom or slavery, order or chaos, and life or death. Since the initial responsibility for activating the territorial government and setting its course lay with the legislature, an examination of its character and acts is called for.

During the territorial period of nearly seven years there were six legislative sessions.[19] As a result of extraordinary conditions prevailing at elections, only the proslavery faction was represented in the first two sessions. Thereafter, members of the Free State party were in the ascendancy. Territorial legislators were uniformly white, Anglo-Saxon, and male. From the standpoints of age and occupational interests they were fairly representative of the settlers. Politics was their preoccupation. Most adhered unswervingly to the party line. Because my present interest is limited to race relations in public education, acts of only two of the six sessions seem relevant.

The territory's first legislative session assembled in July 1855. Its task was to create a complete framework of law for the government of the new constituency. Often called the "Bogus Legislature," its members had been chosen in an election tainted by claims of massive fraud. The few elected Free State party members had been rejected at the beginning of the session. Many of those who sat were mere sojourners who actually resided in the state of Missouri. Predictably, the laws passed at that session were essentially a verbatim enactment of the Missouri state code—a code that reflected the pre–Civil War proslavery attitude and denied all civil and political rights to Negroes.

Provision was made by law for creating, governing, and financing a system of district schools that should be free and open to every class of *white* citizens of appropriate age.[20] No provision was made for the education of children who were not white. The policy declared by the Bogus Legislature remained until 1858 when a Free State party majority took control. A revision of the school code eliminated the word "white" as a condition of access to the public schools.[21]

Common to both the 1855 law and the 1858 revision was the concept of local control. A procedure for the creation of school districts was prescribed. It was the further intent of the law that upon organization each common school district would be autonomous within the boundaries of broad statutory grants of power. Few municipalities have enjoyed the autonomy accorded to the nineteenth-century common-school district and few were more striking examples of the town-meeting kind of democracy. This tradition was carried forward into the era of statehood and continues to influence the law governing the public schools.

The significance of the omission of blacks from the first law governing admissions to the territorial public schools and their later inclusion was probably more symbolic than real. Few blacks lived in Kansas territory. Delays and uncertainties inherent in the beginnings of new public institutions and programs were compounded by the political unrest in territorial Kansas. The first school district in the territory was organized in July 1858. Until after that date no child in the territory, black or white, had the benefit of common-school training. In most communities private or select schools supported by subscription and tuition supplied the response to the educational need. There is no record of the number of black children in the territorial schools, but we can reasonably infer from other circumstances that there were few—perhaps none. The bases for the inference are threefold: first, there were few blacks of school age in the territory; second, private charities had traditionally borne the burden of black education; and third, the prevailing attitudes in most communities would have favored their exclusion. The territorial government was largely uninterested in Negro education.

STATEHOOD

Statehood, as opposed to territorial status, brought greater autonomy, enlarged powers for political leaders, and full representation in the national Congress to Kansas, but it caused little change in the personnel and policies of government. The Republican party into which the earlier Free State party had been merged continued to control the three branches of government. As I attempt to distill intent from legislative debates and other sources, I conclude that the early Kansas thinking about black education followed this line: to foster a uniform system of free public education is a primary responsibility of state government; within broad statutory limits local schools should be subject to local control; all children should have access to education of equal quality, but the teaching of persons of different ethnic and cultural backgrounds requires different treatment in the public schools; local school districts and their officials should have power to classify and separate students according to their special needs; blacks are sufficiently different from whites to justify their segregation in separate schools if locally determined to be in the public interest. This thinking, with later modification, prevailed in Kansas during the first ninety years of statehood.

Legislative History

From the beginning Kansas took the position that the power to classify students for public school attendance on the basis of race was a special one to be exercised only by those local districts to which the power had been expressly granted by the legislature. In the absence of a clear statutory grant the power did not exist.[22] Thus an examination of the pre-*Brown* history of public school segregation in Kansas begins with the legislature.

Although often expressing political disagreement, Kansas state legislators during the period of 1861 to 1951 displayed a remarkable ethnic and cultural homogeneity. With few exceptions they were white, Anglo-Saxon, and male. Most were Protestants. Farmers and farm-oriented business and professional people supplied the majorities and filled most of the positions of leadership. Except for the last decade of the nineteenth century, when Populism flourished in Kansas, and the year 1912, when Democrats won control of state government, Kansans consistently sent Republican majorities to both the Senate and the House of Representatives.

In 1861 Kansas was almost wholly rural. The cities and towns that had been established during the territorial period were economically and culturally parts of the agrarian communities that they served. Between 1861 and 1951 the state's population increased from just over 100,000 to almost 2 million. Geographically, the growth was not evenly distributed. While urban communities were developing, much of the state remained rural and sparsely populated. In fixing the boundaries of legislative districts the Kansas legislature has traditionally been influenced by geography as well as by demographic considerations. A result was that for many years prior to *Brown* the membership of the Kansas legislature was weighted in favor of the rural districts. Most rural legislators had few black constituents. Notwithstanding the rural bias, I cannot say that a different state policy toward segregated schools in cities would have been pursued if legislative apportionment had been more sensitive to demographic changes. The earliest school segregation laws were passed by legislatures that were overwhelmingly rural. Traditionally, most Kansas legislators' interests have been limited to the concerns of their constituents, and the western Kansas legislator who represented no black and no urban communities was indifferent as to whether the law permitted the Topeka Board of Education to segregate its elementary schools. In matters of school policy in cities of the first class he looked for leadership to the representatives of the communities affected and voted with deference to their views. The necessary inference is that racially separated schools were authorized and existed in Topeka because they were agreeable to a majority of Topekans and their representatives.

To provide a basic framework for government under state law the governor called the first legislature into session two months after statehood. Its agenda included the enactment of a body of school laws to supersede the territorial statutes on the subject.[23] The code enacted at the session provided for the organization of common school districts to be supervised by the county superintendent of public instruction. The inhabitants of the district who voted in the annual district meeting were designated as the district's governing body, and they were expressly empowered "to make such order as they deem proper for the separate education of white and colored children, securing to them equal education advantages."[24] Elsewhere in the act it was provided that the district schools should be "equally free to all children resident therein."

Later in the decade general laws for the incorporation and classification of cities were passed. Cities with more than 15,000 population were designated as cities of the first class while those with more than 2,000 and not more than 15,000 could be incorporated as cities of the second class. In cities of each class, boards of education were created with jurisdiction over the public schools of the city, and boards on each level were expressly empowered to organize and maintain racially separate schools.[25] Thus, during the first fifteen years of Kansas history, segregated schools were permitted in all school districts of the state. Whether such schools would exist in fact was a determination to be made on the local level.

Early in the 1867 session the legislature passed, without debate, a resolution ratifying the Fourteenth Amendment to the Constitution of the United States,[26] which, a century later, was used as a weapon to strike down separate schools in Kansas. Six weeks after the 1867 ratification resolution, the legislators expressly empowered cities of the second class to segregate their elementary schools.[27] Still later the same session sought to strengthen the assurance of equality by providing that school board members who denied admission of any eligible child to schools under their jurisdiction should be subject to fines and, in default of payment, to imprisonment in the county jail.[28] By some this provision was read to prohibit separate schools. It seems more likely that the law was particularly aimed at those districts that had no separate facilities for blacks and denied them admission to schools established for other students.

During and following the Civil War the black population of Kansas grew. The 1870 census reported more than 17,000 black residents of the state. That year a bill was introduced to require racially separate schools.[29] Sponsors of the bill argued that equality of opportunity for black students could be assured only in separate black schools subject to the same standards and supervision as other schools. It was contended that in mixed schools discrimination was inevitable. The committee to which the bill was referred recommended its rejection, expressing the view that such determinations should be made by local officers on the basis of local needs and attitudes. There was also a minority report. In part it states: "It is a notorious fact that in many districts of the State, the public schools have been broken up and discontinued the moment that an attempt was made to force colored children into such schools with white children, and that in such districts the schools have been discontinued entirely, or replaced by subscription schools."[30]

During the second decade of the state's history there appears to have been an increasing sensitivity to the civil rights of ex-slaves. The black population of Kansas was increasing, and its leaders becoming more articulate. Voices of dissent from traditional views were heard with greater frequency in the white community. Journalists, political leaders, and administrative officers questioned whether racially separated public schools were necessary or feasible. Responses came from the legislature. In 1874 a civil rights act was overwhelmingly passed. It applied to schools and public institutions on all levels, to common carriers, and to places of public accommodation and entertainment licensed by municipalities; and it prohibited discrimination "on account of race color or previous condition of servitude." Offenders were subject to criminal prosecution and civil damages.[31] This statute remained on the books until 1970, when it was rephrased and reenacted. There is no record that it was ever invoked in a case involving denial of public school admission.

In 1876 the existing school laws were repealed and a new code was enacted that contained no provision for racial separation.[32] The repeal of the power to segregate did not necessarily end the fact of segregated schools. Indeed, there is not sufficient evidence to justify the conclusion that it produced any marked impact on local school practices. Records of later lawsuits indicate that some districts continued to segregate as the result of community pressures and, sometimes, black preference, notwithstanding the absence of statutory authority. Local school officials protested efforts to integrate. At the end of 1876 the Wyandotte County superintendent complained to the state department, "There are a large number of colored pupils in this county, and where they predominate or attend schools in considerable numbers, these mixed schools are not a success."[33]

The decade of the 1870s was a period of growth for the black population. From an 1870 enumeration of about 17,000, the number had increased to more than 43,000 by 1880. The black immigrants were mainly former slaves seeking to escape from the poverty and oppression of the post–Civil War South. Beginning around the middle of the decade, the Negro influx was steady, and the settlements were scattered. Many blacks chose to stay in the cities and larger towns. In 1879 the number of black immigrants increased suddenly and dramatically. Historians have dubbed this vast migration the "Exodus."[34] Within a few weeks some six thousand blacks arrived in Kansas from Louisiana, Mississippi, and Texas. Some of these found their way to the interior towns and farms, but many remained in the points of entry to the state.

The impact of the Exodus fell most heavily on the cities. The newcomers were largely without the skills useful in urban communities. They were poor. Many became the objects of public charity. Their numbers cast a heavy burden on existing public facilities that was particularly felt in the public schools. In 1874 the legislature had passed compulsory attendance legislation requiring that each child between the ages of eight and fourteen years attend school for at least twelve weeks of each year.[35] This provision, although indifferently enforced, intensified the demands upon the schools of growing communities. Taxpayers were required to provide new buildings and additional teachers to meet the increase in school population caused, in part, by the influx of uninvited, nontaxpaying, and unwanted black immigrants from the South. The increase and concentration of black populations in cities made segregation affordable. These facts, coupled with the unexpressed but pervasive racism of the late nineteenth century resulted in a new policy after three years of nonsegregation.

An 1879 amendment to the school code permitted but did not require boards of education in cities of the first class to establish and maintain racial segregation in the elementary schools only.[36] Although the power to segregate was limited to elementary schools in cities of more than 15,000 inhabitants, its impact may have been greater than the limitations suggest. Historically, 90 percent of the black population of Kansas has lived in urban areas that either were or aspired to be cities of the first class. In 1879, secondary schools in public education were in their incubative state. Few Kansans, either black or white, went to high school. Thus, the 1879 amendment and the policy that it reflected had potential consequences for most black education in Kansas. In 1905 the law was amended to permit segregated high schools in Kansas City.

Analysis of the pre-*Brown* history of Kansas public school legislation leads to these conclusions: First, the historical policy of the state favored the universality and equality of educational opportunity of all the state's children, including access by all to the state's public schools; second, in those cities and schools where the black population was sufficiently large to make racially separated schools economically feasible, the state policy could yield to local political determinations favoring separate schools for blacks and whites.

In 1879 three Kansas cities came within the law's exception.[37] By the time of the *Brown* decision the number had grown to twelve. One had never practiced segregation.[38] One was only partially segregated.[39] By 1952 segregation had been terminated in two cities.[40] In two others[41] boards of education had begun the process of desegregation. In the remaining six,[42] including Kansas City, where both elementary and high schools were separate, about 7,000 black students remained in segregated schools.

A review of the Kansas statutes does not disclose the full extent of school segregation. Without authority but in response to community pressures, boards of education and school administrators outside of cities of the first class devised and carried out plans for racial separation of students in separate buildings or classrooms. These plans often existed with black acquiescence. Occasionally, they were challenged in the courts.

Judicial History

The state supreme court sits at the apex of the judicial hierarchy. Between 1881 and 1941 the court heard and decided twelve cases involving public school segregation. Taken together the cases show a disposition of the court to construe the segregation statute narrowly against the school districts and limit its operation to its plain terms. On six occasions the court struck down segregated schools not located in cities of the first class, declaring and confirming the rule that racially segregated public schools were permitted only when and to the extent that the power to segregate had been clearly conferred by the legislature.[43] Two cases saw travel hazards encountered by black students en route to and from their assigned schools as relevant to the issue of equality.[44] Two other cases found that junior high schools, in which seventh-, eighth-, and ninth-grade students were enrolled, were not elementary schools within the meaning of the law.[45] One case in which the plaintiff failed to pursue the inequality issue was decided adversely to her on unrelated technical grounds.[46] Only one plaintiff asserted the federal constitutional objection later raised successfully in *Brown*.

From the standpoint of the state's position in *Brown* the 1903 case of *Reynolds v. Board of Education of Topeka* was the most important Kansas precedent.[47] Like Oliver Brown, William Reynolds, a black resident of Topeka, attempted to enroll his child in the neighborhood school. The son was denied admission solely on the basis of his color. Reynolds sued, claiming that the statute that purported to empower

Topeka to segregate its elementary schools was invalid because it denied the equal protection of the laws guaranteed by the Fourteenth Amendment. He lost. The opinion was written by Justice Rousseau A. Burch, who was widely respected as a jurist and scholar. Justice Burch considered the claimed denial of equal protection. He found no authority to support Reynolds's claim. He found much contrary to it. He found no evidence in the record to show substantial inequality. He considered cases from other jurisdictions with emphasis on *Plessy v. Ferguson*. He found the separate-but-equal doctrine of *Plessy* to be controlling. Had the quantum of precedent been less or had it weighed less heavily on Justice Burch's judicial conscience, one wonders what his decision might have been. Perhaps his own comment may provide an inkling as to his feeling: "The question is solely one of power and not of policy. Whether, in view of the history of this state, the traditions of its people, the composition and quality of its citizenship, its political and social ideals, and the relations of the white and colored people of large cities to each other, such a law is wise and beneficent this court is forbidden to investigate."[48]

An overview of the judicial history of the Kansas school segregation law leads to the following general conclusions: first, the separate-but-equal doctrine was accepted as valid law; second, the general policy of the state favored unrestricted admission of all students to the public schools; third, the legislature might permit variations from the general rule by clearly expressed exceptions created for defined classes of school districts; fourth, such exceptions were to be construed narrowly against the districts; and fifth, equality of facilities and educational opportunity was critical, and any condition that impinged on equality would vitiate the separation.

Reading between lines I have sensed a measure of personal discomfort felt by the justices as they applied what they understood to be the law. The first case challenging segregation was decided in 1881. The author of the opinion, while expressing doubt, assumes without being required to decide that the 1879 statute was valid. But he asks: "Is it not better for the grand aggregate of human society, as well as for individuals, that all children should mingle together and learn to know each other?" Later he comments: "As a rule, people cannot afford to be ignorant of the society which surrounds them; and as all kinds of people must live together in the same society, it would seem to be better that all should be taught in the same

schools."[49] Thus, at this early stage there emerges evidence of the recurring dilemma in the history of school segregation in Kansas—the
conflict between the law and the reason and conscience of many of
those bound to implement its commands.

The View of the People

To focus attention on the law as enacted by the legislature and interpreted by the courts is to present an incomplete picture of the history of school segregation in Kansas. Half of the cases reaching the
Supreme Court prior to 1954 involved attempts by unauthorized
school districts to separate students on the basis of race. Uniformly,
those efforts failed, but similar practices prevailed in other communities outside first-class cities and continued with the approval of the
people or the want of challenge by the black residents. It is a fact of
history that black schools were often inferior to those open to whites
but that inequality existed because no legal remedy was sought. In
other cases demography and economics combined to produce
schools that were both separate and inferior. Traditionally, the Kansas
common schools derived their support from the taxation of property
within the districts. Black neighborhoods were seldom affluent. As
then understood, equality meant equality within the district; thus, an
all-black common-school district with meager resources might maintain an all-black inferior school in violation of no federal or state law.

From the earliest days of statehood few Kansans denied the need
for black education. Education of freedmen was said to benefit the
state in that it helped them to become self-sufficient and lessened the
likelihood of their becoming public charges or resorting to crime. If
we can rely upon the statements of public figures, it was also believed that all students, regardless of color, should enjoy equal educational opportunity. At the same time they believed that local circumstances might favor separate schools and that local officials should
have the power to determine whether such circumstances existed.
Few found the idea of separate schools offensive. Most early Kansans
were the inheritors of a tradition that sanctioned separate schools,
and their attitudes had been conditioned by their history. Some were
motivated by prejudice—a belief in the inferiority of the black race.
Others took a more benign view: they believed that the cultural and
intellectual experiences of the freed slaves were so different from

those of the white community that equality of opportunity could be assured only by separate and special educational programs. Most probably had thought little and formulated few opinions about the issue. They were uncomfortable when too close to people who were different; hence, they accepted the idea of separateness and enacted it into law.

Although the law demanded equality of opportunity for black children, the people were lethargic in their responses. During the early years almost all public school students were white. The few black children who attended school were taught in programs supported by private charity. Many received no schooling. Few whites were concerned. Little attention was given to the education of black children.

During the latter part of the Civil War, as black migration to Kansas began to accelerate, it became clear that the private freedmen's or charity schools lacked resources to cope with the demands for black education. In 1866 a move to enlarge the opportunities for Negro education was initiated by the teachers in the public schools. At the meeting of the State Teachers Association in July it was resolved "that we as teachers use our best endeavors to overcome unreasonable prejudice existing in certain localities against the admission of colored children upon equal terms with the white children as guaranteed by the spirit of the law of our state."[50] In 1867 the state superintendent of public instruction complained that of 4,535 resident Negro children of school age, only half were enrolled in the public schools.[51]

In what was apparently an effort to remedy the condition about which the superintendent complained, the 1867 legislature imposed penalties on district boards refusing admission of any eligible child to the common schools of the district.[52] Whether the prescribed penalties were enforced or effective is not a matter of record. The following year a decrease in the number of colored students enrolled in public schools was reported. Part of the decrease may be attributed to changed methods of reporting, but the report adds:

In some localities, a very great prejudice against the co-education of the races, still exists. It is noticeable, also, that the greater prejudice prevails in communities less advanced in general intelligence. In a few districts, schools for the white children, even, were entirely suspended, in order to deprive a few colored children of the equal educational advantages which the law guarantees to all the children of the State, irrespective of caste or color.[53]

In 1870 the legislature was informed that the closing of public schools to avoid racial mixing was a "notorious fact."[54]

Most of those who protested the absence or inequality of facilities for black education seem to have approved or accepted racially segregated schools in districts where it was locally determined that such separation was feasible and could assure equality of opportunity. A minority, including many with special responsibility for education, questioned whether equality was possible in a segregated system. Early dissents from the prevailing view were expressed by teachers, journalists, and educational administrators.[55] During the economically depressed 1870s the cost of maintaining separate schools was a matter of concern to many. Deeming racially separate schools to be the result of "costly prejudice," thoughtful journalists asked their readers if their prejudice was worth the cost.[56] White leaders in the educational community raised similar questions. The state superintendent inquired: "Why should a small district struggle to maintain separate schools, when the thing is impracticable, and cannot be done without injury to all classes. Why not permit all the children of the community, without distinction of condition or color, to enter our public schools together. . . . And I submit, that the course which I have indicated, is the only course worthy a citizen of Kansas."[57]

With numbers never exceeding 5 percent of the state's population, the blacks were hardly a significant political force in Kansas. However, their voices were sometimes heard to protest against racial segregation. Black organizations and black newspapers were unanimous in their demands for equal educational opportunity. The African-American press of the time, consisting of only a handful of publications, had little influence outside the black community, but it was unified and vigorous in its opposition to racially separate schools. It argued that such separation inevitably resulted in an inequality disadvantageous to the black students and tended to perpetuate racial prejudice.[58]

Regardless of their intellectual and moral quality, the arguments of the antisegregationists were rejected by an unsympathetic majority. To many the integration of education was a step toward social integration and to eventual mongrelization and the loss of racial identity. One editor put it thus:

> This idea of social Negro equality can never be engrafted in the American people. And why should it be? Has not the maker of the Universe placed an unmistakable mark on the two races, the nature of which is to forbid social alliances, and consequently social contact. The Negro may be the superior of the two races, but admitting that he is, does not justify his amalgamating with the white. We have fought for, and advocated equal rights for every human being under this government, but we are not yet ready to array ourselves in antagonism to the immutable laws of nature.[59]

The 1870s were years of growth and optimism in Kansas. There remained millions of unclaimed and unsettled acres in the public domain and in the hands of railroad companies to whom grants had been made. Elaborate promotional campaigns were undertaken to attract immigrants of "the better sort" from Europe and the eastern United States. The most desired new settlers were those who were ethnically, politically, and philosophically compatible with other Kansans and who had the means and industry to be self-supporting and contribute to the economy of the state upon their arrival. The freedmen of the South did not fit this pattern.

Negro migration to Kansas had begun during the Civil War and continued through the seventies. So long as the growth of the black population was moderate, steady, and predictable, and the migrants were sufficiently propertied or skilled to be self-sustaining, interracial tension appears not to have been aggravated. Indeed, the Civil Rights Act of 1874 and the repeal of the school segregation provisions in 1876 might cause one to infer that the acceptance and assimilation of blacks was progressing. Near the end of the decade the trend changed abruptly and dramatically. Extreme poverty and unsettled political conditions combined with the exhortations of black leaders to produce a frantic, unplanned, unorganized, and greatly accelerated migration of former slaves from their southern homelands to the more benign frontier states further north. Kansas, unrealistically perceived to be a land of freedom, equality, and opportunity, became the destination of many, perhaps most, of those who sought new homes. These migrants became known to history as the Exodusters.

No one knows how many blacks moved to Kansas during the period 1878–1881. The 1880 federal census shows an increase of about 26,000 during the preceding decade. This figure may be low since some Exodusters did not remain in Kansas but returned to their homes in the South or moved on to other states. Whatever their number, the arrival of the Exodusters is a significant episode in the history of interracial relationships in Kansas.

Unlike the earlier migrants, many of the Exodusters were destitute and unable to complete their trip to Kansas without financial help. No public funds were available for this purpose. Philanthropists and private charities en route provided limited and grudging assistance, largely for the purpose of enabling the unwanted travelers to keep moving. A similar lack of enthusiasm met the black home seekers at the towns where they disembarked on the eastern edge of Kansas. Having neither the resources nor the desire to absorb them, local relief groups seem to have emphasized efforts to assist the black newcomers to settle elsewhere. Topeka was the place where many Exoduster trails converged.

John P. St. John was governor of Kansas during the time of the Exodus. When urged to take steps to bar the Exodusters from the state, he declined, saying that "so long as I am governor of the state, there shall never be placed at the portals of Kansas a sentinel to make politics, religion, race or color a condition precedent to the right of any human being to come within its borders."[60] Denied federal, state, and local financial assistance, he sought relief funds from other states and philanthropists living elsewhere. It is reported that about $150,000 were raised for the assistance of freedmen during the first year of the Exodus.[61] Under St. John's leadership the Kansas Freedman's Relief Association found employment for many of the migrants and assisted in resettling them in other parts of the state.

Did Governor St. John's sympathetic view of the Exodusters represent the attitudes of the people of Kansas who were his constituents? Obviously, when cast in those terms the question cannot be answered. Political unanimity does not often appear in the pages of Kansas history. Many were in abstract agreement with his position, but few were willing to lend concrete support. Most of the financial support for the Kansas Freedman's Relief Association came from sources outside the state. Local contributions were not substantial. The governor was subjected to much adverse criticism and personal abuse. He was burned in effigy, called "nigger lover St. John," accused of inviting the Exodusters to increase his political following, with diverting relief funds to campaign purposes, and with hurting the state's image by pleas for outside aid.[62] Although his critics were not in the majority, they were numerous enough to be heard loudly and often. In 1882 Governor St. John became the state's first Republican governor to be denied reelection. His role in dealing with the Exodus was overshadowed by other issues, but his benign attitude toward the black invaders from the South compounded the case against his candidacy.

By the end of 1880 the Exodus was over. Historians may speculate as to whether the Exodus had an effect on later race relations in Kansas. In my view, its impact was significant. When the first Exodusters arrived, Kansas was in its seventeenth year of statehood. It had survived war, drought, grasshopper invasions, near famine, and financial panic. Economic and political stability were among the things hoped for but not yet achieved. Most Kansans were struggling to overcome poverty and hardship. Their public institutions and services were less than sufficient. It was inevitable that the arrival of uninvited and unwanted masses to compete for economic advantage and to place additional strains on community services and public and private charities should arouse resentment. Among white Kansans, conscious of the different color, manner of speaking, ethnic origins, and cultural values of the Exodusters, waning, perhaps latent, prejudices were revived and reinforced. While conceding the basic rights of blacks, the white majority set up and continued barriers, legal and otherwise, to prevent their full integration into Kansas society. Its unarticulated objective seemed the creation of a separate but equal world for Negroes. Because whites thought blacks were "immoral," it was assumed that the mixing of black and white children in the schools would be harmful to the whites.[63] One result was the 1879 law permitting segregation in cities with the largest black populations, and the existence of separate schools in other communities without benefit of law but with the people's approval.

During the 1880s and 1890s the people of the state settled into a pattern of racial separation—so long as it violated no constitutional or statutory restraint nor cost too much. Protests were heard from black organizations and black journalists, but they evoked few responses. By 1900 most blacks seem to have acquiesced in the roles to which they were assigned. When in 1905 the legislature enlarged the segregated schools of Kansas City by permitting the board of education to classify high school students on the basis of race,[64] the governor, in advising the legislature of his approval of the amendment, expressed grave personal misgivings, citing his belief in equality before the law and his abhorrence of race-based discrimination. He concluded, however, that to permit the bill to become law would be in the interests of blacks and whites alike, commenting that "in this opinion I seem to be sustained by an overwhelming majority of the people on the ground, as well as by a very large majority of the many able and conservative men with whom I have counseled from other parts of the state."[65] Again, the voice of the people was heard above the whisperings of conscience and reason.

After 1905 there was no significant change in the law of Kansas relating to segregated schools. Most cities of the first class segregated their students. A few other communities practiced segregation without legal sanction but with public approval. Districts with fewer black students, less sensitive to the fancied Negro menace and finding dual schools too costly, admitted students to all schools without reference to color. Regardless of place of residence or political preference, most Kansans accepted and gave lip service to the principle of separate but equal as ordained by the Kansas legislature and affirmed by the supreme court of the state.

AGAIN—WHY KANSAS?

As a Kansan and a traditionalist I honor the history of my state. During the more than eight decades that I have been a Kansan, history has often helped me to understand and to explain public issues of current concern. At the same time, I am not unmindful of two basic premises: first, to explain is not to justify; and second, change is pervasive, and the assumptions of history are subject to a continuous process of evaluation. Hence, when confronted with the question, Why Kansas? I am hardly satisfied with a response that refers only to events that occurred generations before *Brown*. In 1859 most black residents of the United States were slaves. Most of the few that had gained the status of "free Negroes" were only a generation or two removed from slavery. Among the Wyandotte delegates who were the most vigorous opponents of slavery, questions were raised as to whether a people whose intellectual and cultural development had been arrested by centuries of slavery were capable of self-government or of responding to education in the same manner and to the same extent as others who were less disadvantaged. Thus, many delegates justified the exclusion of blacks from the mainstream of the state's political and cultural life.

By mid-twentieth century the dubious assumptions of 1859 clearly could no longer be supported. The black population of Kansas had increased one hundredfold by 1950. Black students were performing competently in racially mixed common and secondary schools in most areas of Kansas and were pursuing courses of higher education in the state's colleges and universities. Granted the suffrage by the Fifteenth Amendment to the Constitution of the United States, blacks voted responsibly in elections and had served in public office on state, county, and local levels. At the same time, education had become one of the most important activities of state and local government. Knowledge of the world and its ways had become critical to survival and success. In every community the physical facilities for education represented a major public investment. Compulsory school attendance laws applied to whites and blacks alike.

On the national level, an increased concern for equality of opportunity to participate fully in the educational process was reflected in a series of Supreme Court cases dealing with higher education. Although each of these cases was decided on a finding of inequality, all involved separate facilities and tended to raise the issue of whether, in public education, separate facilities can be equal.

If the question, Why Kansas? had been framed differently (or if I had interpreted it differently)—if the inquiry had been For what reasons in 1951 did racially segregated schools exist in Topeka, Kansas?—I could not have answered. Now, forty years after the fact and no longer subject to the constraints of advocacy, I say without equivocation that to me the Topeka policy represented neither good government, good morals, nor good sense. However, I cannot confidently say whether four decades ago my feeling was or was not different from now. I was then a lawyer representing a litigant and concerned with a question of constitutional law. The Fourteenth

Amendment, the statutes of Kansas, and the policies of the Topeka Board of Education are not enactments of my personal predilections. Hence, my personal feeling was not relevant. In the role in which I was cast by circumstance I believed it was my duty to analyze, understand, and present the legal posture of Kansas in its most favorable light. Some have said the view that I have taken is simplistic, unimaginative, and even cynical. My response is that the belief is mine, and it is honest.

Before the Supreme Court, Kansas appeared neither as a penitent transgressor nor as an intransigent member of the family of states. It appeared to inform the Court of the history and traditional cultural patterns of Kansans and its understanding of the relevant judicial precedents. It appeared to support what its people believed to be the strength and fiber of the federal system—that local self-government should prevail in those matters in which it is competent to be effective, and that government of local schools is within that competence. A sound disposition of the issue raised in *Brown* required that the Supreme Court be informed of these concerns along with the other relevant contentions. Patently, the views of Kansans could best be expressed by the officers enjoined by law to represent the state. That is why Kansas and its counsel were there.

3

Why Me?

I first saw Topeka when I was eight or nine years old and visited there at the home of a friend. After more than seventy years I remember few particulars of that visit—only the excitement that I felt at being in a city of nearly 50,000 people. Later events have refreshed my recollection of one part of the experience. My friend's family lived in a racially mixed neighborhood, not far from Sumner School. Thirty years later a newer Sumner gained a place in history when its principal denied enrollment to Linda Brown. As a child I did not have the word "racism" in my vocabulary, and I was not then aware of the barrier that is supposed to separate white people from black people. Hence, I saw nothing remarkable in the mutual respect and cordiality between my friend's family and their black neighbors.

GROWING UP

My first two decades—nearly one-fourth of my life—were spent on a Kansas farm near the rural village of Quenemo, about forty miles southeast of Topeka. It was a pleasant neighborhood of farms

51

and families. Located in the valley of a crooked, sluggish stream euphemistically called the Marais des Cygnes River, it was a place of modest homes, fertile fields, and green pastures.

There was little ethnic or cultural diversity in our neighborhood. Indeed, we were inclined to suspect those who looked and thought differently than we. The surnames in the telephone book and on the roadside mailboxes were mainly of English, German, or Scandinavian origins. Exceptions to the neighborhood homogeneity were few. Four or five Hispanic families, immigrants from Mexico, lived on the edge of town on land adjacent to the railroad right-of-way and supplied labor for the maintenance of the Santa Fe tracks. The Mexican adults spoke little or no English. They were Roman Catholic. I assumed that it was by their own choice that they lived aloof from the Anglo community. At the same time, I am not aware that the community made any effort to involve them in its affairs.

Three residents of the community were black, and I knew them only by sight and report. An elderly black couple lived in town. Both worked regularly, he as a handy man with skills as a carpenter, stonemason, and mechanic; she did household service. Their children, who had attended the public schools, had gone elsewhere to pursue careers. The parents continued to live in, but were not quite members of, the community. They were respected as honest, industrious, dependable, and law-abiding people. Moreover, it was said that they "knew their place." The third black resident of the township was a man of middle age who lived on a small farm outside of town. He was single and was seldom seen at community events. I had no personal acquaintance with any of our black neighbors. In fact, I never spoke with a black person until I entered the university at the age of nineteen years.

Residents of our neighborhood, like most rural Kansans, knew little and thought little about interracial problems. In a community of people that are ethnically and culturally alike, where there are no criteria for discrimination, such problems do not exist. However, there was an implicit assumption of white superiority. If the minority population had been sufficient to make racially separate schools economically feasible and if the law had permitted it, I suspect that most of my neighbors would have approved. Although they recognized the rights and aspirations of all, they were more comfortable with people of their own kind. To that extent, they were probably nonpracticing racists. Whether they were blameworthy should be judged, I suggest, by the standards of their own time.

I cannot say when my awareness of Topeka began, but it was early in my life. As a youngster I knew that Topeka was the capital city where the state officers lived and the laws were made. News from the outside came to us through the columns of the *Topeka Daily Capital*. We also read *Capper's Weekly, Kansas Farmer Mail and Breeze,* and *Household Magazine*, all Topeka-based publications. In the late twenties radio came into our home. Most often we were tuned to station WIBW in Topeka.

Most of my rare boyhood visits to Topeka happened at fair time. The annual Kansas Free Fair at the end of summer was an important cultural event of northeast Kansas. For a full week the fairgrounds teemed with Kansans viewing exhibitions of livestock, farm produce, domestic and fine arts, crafts, and a wide range of business, educational, and political promotions. A huge carnival with rides, games, sideshows, and other attractions was designed to insure that few left the fair with his or her purse intact. Added entertainment included fireworks, horse racing, and performances by stars imported from Hollywood, Broadway, and Nashville. For us the fair was a daylong adventure. Although time has consigned the fair to history, it remains a vivid part of my remembrance of Topeka.

As my personal horizons expanded, my interest in Topeka began to reach beyond the fairgrounds. On several trips I walked the mile or so to the Statehouse, the center of Kansas government. At the Statehouse I visited the governor's office, saw the chambers of the Senate and the House of Representatives, and even rested in the room where the Kansas Supreme Court sat to hear arguments. From the fifth floor I climbed the 200 or so steps to the dome, which rose 281 feet above the surrounding lawns, and from which, on a clear day, one could see far beyond Topeka's outer boundaries. Leaving the building, I descended the broad south steps, leading down from the second floor, where governors and other elected state officials have traditionally stood while taking the oath of office. In September 1932, I stood at the foot of the steps to hear Franklin D. Roosevelt deliver a major campaign speech, addressed to the farmers of America. Four years later I watched and heard Alf Landon, then governor of Kansas, speak from the same rostrum to accept the Republican nomination to oppose FDR's reelection.

The Memorial Building across the street from the Statehouse was the home of the Kansas State Historical Society. Several of my early visits to Topeka included visits to the Museum of History and hours of immersion in the history and traditions of my state. The things that I learned there and the views that I formed were hardly profound and seldom tested by criticism, but they were important parts of my early Topeka experience. By that experience I was persuaded that Kansas was my place and that elsewhere I would be a stranger.

At the age of sixteen I was graduated from Quenemo High School. It was 1930, the first year of the Great Depression. I had begun to think of a career in law and, maybe, politics, but bank failure, drought, and impending foreclosure made college impossible. For three years I worked, waited, and looked for the light at the end of the tunnel. Finally, in 1933, a few summer showers passed through our neighborhood, and government-encouraged restrictions on agricultural production triggered a mild rise in hog prices. I had acquired forty acres of harvestable corn and a dozen shoats, so I cashed in at the end of summer, and with the promise of a job for room and board, I enrolled at the University of Kansas.

LAWRENCE—THE UNIVERSITY

Kansans know that the University of Kansas, usually called KU, is at Lawrence, situated on a high (for Kansas) elevation that overlooks the city and the valley where the Wakarusa River flows into the Kansas or Kaw. The site and the campus that sits upon it are known to Jayhawkers as Mount Oread but often less romantically spoken of as "the hill." Lawrence is about forty miles northeast of Quenemo and twenty-five miles east of Topeka. Within the area enclosed by an upside-down isosceles triangle, with Quenemo, Topeka, and Lawrence marking its three angles, is my home country. Although I have sojourned in New York and in the far West and have wandered from Turkey to Tokyo, from Tangier to Zamboanga and places between and beyond, my heart has never left Kansas. Here is my world, warts and all. Perhaps this helps to explain Richard Kluger's assertion that "by eastern standards, Paul Wilson was a hayseed."[1]

In 1933 Lawrence had fewer than 15,000 residents, exclusive of university students whose homes were elsewhere. Founded in 1854

by New Englanders under the aegis of the New England Emigrant
Aid Company, the town had been an important center of free-state
activity during the territorial period. Eighty years later Lawrencians
still thought of themselves as the spiritual and cultural heirs of New
England. The main commercial street is called Massachusetts, and
other public ways in the original town bear the names of the New England colonies. The people of Lawrence were mostly white, Protestant, Republican, and of northern European stock. A few hundred
black citizens were largely concentrated in neighborhoods north of
the Kaw or east of Massachusetts and maintained low profiles elsewhere.

Four thousand and six students were enrolled at KU during the
academic year 1933–1934. Ninety-nine Kansas counties contributed
about 80 percent of the enrollees, and the balance came from other
states and foreign countries. Men outnumbered women by about two
to one. Whites outnumbered blacks twenty to one. My first year at
KU was probably the most exciting period of my life. The ascent from
a hardscrabble farm in Osage County to the world of books and
scholars, libraries and laboratories atop Mount Oread was, for me,
something like a trip to the moon. As I now reflect, I am uncomforta-
bly aware that the euphoria that I experienced was not pervasive. The
black student beside whom I sat during English History lectures left
the classroom to enter a world quite different from the one I enjoyed.

The university had enrolled its first students in 1866. In the beginning only preparatory classes were offered, and in 1870 the first
black student, a woman, entered the preparatory class. Although
blacks were enrolled in each succeeding year, most dropped out before graduation. In 1885 the first black graduate was awarded the degree Bachelor of Didactics.[2] Negro enrollment grew slowly, and by
1933 the number had not reached 200. Racial discrimination in state
institutions had been expressly prohibited by law since 1874, and so
far as I know, there was no discrimination in the academic programs
at KU. Beyond the narrow limits of academe, blacks and whites lived
in separate and different environments. In the university cafeteria
blacks were permitted to sit only in a restricted section of the dining
room. Although white students might take meals in the black section
if they desired, black students could not sit elsewhere. At university
concerts and athletic contests blacks were seated only in sections reserved for them. Economic arguments were advanced to justify these

policies. It was claimed that the specter of racially mixed seating would discourage white patronage.[3]

In the early 1930s there was no black participation in intercollegiate sports at KU. University officials rationalized their exclusion by shifting the responsibility to other institutions. Kansas was a member of the Big Six Athletic Conference, which later expanded to become the Big Eight. Then, as now, the Universities of Missouri and Oklahoma were members of the conference. Neither admitted black students, and neither permitted their athletic teams to compete against black opponents. Other schools in the conference in deference to their Tiger and Sooner brethren entered into a "gentlemen's agreement" that no member of the conference would field black athletes in intercollegiate games. An interesting problem was created by the restriction on access to the university swimming pool. The catalog stated that every student must be able to swim by the time of graduation.[4] At the same time admission to the university pool was limited to whites only. Although the swimming requirement might be waived at the request of the student, some black students declined to make that request. In such cases it was apparently necessary for the Negro student to arrange specially to be admitted to the pool for swimming instruction at times when there were no white swimmers.[5]

Most student organizations were lily-white, the notable exception being the KU-Y, which coordinated the programs of the campus Young Men's and Women's Christian Associations and which actively sought black members. Negroes were not members of the glee clubs, the band, the orchestra, and other student musical organizations. They were not admitted to ROTC. They did not participate in debate and forensics. I cannot say whether they were always deliberately excluded, but I know from observation that no black faces appeared in group photos of students engaged in those activities.

The campus social and political life in that day was dominated by the Greek-letter societies. In 1933 fifteen national fraternities and ten sororities had chapters and houses at KU. None admitted Negroes to membership. In addition three or four all-black living groups occupied their own houses and identified themselves by Greek letters. The men's and women's Panhellenic councils, which fixed standards and adopted rules for the governance of the Greek societies, were composed of representatives of only the white organizations. The Greek-letter organizations dominated student politics. During my student years no Negro was ever elected to a position in campus government or to a class office.

Student living was segregated. Racially mixed housing was virtually unknown. The house where I lived for three years was the home of a Christian widow of mature years and benign disposition. Six white, male students occupied the second floor of her two-story house. At a time when she needed help for house maintenance, a black graduate student came to her door seeking to exchange work for a place to live. He was permitted to move into improvised quarters in the basement only after the widow had secured the express approval of each white occupant of the house, assuring them that he would use separate bathroom facilities and would enter the house only through a side door leading directly to the basement.

The 1930s was a time of big bands, and much of the student social activity consisted of ballroom dancing. To the frequent all-university parties held in the Kansas Memorial Union building all students, except blacks, were invited. Black students had their own parties in rented halls at off-campus locations. A few years earlier a white student writer in a campus publication had expressed the prevailing white student attitude thus: "To permit the Negro to attend the Junior Prom and the Varsity dances and to give him representation in the Inter-Fraternity Council is to break down social segregation. . . . We do not wish to deny the Negro an opportunity for justice and a happy life, but we do ask that he obtain his justice and live his own life among his own people."[6] Was this what was meant by separate but equal?

Although many Kansans regarded KU as an elitist school and referred to Mount Oread as "Snob Hill," the discrimination on the campus differed little from that experienced by blacks in other places. Students came to KU from all parts of the state, and their attitudes were those of the families and communities back home. In the city of Lawrence, known historically as a citadel of freedom, Negroes were either segregated or excluded by restaurants, hotels, theaters, swimming pools, barber shops, pool halls, golf courses, and most other places of public accommodation and entertainment. Few of the amenities mentioned by the chamber of commerce when boasting of the quality of life in Lawrence were enjoyed by black residents. Even in their worship of their common God, blacks and whites were separated. There were Negro churches and white churches, black congregations and white congregations, all seeking the same salvation.

As a student, I knew few of my black counterparts, and I can claim a close friendship with none. In 1934 I took a beginning course in public speaking. Twenty-eight white and two black students were enrolled in the class. Most of the classroom work consisted of oral presentations by students followed by teacher and student critiques. Of the dozens of student speeches that I heard I remember only one. A young black woman spoke of her experience as a black member of a white society. She spoke simply but with feeling that approached eloquence. The class listened. This would be a better story if I could say that then and there I resolved that I would use whatever clout I might acquire to end the condition that she described. But as I try to recall my reaction, it was something like this: I'm sorry; it isn't right; but that's the way the world is; and things will be better later on. I did not foresee that twenty years later chance would cast upon me the responsibility to defend the power of the state of Kansas to contribute to the condition about which she spoke. Still, after sixty years I remember the speech, and the questions it raised still trouble me. Perhaps the impact of her words was greater than I knew.

TOPEKA—1940

I was a student on Mount Oread for five years. During that time I earned bachelor's and master's degrees in political science and completed one year of law school. In the summer of 1938 I was appointed to a position in the Statehouse, where I worked until December 1940. While living in Topeka, I enrolled in the law school at Washburn College, now Washburn University, and completed the work for my LL.B. I was admitted to the Kansas bar in February 1940.

In 1938 the population of Topeka was pushing 65,000 and at least 10,000 people lived in adjacent unincorporated suburbs. The city consisted of three distinct areas, each having its own identifiable geographic, demographic, economic, and social characteristics. The area north of the Kansas River was a community of wage earners, retired persons, and small businesses. Kansas Avenue, the main commercial street, divided the much larger part of the city that was south of the Kaw. East of Kansas Avenue were some of Topeka's major industries.

The people who lived there were mainly blue-collar workers who lived in modest houses in unpretentious neighborhoods. Topeka's Mexican residents, many of whom worked for the Santa Fe railroad, were concentrated there. More blacks lived on the east side than elsewhere in the city. The Topekans who counted (as they viewed it) lived west of the Avenue. In this section one found the rich and those who aspired to be rich, leaders in business and the professions, the biggest houses, the most attractive yards, and the most coveted street addresses. Although many working people, including blacks, lived on the west side, it was not they who set the tone of the area. Gage Park, the showpiece of the city's recreation system, was on the west side, as were Washburn College, Topeka High School, the public library, and the finest churches.

The Topeka of which I had actual knowledge in my student days was the Statehouse, the campus, and the twenty or so blocks that lay between. Other parts of the city I knew by casual observation, hearsay, and report. From the Topeka Avenue bridge that spanned the Kaw and carried traffic high above the railroad tracks and riverfront industries, I could see a cluster of improvised shanties that sheltered the homeless between the tracks and the river's edge. There were ethnic neighborhoods, some of which I was never able to identify. Topekans spoke of Little Russia, of the Germans of St. Joseph's parish, and other concentrations of people with common national heritage. By my time, however, the ancestral ways were being discarded, and dwellers in the former ethnic communities were becoming conforming Kansans. Two groups remained apart. The considerable Mexican community consisted of fairly recent immigrants and kept its separate identity. Older members continued to speak the Spanish language. Held together by Catholicism and the Hispanic tradition, their neighborhood was one of Topeka's more vibrant and interesting ones. The Mexican children were admitted to the white public schools, although many attended parochial institutions.

The few thousand blacks of Topeka were scattered throughout several parts of the city. There were black neighborhoods, such as the Bottoms, east of Kansas Avenue, and Tennessee Town, a few blocks west, but other blacks lived in neighborhoods that were racially mixed. I knew little of black Topeka. The black state employees that I encountered were mainly on the building- and grounds-maintenance staffs. A black person operated the elevator. Another shined shoes. A few clerks and an occasional token professional completed the black Statehouse contingent. During the legislative sessions a few blacks worked as doorkeepers and cloakroom attendants. Of the 165 legislators only 1, a representative from Kansas City, was black. I cannot say why so few black faces appeared in the Statehouse. Whatever the reason, blacks were hardly in a position to have a real role in state government and policy.

It was probably my interest in my job and the study of law that precluded my becoming more aware of Topeka's black community. Indeed, I was hardly conscious of its existence. More than 7 percent of the total population was black, and if I had been less preoccupied and more curious, I might have learned more about their part in the life of the city. As I now reflect, I recall that there were black schools and white schools, black churches and white churches, black neighborhoods and white neighborhoods, and so on. In nonbusiness activities blacks and whites were generally isolated from one another. Places of public entertainment and accommodation were segregated—not by law, but by custom. The restaurant where I took many of my meals displayed a sign that read, "Colored and Mexicans served in sacks only." Movie houses were segregated—one for blacks and five or six for whites—although in the Grand, one of the city's top theaters, I remember a section in the balcony, sometimes called "nigger heaven," reserved for black moviegoers.

At Washburn I knew no black students. My impression is that the white students at Washburn were more tolerant of their black colleagues than those at KU. Several circumstances may have contributed to the different attitude. First, Washburn, originally called Lincoln College, had an early relationship with the Congregational Church, and vestiges of New England Puritanism lingered. Second, Washburn was largely an urban institution. Its white students were more familiar and thus more comfortable with their nonwhite counterparts than most rural Kansas youth who came from communities in which blacks were strangers and suspect. Occasionally, some of my more adventuresome colleagues spoke suggestively of real or imagined Saturday night forays among the fleshpots of the East Bottoms, where the color line grew indistinct. Being of a less daring disposition, I remained innocent of such activities.

"Whatever else it was in 1951, Topeka was a Jim Crow town. It had been as long as anyone could remember.'"[7] Thus writes Richard Kluger. I suggest that author's pontifical declaration needs further examination. The phrase "Jim Crow" is an epithet of uncertain meaning. Presumably, it refers to discrimination against Negroes enforced by legal or traditional sanctions. Except for the board of education policy requiring racially separated elementary schools (a policy that many Topekans regarded as benign), there were no legal or institutional distinctions based on color. In railroad and bus stations blacks and whites used the same waiting areas, drinking fountains, food services, and toilet facilities. On public conveyances blacks sat wherever they chose. No law restricted the access of blacks to the services and facilities of state and local government.

At the same time, candor requires recognition that Topeka was not an integrated community. Black faces did not appear among Topeka's business and civic leaders. There were few black entrepreneurs. Black professionals served mainly black clienteles. Homes in black neighborhoods were usually modest and often indifferently maintained. Black churches, clubs, and lodges served the religious, social, and recreational needs of black Topekans. Custom and tradition had placed blacks outside the mainstream of community life. But in these respects, Topeka was hardly unique. Topeka was representative of mid-century, middle-American cities. The racial separation that existed in Topeka was not the product of a studied and deliberate intention to discriminate. Instead, it was the result of history, indifference, and unexamined assumptions. Perhaps the distinction is too subtle to be meaningful, but I think it is reflected in the Topeka decision not to resist the Supreme Court challenge to its segregated schools.

HERE AND THERE

The 1940s was a decade when the best laid plans of America and Americans went awry. War and readjustment provided the milieu for a reexamination of traditional assumptions and values and may have accelerated maturing concepts of racial equality and civil rights. If my premise is correct, my experience during that time is a part of my story of *Brown* and Topeka and me.

In 1940 I was admitted to the bar of Kansas. In 1941 I married. A few months after my admission to the bar I left Kansas to pursue a career in the Chicago office of a large corporation, but nine months of urban living reinforced my conviction that I am a Kansan and that my roots are too deeply imbedded in the Kansas soil to permit transplanting. In September of 1941 I and my newly pregnant bride set up housekeeping in Ashland, a southwestern Kansas county-seat town whose population just exceeded a thousand. On Sunday morning, December 7, we heard the news of the Japanese attack on Pearl Harbor. As I now reflect, we were then unable to comprehend the impact that the events of that Sunday morning would have on our lives. The next few weeks brought the sobering realization that our world was in a state of convulsion and that our plans and expectations were no longer realistic. On April 9, 1942, our first child was born. Two days later my draft board informed me that my status was being reviewed for possible reclassification. My inference was that my marriage and the birth of our child had occurred too late to support a claim for deferment. Two months later I closed my law office and left Ashland to enter the army with some assurance of an early commission.

Neither the Chicago nor the Ashland experience was of a kind that directed my attention to America's interracial problems. In Chicago I lived in an all-white neighborhood, was a member of an all-white staff serving a mainly white clientele. I knew that on the south side of the city there were many blocks inhabited only by blacks. Friends advised me that in the interest of personal safety I should never venture into that part of the city alone. In Ashland my concerns were limited to the community and my efforts to attract and represent clients; although the census rolls showed four black residents of the county, I knew none of them.

My active military service included about twenty months of stateside training—basic training, Officer Candidate School, and training for overseas combat duty—and a like period of service in the Pacific. Duty assignments in the United States included posts in Arkansas, Georgia, and Florida. There, I had my first impressions of Jim Crow America as I conceived of it. Both rural and urban blacks were concentrated in apparently impoverished neighborhoods. Public facilities and accommodations were totally segregated. Although I had no personal knowledge of the quality of the separate black educational programs, the visible facilities—buildings, landscaping, playground equipment, and so on—led me to the conclusion that they were substantially inferior. I was not insensitive to this pervasive evidence of discrimination, but my feeling was hardly one of outrage. Instead, I was inclined toward an attitude of self-righteousness. In Kansas, I thought, our Negro citizens enjoy more favorable treatment than their counterparts in the South. Fifty years later I recognize the flaw in my thinking. Instead of comparing the status of Kansas blacks and southern blacks, the comparison should have arrayed the condition of black Americans beside that of their white countrymen.

The army into which I was inducted had practiced racial segregation from its beginning. Although there was much evidence to the contrary, there was a persistent and often expressed belief that Negro soldiers lacked the courage and resourcefulness to function effectively in combat. Whereas the World War II draft conscripted blacks to the same extent as whites, most black soldiers were assigned to service rather than combat branches. They handled supplies, drove trucks, operated construction equipment, maintained laundry and sanitation facilities, and provided other indispensable services not involving contact with enemy troops. Although there were no black troops in the command to which I belonged, our efforts were often coordinated with and complemented by those of black units. To my best recollection, their performance was comparable to that of our white troops. Some were good; some were bad; most were satisfactory.

To the extent that I was able to observe them, black units were usually commanded by whites. The army was beginning to commission black officers, but few were assigned to positions of troop leadership. I wondered why. To my unmilitary mind, the idea of black soldiers commanded by white officers was reminiscent of black slavery. I saw many black noncommissioned officers who could competently have commanded platoons and companies. Why, I wondered, were they denied that opportunity? The answer often given by my white colleagues was that black soldiers needed white leadership; that they did not sufficiently respect members of their own race to submit to military discipline imposed by black officers. To me, the answer was not persuasive. My conclusion was that the policy of thrusting white leadership on black troops was the result of history and the military's reluctance to accept change—a reluctance shared by most who find the status quo agreeable.

In the Civil War the blacks recruited for Union service were mainly slaves and others who had recently fled or been emancipated from slavery. Lacking in military experience and skills and without demonstrated capacity for leadership, they seemed to require organization into units under experienced white commanders for proper utilization. The pattern thus established continued far into the twentieth century. By the time of World War II black youths eligible for military service were no longer illiterate. Many had demonstrated the skills and maturity necessary for effective troop leadership. That they were denied this opportunity gave concern to many thoughtful persons. Finally, more than two years after the war's end, equality of treatment and opportunity was decreed.[8] Still, I conclude that the long denial of opportunity to command was not the result of a deliberate purpose of black suppression. It had its origin in the facts of history and owed its continuation to human lethargy—the same causes that in 1951 produced segregated education in Topeka, Kansas.

Unlike the wars in Europe, the Pacific phase of World War II was interracial. I cannot say that an enemy of a different color increases the intensity of feeling and the bitterness of the attack, but, facts and happenings that I observed and inferences that I drew may be relevant to my present views of racism in my world. Our soldiers' first contacts overseas were with the Anzacs—Australians and New Zealanders. They were our allies, and we shared a common cultural heritage. They were our friends. They were white. Next, we met the Papuans and the Melanesian people of the Southwest Pacific. They were friendly but black and, by our standards, primitive. Their villages were off-limits to American GIs, and we seldom encountered them on the beaches and along jungle trails, so our person-to-person contacts were few. As I now recall, our interest in them was mainly curiosity. Whether for racial or cultural reasons, we regarded them as something less than people. They were simply an interesting part of the fauna of the region.

The Japanese were of a different color than we. They were also our enemy. We hated them. Although I have assumed that our hostility was the product of our respective military postures, it may have contained an element of racism. Nearly fifty years later I almost instinctively associate all things Japanese with nights spent in water-filled foxholes on the beaches of New Guinea, with exploding mortar shells and the reports of snipers' rifles. The war's end and our occupation of Japanese cities brought us into contact with Japanese civilians. Then, race was irrelevant. We were the victors; they, the vanquished. By virtue of our military dominance our bidding was their law. We demanded and enjoyed privileges that we denied to the Japanese. Notwithstanding the residue of hostility, and contrary to command directive forbidding fraternization, the GIs quickly established friendly relationships in the Japanese community. As a line officer I occasionally was detailed as Officer of the Day. This duty often required nighttime patrolling of streets where the action was said to be. The sight of a row of GI combat boots beside the doorway of a Japanese house of assignation taught me, a still-naive, white Protestant Kansan, something about humanity. Politics and color are only skin deep.

Between the southwestern islands and Japan there had been a nine-month interlude in the Philippines. The Filipinos were our military allies; they had fought beside American troops in resisting the Japanese invasion. To recover control of the Philippine Islands had been a major objective of the war in the Southwest Pacific. They were our friends. For more than four hundred years they had been ruled by Western powers and exposed to Western civilization. For more than forty years the islanders had been subject to the sovereignty of the United States. They had built cities and universities and cathedrals. They had embraced Western religions and accepted Western ways. My first impressions of the Philippines came at daybreak on a morning in early January 1945, when I waded ashore at Lingayen Gulf with full combat equipment, under the protective cover of artillery fire from warships lying in the harbor. Crossing the beach that had for three days undergone preattack bombing and strafing, we moved along the road leading toward the distant town. Standing among the roadside shambles was a sign announcing that the Rotary Club met each Thursday. Nearby was a Filipino entrepreneur bartering nipa wine to the arriving GIs for cigarettes and chocolate bars. This was like home. Still, the Filipinos had dark faces. Their culture had its roots in the mountain villages and the coconut groves and the rice paddies of their islands. They were not like us. Hence, we could not or did not accept them as peers.

A wartime environment may hardly be the place to observe social interaction. Yet it may say more about basic feelings and instincts than a more thoughtfully contrived environment. News stories reported in the GI media indicated that the relationship between the returning Philippine government-in-exile and the American Supreme Command was wholly amicable—that General MacArthur and President Osmeña met and negotiated as equals. From my vantage point near the bottom of the hierarchy the view was a different one. Our return to the islands and the expulsion of the Japanese had been met with enthusiasm. We came as heroes. We accepted the role, but the conduct of some of us was not always heroic. We claimed the privileges of heroes, but too often, we failed to be sensitive to conflicting claims. Misunderstandings and resentments were inevitable. The Filipinos that we saw most often after the fighting ended were those that worked on the docks or loitered in the streets or sold bad liquor and sleazy merchandise to GIs. Among the Filipinos as in all populations there were thieves and sluggards. Unhappily, people are disposed to overgeneralize about other people and to ascribe to all members of a group the characteristics exhibited by a few. Most Filipinos believed that Americans were rude, arrogant, and insensitive. Most GIs believed that Filipinos were knaves and blackguards. Whether right or wrong, belief and not fact, myth and not reality, determine how people treat one another. We saw the Filipinos as different in color and culture—hence, inferior.

In mid-August 1945 the war ended. Five months later I was home, ready to resume my role as a Kansas country lawyer. I chose to locate my home and launch my career in Lyndon, the county seat of Osage County, where I had begun life and with which I had long been emotionally involved. Osage County in 1946 had a population of 13,009, which included a dozen blacks. Seven hundred people lived in Lyndon. All were white. It was commonly said that no Negro could remain in town overnight unless he was in jail. Service was not available to blacks in the dining rooms of either of the town's two restaurants. Other places of public accommodations served only whites.

I remained in Lyndon four years, engaging in general civil practice and serving as prosecuting attorney. In addition to prosecuting violators of state law, I helped farmers and townspeople who sought my assistance and advice with a wide range of problems, personal, financial, and political, as well as legal. In rural communities where there is a dearth of social services, the country lawyer acts as priest, psychiatrist, social worker, and friend, as well as an advocate before the bar.

In my four years in Lyndon I represented no black plaintiffs. I appeared for no black defendants, nor did I prosecute any black offenders. I examined no black witnesses and faced no black jurors. Mine was a world of white people. Blacks inhabited other places. I felt no urge that it should be otherwise.

TOPEKA AGAIN

Late in 1949 a call from the governor's office invited me to consider a position in state government. The invitation came at a time when I had just lost a case in court, when my family responsibilities were increasing more rapidly than my income, and when the idyllic life of a country lawyer was beginning to lose its charm. Also, I then had a vague interest in state politics. A few weeks later I closed my Lyndon office, and shortly after January 1, 1950, we moved to Topeka. Our new home was in Highland Park, an unincorporated suburb adjacent to the city. The Highland Park School District was then a common-school district not within the jurisdiction of the Topeka Board of Education. Hence, the schools attended by my eight- and six-year-old daughters were not racially segregated. For the first time they became acquainted with children of another race. As I recall, the fact of race was never mentioned by our children. Their friends, both white and black, were just "kids" with whom they went to school.

In spite of the impact of war, the 1940s had been good years in Topeka. New federal programs and projects combined with growth of war-related industries to accelerate the growth of population and the tempo of the economy. The 1950 census listed nearly 90,000 residents of the city with another 20,000 living in the environs. Business was good. People were gainfully employed. Social services were being expanded. New cultural opportunities were emerging. From my perspective as one who was young, strong, well-educated, agreeably employed, and white, Topeka in 1950 was a good place to live. Unhappily, there were others who saw it differently. It was in the fall of 1950 that Oliver Brown attempted to enroll his daughter Linda in Sumner School and was rebuffed. At the church we attended I encountered a black man of my own age whom I had known at the university, where he was recognized as a good student, ambitious for a professional career. In 1950 he was the church janitor.

Young blacks returning to Topeka from the military service and from colleges and universities were beginning to ask questions about their status in the community. More confident, more articulate, better informed, and less acquiescent than their parents, they were beginning to reject the status quo. Their first concern was their inability to find suitable employment. To many employers, the color of an applicant's skin determined the job for which he would be considered and his chance for promotion. Blacks were often employed as household workers and window washers. They seldom were considered for skilled, managerial, or professional positions. By 1950 most Topekans were aware of the restiveness in the black community. There were few strident protests and, so far as I know, no demonstrations in the streets, but the newspapers began to report increased activity by the National Association for the Advancement of Colored People and other civil rights groups. Black Topekans, these groups contended, did not have the same opportunity to enjoy the good life that Topeka offered to its white citizens. Topeka, they argued, ought to do better. As a mildly interested bystander with no chips in the game, I was inclined to agree with their contentions.

By 1951 I was becoming an experienced lawyer. I had advised and represented both private litigants and public officers. I had appeared for clients in the trial courts of at least two dozen counties of the state and in the federal courts for the district of Kansas. However, my experience was deficient in that I had never argued a case before an appellate court. Conscious of my lack of appellate experience, I sought and was appointed to a position on the staff of the attorney general of Kansas. A year later I argued my first case before an appellate tribunal. The tribunal was the Supreme Court of the United States. The case was *Brown v. Board of Education of Topeka*.

THE FICKLE FINGER OF FATE

Traditionally, the attorney general of Kansas has been a politically sensitive officer. Election to the office was often regarded as a stepping stone to a higher position in state government. In 1951 the incumbent was Harold R. Fatzer, commonly known as "Dick," an able and ambitious officer who later became chief justice of the Kan-

Paul E. Wilson, assistant attorney general of Kansas (1951–1957), wrote the appellee's briefs and represented Kansas at oral argument of *Brown v. Board of Education* in the Supreme Court on December 9, 1952, and December 8, 1953.

sas Supreme Court. When I joined his staff in December 1951, without design or intent, I moved a step closer to a role in the *Brown* cast.

The duties of the Kansas attorney general were then and are now defined by law.[9] They include representing the state before the Kansas Supreme Court in cases where the state is a party or interested. Most cases in that court are appeals from lower courts. Other specific duties are imposed by the statutes but are not important to this commentary. In addition to the powers and duties prescribed by statute, the attorney general, as a constitutional officer with common law antecedents, possesses a residue of inherent but undefined power that enables him to take such legal action as may be necessary to defend and protect the integrity of his sovereign—the state of Kansas.

The internal organization of the 1951 Kansas attorney general's office was not complex. Each of the six assistants was assigned a group of agencies or activities for which he had primary responsibility. Each reported directly to the attorney general. Ad hoc assignments were made when cases raised extraordinary questions or involved situations of special public concern. Among the departments assigned to me were the Office of the Governor and the Department of Public Instruction. Also, my duties were to include advising state law enforcement agencies and local prosecutors. The files in the *Brown* case were on the desk of Willis McQueary, the first assistant, who had appeared for the state in the pretrial and trial proceedings in the district court. I had no particular interest in the case, and it seemed quite unlikely that there would be an occasion for me to become interested.

Historically, ambitious young lawyers who join the staff of the Kansas attorney general do not remain in the office for long periods. The modest salaries and uncertainty of tenure have made the positions unattractive as careers. At the same time, the office has provided an unparalleled opportunity to gain useful experience and broaden one's acquaintance. In January 1951 Willis McQueary decided it was time to move on. He resigned his position to return to private practice in his home community. His departure required the reassignment of his pending files. A few days later Attorney General Fatzer called me to his office. Handing me the *Brown* file, he explained that the district court's decision upholding Topeka's segregated schools had been appealed, and the appeal would probably be argued before the Supreme Court late in 1952. He told me that he planned to present the argument, but he wanted me to assist in his preparation. He instructed me to become acquainted with the trial record, to identify the issues to be argued, and to assemble and analyze all of the relevant legal authorities, both favorable and unfavorable. It was his wish that I should write the first draft of the brief in support of the state's position. He emphasized that he did not intend to support the segregation policy of the Topeka Board of Education. He would argue only that the Kansas statute was not unconstitutional—that *Plessy v. Ferguson* and *Gong Lum v. Rice* remained the law of the land. His final suggestion excited me most. He said: "When I [Fatzer] go to Washington I want you [Wilson] to go with me. We will get you [Wilson] admitted to the Supreme Court bar." It was his thought that I would be present during the argument, that I would not speak but would sit at the counsel table, and that my name would appear as one of the attorneys of record. I was overjoyed.

In 1951 few Kansas lawyers were licensed to practice before the Supreme Court of the United States. That I should join that elite circle strained the limits of belief. With that prospect in view my interest in the case markedly increased. By early summer I had found time to digest the trial record, study the briefs filed in the trial court, and read the authorities cited on both sides. I had begun to explore the broader aspects of the black experience in Kansas with special attention to the quality and accessibility of public education for black children. I would be ready to write the state's brief when the signal was given.

4

In the Trial Court

Claiming denials of the equal protection of the laws guaranteed by the Fourteenth Amendment to the Constitution of the United States, Oliver Brown and his coplaintiffs launched their attack in the United States District Court for the District of Kansas. The defendants were the Topeka Board of Education, Superintendent McFarland, and Sumner Principal Wilson. The state of Kansas was not sued. The relief sought included (1) an adjudication that the state law that permitted the Topeka Board of Education to maintain segregated elementary schools was unconstitutional; (2) a declaration that the policy of the Topeka Board of Education to segregate elementary school students on the basis of race was unconstitutional and void; and (3) a judgment enjoining the board from maintaining and operating racially segregated elementary schools. As required by the statute[1] then applicable to such cases, the plaintiffs asked that three judges be designated to hear the case.

THE ACTORS

The federal judicial district of Kansas is coterminous with the state. In 1951 its two district judges heard cases principally in Kansas

City, Topeka, and Wichita, with occasional sittings in other cities. The chief judge, Arthur J. Mellott, lived in Kansas City and maintained his principal chambers there, while his associate, Judge Delmas C. Hill, lived and had his judicial base in Wichita. Both judges heard cases in Topeka and the other cities designated for sittings of the court. Judge Walter A. Huxman of the United States Court of Appeals for the Tenth Circuit was a resident of Topeka and kept his headquarters there in the Federal Court House. When the *Brown* case was filed in Topeka, the clerk immediately advised Judge Mellott of the filing. Judge Mellott communicated with Judge Orie L. Phillips, chief judge of the Tenth Circuit, requesting that three judges be designated to try the case. Judge Phillips's response was to name Judges Huxman, Mellott, and Hill as members of the three-judge court. Although the state of Kansas was not a named defendant, since the constitutionality of a state statute was being challenged, Judge Mellott ordered that notice of the filing and copies of the complaint be delivered to the governor and the attorney general.

Judges Huxman, Mellott, and Hill, members of the three-judge district court, were all native-born Kansans. All were white, Protestant, and male. All were Democrats who had attained a considerable amount of professional and political experience before ascending to the bench. Lawyers who practiced before them regarded each as an able, fair-minded judge.

Judge Huxman was a graduate of the University of Kansas School of Law. He had practiced in Hutchinson, Kansas, and had served there in county and city offices. Hutchinson schools were not segregated. After serving on the State Tax Commission, he was elected governor in 1936, serving one two-year term. In 1939 he was appointed by President Roosevelt to the court of appeals. He was sixty-four years old when he presided at *Brown*. Judge Huxman was a preeminently humane jurist. He never succumbed to the God complex that affects many judges. Devoid of pomposity, he ascribed his ascent to the court of appeals to his being "the right rat at the right rat hole at the right time." His opinions reflect compassion, an understanding of human problems, and a sense of justice that sometimes reached beyond the limits of stare decisis.

Judge Mellott was a Kansas Citian. He had taught and been engaged in the administration of the rural (hence unsegregated) public schools of Wyandotte County. After studying law at the Kansas City

Members of the three-judge United States District Court that heard *Brown v. Board of Education* in Topeka, June 1951: *(left to right)* Arthur J. Mellott, Delmas C. Hill, and Walter A. Huxman. (Courtesy of the Library, United States Court of Appeals for the Tenth Circuit, Denver, Colorado)

(Missouri) School of Law, he had practiced law, served as judge of a magistrate-level court, and served as county attorney, all in Kansas City. After serving as judge of the United States Tax Court (formerly U.S. Board of Tax Appeals) for ten years, he was appointed to the district bench by President Truman. The black population of Kansas City, Kansas, was about 20 percent of the city's total. Its school system, unlike Topeka's, was segregated on both elementary and secondary levels. We can thus assume that Judge Mellott, who had been a city judge and county prosecutor, had a greater awareness of interracial conflict and accommodation than either of his colleagues on the three-judge court. As a judge, he dominated his courtroom by his personality. Distinguished in manner and deliberate in speech, he exhibited an impeccable courtroom demeanor. Lawyers appearing before him were held to high standards of decorum and conduct. He was sixty-three years of age when he sat in the *Brown* case.

Judge Hill, at the age of forty-five, was the youngest of the trio in both age and years of judicial service. He was appointed to the federal district bench by President Truman in 1949. He was a graduate of the Washburn Law School and had practiced and served as county attorney in rural Pottawatomie County, Kansas. The county had fewer than twenty black residents. Judge Hill served as counsel for the state tax commission, presided as chairman of the Democratic State Committee, and was in the Army Judge Advocate General's Corps during World War II. He was a gracious person, reputed to be a somewhat conservative judge, fair minded, sound thinking, and wholly competent. In 1961, Judge Hill was elevated to the Tenth Circuit bench by President Kennedy.

The plaintiffs' attorneys of record at the pleading and pretrial stages were Charles E. Bledsoe and Charles S. Scott and John J. Scott of the Topeka firm of Scott, Scott, and Scott. For the trial they were joined by Robert L. Carter and Jack Greenberg, of New York, staff attorneys for the Legal Defense Fund. Bledsoe was a former Topeka fireman who, by part-time study at Washburn Law School, had earned a degree and admission to the bar. Although he was in practice in Topeka, he was not particularly visible as a lawyer. He must be credited, however, with being an initiator of the *Brown* litigation and one of the black Topekans who sought and obtained the assistance of the NAACP and its Legal Defense Fund. He was the first Topeka lawyer to correspond with the fund's staff attorneys about the case. Charles Scott related that Bledsoe was chairman of the legal redress committee of the local branch of the NAACP and that the case belonged to him. Sensing the need for local help, he solicited and received the assistance of members of the Scott firm, who appeared as cocounsel and assumed a major role in the pretrial and trial proceedings.

The Scott law office had served the black population of Topeka for nearly thirty-five years. Elisha Scott, its founder, was a native Topekan, a descendant of Exodusters, and a Washburn Law School graduate in the class of 1916. At a time when there were few black lawyers in Kansas, his race, combined with his extraordinary flamboyance, gained him a special place in the Topeka bar. His clients were drawn from Topeka's minority population and whites in the lower economic strata. He was known as an attorney who would go to bat for people who could not find representation elsewhere. Thirty years after his death he remains a legend among Topeka lawyers.

Topeka counsel for the plaintiffs, *Brown v. Board of Education:* (*top left*) John J. Scott, (*top right*) Charles S. Scott, and (*below*) Charles E. Bledsoe. (Courtesy of *Washburn Alumni Review*, December 1989, Topeka.)

Elisha Scott (*opposite*) was a senior member of the law firm of Scott, Scott, and Scott and for more than forty years was the spokesman for many black Topekans. (Courtesy of the Kansas State Historical Society)

An advocate of black equality, Elisha was not a visibly angry militant. He preferred to rely on persuasion and to work within the established power structure. In his time Republicans usually controlled the governments of Kansas and Shawnee County. Elisha was a Republican. In 1930 he ran for the Republican nomination for attorney general. He did not win the nomination, but his vote showed him to have been a serious contender. He continued to be a Republican activist.

By the time of the *Brown* trial Elisha had passed his prime, and the firm's practice was being carried on by his sons, John and Charles. The trial record shows Elisha's presence only once, when he appeared in the courtroom while the trial was in progress and interposed an objection to the testimony of one of plaintiffs' witnesses. The objection was promptly overruled.[2] Some who were present suspected that he was not entirely sober.

John and Charles Scott were, respectively, thirty-two and thirty years old in 1951. John had been admitted to the bar in 1947, and Charles, a year later. Both were graduates of the Washburn Law School and veterans of World War II. After admission to the bar, each had begun to practice in his father's office. Although neither had inherited Elisha's flair for showmanship, they were regarded as sound and competent lawyers and were generally respected by the Topeka bench and bar. Neither was inclined toward militancy, but both were active in the NAACP and shared the concerns of Topeka's blacks. When Charles Bledsoe sought their help they were ready, willing, and able to move.

At the trial the Topeka lawyers were joined by Robert L. Carter and Jack Greenberg. Both were members of the New York bar and staff lawyers for the NAACP Legal Defense Fund. It is my impression that they had masterminded the lawsuit from its earliest stages, advising the local lawyers concerning the plan of attack, preparation of pleadings, assembling of evidence, and other pretrial stages. In the words of Charles Scott, "it was coordinated from the local up to the top level, national level."[3] Carter, thirty-four years old, was a graduate of the Howard University School of Law, whereas Greenberg, twenty-seven, had received his legal education at Columbia University. Despite their youth, both had had substantial experience in public law and civil rights cases. Their post-*Brown* careers led to Carter's appointment to the federal district bench in the Southern District of New York and Greenberg's appointment to the faculty of the Columbia University School of Law and a deanship. Neither had been in Topeka before their appearance in the trial of *Brown v. Board of Education*.

The defendants in the case were represented at the pretrial and trial stages by Lester M. Goodell and George M. Brewster, Topeka attorneys who were partners in the firm of Wheeler, Brewster, Hunt, and Goodell. The firm was an old and respected one engaged in the general civil practice and had represented the board of education for many years. Goodell, known by his clients and associates as "Les," was the senior among the firm's active members. He was fifty-two years old and had practiced law for twenty-six years. In his early years at the bar he had been a prosecutor, serving as assistant county attorney and county attorney and had established a reputation for fairness and compassion. He was not an establishment type. Tall, dark-complexioned, somewhat Lincolnesque in appearance, he was vigorous and forceful. He tried a good lawsuit. Elisha Scott regarded him as a friend. George Brewster was a member of a prominent Kansas family of lawyers, his father having served as United States district attorney when that office represented high professional accomplishment. When he appeared in *Brown*, George Brewster was middle-aged and had been a member of the bar for twenty-two years, practicing in the firm of which his father was a founder. He was a competent and respected lawyer whose practice was largely business oriented. In the *Brown* case he second-chaired Les Goodell, his senior partner.

PRELUDE TO TRIAL

Three-judge cases are rare in the federal district of Kansas. On March 5 Judge Mellott wrote to Judge Huxman noting that the two of them with Judge Hill had been designated to man the three-judge bench. He added, "The experience of both Judge Hill and me in the work of a three-judge court is quite limited, so we will have to depend upon you for appropriate guidance."[4] Presumably, Judge Huxman's experience was greater than that of his colleagues. The statute that then governed three-judge courts provided "any one of the three judges of the court may perform all functions, conduct all proceedings except the trial, enter all orders required or permitted by the rules of civil procedure."[5] The statute did not supply guidelines for avoiding or resolving conflicting orders or determining which judge should ex-

Lester M. Goodell, chief trial counsel for the Topeka Board of Education in the proceedings before the three-judge federal court in June 1951. (Courtesy of Gerald L. Goodell)

ercise administrative control of the case. Judge Mellott was the chief judge of the District of Kansas and exercised general administrative supervision of the docket. Judge Huxman, as a court of appeals judge, outranked Judge Mellott in the judicial hierarchy. In a letter dated March 5, Judge Mellott requested that because of Judge Huxman's location in Topeka, where the case was pending and where all of the attorneys maintained their offices, Judge Huxman take charge of the case and proceedings prior to trial.[6] In his reply, Judge Huxman accepted the responsibility.

Brown v. Board of Education was commenced on February 28, 1951, when the plaintiffs' complaint was filed and a summons was issued to each defendant. Amendments, motions, hearing, and further amendment followed. Finally, on June 7 the defendants answered the twice-amended complaint. The answer admitted some of the plaintiffs' claims, denied others, and placed squarely in issue the lawfulness of Topeka's segregated elementary schools. In cases where the facts in dispute are extensive and complex there is ordinarily a period for discovery or investigation by the parties. *Brown* was a simple case, and no extensive discovery was deemed necessary; the proceeding moved to its next stage, the pretrial conference. The date for the conference was fixed for June 22.

At the pretrial conference the attorneys representing the contending parties appear before the court and determine what issues of fact raised by the complaint and answer are in actual dispute, and what facts may be agreed upon and stipulated to. The purpose of the conference is to expedite the trial or other disposition of the case by restricting proof to those facts actually in controversy. Attorneys for the board of education were apprehensive that the plaintiff's counsel might be uncooperative and seek to burden the record with spurious issues. Lawyers in mid-America—based on experience—are often chary of their more sophisticated brethren from the big cities. Les Goodell thought that, in order to assist the judges to avoid a protracted pretrial hearing, a special master or hearing officer might be appointed to hear the evidence and make suggested findings to the court. Judge Huxman thought otherwise. He wrote to his colleagues, "I doubt whether we will have any difficulty with the local attorneys. What the situation will be with the foreign counsel and there will be foreign counsel, remains to be seen, but we ought to have no difficulty in handling that."[7] At the same time he and Goodell agreed that the parties should each prepare copies of documents and other data on which they wished to rely and submit them to opposing counsel for study before the pretrial conference. Local attorneys for the NAACP approved the plan and agreed to comply. A more serious concern of the judges was the posture of the state of Kansas. A state statute had been attacked as unconstitutional. Assuming that the state had an interest in sustaining the validity of its laws, how, the judges wondered, could that interest be best protected?

THE UNCERTAIN ROLE OF THE STATE OF KANSAS

The *Brown* lawsuit was against the Topeka Board of Education and certain district officials. Neither the state of Kansas nor any of its officers was made a defendant. At the heart of the plaintiffs' claim was the question of whether a Kansas statute was constitutional.

At the outset the issue of constitutionality was one between Oliver Brown and his coplaintiffs and the Topeka Board of Education. Had the state not intervened the issue of constitutionality could have and would have been determined in the state's absence. The state of Kansas was not a necessary party nor the attorney general a necessary participant in the case. Still, the judges reasoned, the state had an interest in upholding its laws, and the appropriate state officers should have the opportunity to be heard. Hence, when *Brown* was filed, Judge Mellott directed that notices of the filing and copies of the complaint be delivered to the governor and the attorney general.

Edward F. Arn, the then-Governor of Kansas, at forty-five, was personable, vigorous, and politically ambitious. A Republican, he had been twice-elected attorney general, where he gained a reputation as a vigorous prosecutor, but had resigned during his second term to accept an appointment to the Kansas Supreme Court. After a year on the court he put aside his judicial robe to become a candidate for governor. He had held the office for less than two months when the Brown complaint was delivered to his office. Arn had been succeeded as attorney general by Dick Fatzer. Also young, a Republican, and equally ambitious politically, he had served as county attorney in rural Edwards County, Kansas, and as attorney for the Kansas Department of Social Welfare before becoming an assistant attorney general. After being appointed in 1949 to complete Ed Arn's unexpired term as attorney general, he had been elected to the office in 1950.

The governor, as the state's chief executive officer, has certain statutory duties with respect to cases in court. Whenever he receives notice of the commencement of an action "by which the rights, interests or property of the state" may be affected he shall inform the attorney general and "require the Attorney General to act in conjunction with counsel for the proper party to protect the interests of the state," or he may employ special counsel if he or she determines that the public interest requires it.[8] It is the duty of the attorney general to represent the state before the Supreme Court of Kansas in all cases "in which the state shall be a party or interested" and, "when directed by the governor or either branch of the legislature," to appear in any other court or before any officer in any matter in which the state is interested or a party or "when the constitutionality of any law of this state is at issue."[9]

When the *Brown* case documents were received in the governor's office they were routinely forwarded to the attorney general's office, where they were filed along with the copies of the notice and complaint that had been delivered to the attorney general. A review of the file disclosed that the state was not a party; the case was not before the Supreme Court of Kansas; and the attorney general's appearance had been required neither by the governor nor by either branch of the legislature. His appearance would have been proper, but, absent a request, the decision to appear was for him to make.

In early March 1951 the Kansas legislature was in session, and both Governor Arn and Attorney General Fatzer were preoccupied with the legislative agenda. Neither had an interest or a desire to become embroiled in the affairs of the Topeka Board of Education. Consequently the *Brown* lawsuit went on hold.

The inactivity of the state officers was a cause of concern for both the Topeka Board of Education and the judges. The lawyer board member, Mike Casey, was a personal friend of both Governor Arn and Attorney General Fatzer. So were Les Goodell and George Brewster. Informally yet firmly, they were able to convey the board's feeling that the board's case would be strengthened if the state were to assume a more active role in defense of the statute. Others thought the state should be involved in the defense of its law. As the trial date ap-

Harold R. Fatzer, attorney general of Kansas (1949–1956), represented Kansas in the Supreme Court arguments on the implementation decree in *Brown v. Board of Education*, April 11, 1955. (Courtesy of the Kansas State Historical Society)

proached, evidence of the judges' concern began to appear in the intracourt communications. Writing to his colleagues on June 1, Judge Huxman commented: "Nowhere does the State of Kansas or the Representative of the State of Kansas in the suit appear in the suit as defendant. Since this is an action to have declared illegal a State Statute, should the State of Kansas not be made a party defendant and, if the parties themselves do not do so, should not the court of its own volition take this step?"[10]

On June 4 Judge Mellott wrote to Judge Hill, desiring to compare thoughts with him before replying to Judge Huxman. He wrote: "I see nothing in the statute requiring the State of Kansas or its representatives to be in the suit unless they care to do so."[11] Judge Hill responded on the following day:

> In regard to the three-judge court case, I see no legal necessity for either the Governor or Attorney General being made parties. . . . Referring back to the Governor and Attorney General situation I believe we could probably ask the Attorney General, after we have heard the evidence, to appear as a friend of the Court and either file a brief or orally argue the constitutionality of the statute if he cares to do so.[12]

Next on the intracourt communication log is Judge Mellott's letter to Judge Huxman, written on June 6. He reported his and Judge Hill's opinion that the state should not be required to appear. Pointing out that the board of education was in court, properly represented, that the governor and the attorney general were both given notice and supplied with copies of the complaint when the case was filed, and that both had had notice of the time set for trial, he continued,

> Judge Hill suggests, and I think there is substantial merit in his suggestion, that in the event the governor and attorney general do not see fit to participate in the trial of the case, that we, after the evidence has been heard, ask the attorney general to appear as a friend of the court, and file a brief or participate in argument upon the constitutionality of the statute if he cares to do so.[13]

Dick Fatzer was experiencing a quandary not easy to resolve. Personally, he did not believe in segregation, and he did not condone Topeka's

segregated elementary schools. As a lawyer, he knew that the Kansas segregation law was consistent with and supported by a long line of precedents both judicial and legislative. As attorney general, he was sensitive to
his duty to see that laws passed by the Kansas legislature and approved by
the Kansas courts were properly defended against attack. He also knew
that the board of education represented by able attorneys would, in his absence, make a vigorous defense. Then there were political considerations.
Dick was ambitious and foresaw the possibility of a move to the governor's
suite. He had enjoyed substantial support in the black community, and he
wished to retain that support.

In mid-1951 few Kansans understood and appreciated the magni-
tude and significance of *Brown*. By most it was regarded as a local
case, of interest only to Topekans. The Topeka news media gave it little
attention. Elsewhere in the state, most people knew little and cared
less about the matter. Dick Fatzer's black friends advised him that few
blacks were interested. Most, they said, regarded the Topeka NAACP
group as troublemakers and did not support them. Meanwhile, the
board of education continued to seek his assistance. Statehouse colleagues thought the attorney general should have a more active part.

The decision reached by General Fatzer is reflected in a letter
from Judge Mellott to his colleagues on June 12. He wrote, "The Attorney General appeared in open court before me yesterday following
a brief preliminary conference and orally moved for leave to file an answer within five days. I granted such leave."[14]

The separate answer of the state of Kansas, an intervening defendant, was filed on June 15. The answer raised a single issue in that
"it expressly denies Chapter 72–1724 of the General Statutes is unconstitutional." Other allegations in the complaint were either admitted
or, because of the state's lack of knowledge or information, neither admitted nor denied.[15] Thus, ten days before trial Kansas entered the
case solely for the purpose of defending its statute against the plaintiffs' claim of unconstitutionality. All other issues raised by the pleadings were left to plaintiffs and the Topeka Board of Education.

THE TRIAL

For each of the judges involved, service on the three-judge bench
was extraordinary, unplanned-for judicial duty. Each had a full sched-

ule of other court commitments. Their early intracourt correspondence suggests their concern for reconciling the expeditious disposition of the *Brown* case with their regular docket responsibilities. At the outset the prospect of an early disposition was not good, particularly if the trial was to be a protracted one. In his March 6 letter to Judge Mellott, Judge Huxman suggested that once the issues were formed, a pretrial conference to determine what facts should be agreed to might eliminate a considerable portion of the work, with a resulting saving of court time.[16]

The trial date was set for Monday, June 25. On the preceding Friday the attorneys for the parties appeared before Judges Huxman and Mellott for the conference to determine what facts could be agreed upon and stipulated to. Judge Hill was not present. The plaintiffs were represented by their Topeka counsel, who were joined by attorneys Carter and Greenberg. Goodell and Brewster represented the Topeka Board of Education. Also present were Willis H. McQueary and Charles H. Hobart, assistant attorneys general, who represented the state. After allowing insubstantial amendments to the language of the complaint and recognizing Carter and Greenberg as additional counsel in the case, the judges gave their attention to the expected use of expert witnesses. Mr. Carter stated that the plaintiffs would offer expert testimony and expected to call nine or ten witnesses to prove the deleterious impact of segregation on the plaintiffs' right to equal educational opportunity. The judges felt that five would be enough. A similar limitation was imposed on the defendants.

A thoughtful student once said to me, "Lawyers have ways of making simple things complex." I recall those words as I read the record of the pretrial conference in *Brown*. Nine lawyers and two judges engaged in the colloquy. After hours of argument by counsel and cajoling by the court, a few self-evident facts were agreed to. With respect to others the parties agreed to disagree.

It was agreed that Topeka was a single school district governed by the defendant board of education; that the district was divided into eighteen territories or subdistricts with an elementary school in each territory; that white children were required to attend the schools located in the territories where they lived and that no black children were admitted to those schools; that the district maintained four schools for black elementary students only; that the black schools were located in black neighborhoods; and that black students might attend any of the black schools selected by the students or their parents. It was further agreed that bus transportation was furnished by the district to black students and that no transportation service was supplied to whites; that the same course of study and school textbooks were employed at both black and white schools; and that play supervision, health services, teacher supervision, and other extra-classroom services supplied to white and black schools were of the same quality and extent. By agreement a mass of documents showing territorial boundaries and statistical data concerning schools, teachers, pupils, and other relevant facts was received and made part of the trial record.[17]

Although the representatives of the state were present at the conference, they had made no request for admissions and did not participate in the colloquy. In response to an inquiry by Judge Huxman, Assistant Attorney General McQueary stated:

> If Your Honor please, the position of the State of Kansas, insofar as this lawsuit or this controversy is concerned, is going to be to endeavor to uphold the constitutionality of the statute in question, and our participation will be limited to that field, and so far as equal facilities or the conditions provided by the Board of Education of the City of Topeka or the facilities enjoyed by the Negro, by the plaintiffs, we are not going to make that a matter of issue insofar as we are concerned. We have no knowledge as to that; we haven't investigated it. That will be left solely to the other parties in this matter.[18]

Monday, June 25, the full court convened, with Judge Huxman presiding. The courtroom was hardly half-filled with spectators, most of whom were black. Judge Huxman inquired if there were additional parties or attorneys to be shown by the record. Mr. Goodell announced that attorneys for boards of education in Leavenworth, Coffeyville, and Manhattan had requested that they be entered as attorneys of record and be permitted to file briefs. The request was granted by the court. Judge Huxman stated that the record would show the appearance of each as amicus curiae (friend of the court). Several documents were marked as exhibits, agreed to, and admitted as evidence. Then, after admonishing the attorneys against quarreling and bickering and the spectators against demonstrations, Judge Huxman announced that the case was ready for trial.

Mr. Carter began the plaintiffs' presentation of evidence by calling board member Arthur H. Saville and Dr. Kenneth McFarland, superintendent. Mr. Saville had been defeated for reelection, and Dr. McFarland's resignation had been accepted; hence, both were lame ducks whose tenure would expire in a few weeks. As adverse parties, they were deemed hostile witnesses, but their hostility is not manifest in the record, and their testimony, relating mainly to policy and administrative details, produced no fireworks. Mr. Carter's examination of his first two witnesses seemed only minimally productive.[19] Topeka lawyers Bledsoe and John Scott then came forward with the testimony of a dozen friendlier witnesses.

Of the twelve witnesses next called, eleven were plaintiffs in the lawsuit. Their grievances were similar and their complaints were generally not about classrooms, teaching personnel, or facilities but were aimed at the hardships experienced by their children in traveling between their homes and the schools they attended. Many, perhaps most, of the black children of Topeka lived within easy walking of their schools. At the same time, other black families lived in racially mixed neighborhoods, scattered throughout the city, often a long way from the schools their children were required to attend. It was a concern for these families that motivated the board to establish a system of free school transportation for all black children in the district. From this group the plaintiffs had been recruited.

Children of the plaintiffs who testified attended black schools located from six to thirty blocks from their homes. It was their claim that students using the bus were forced to spend excessive amounts of time en route to and from school. All lived significantly closer to white schools. Stations at which the school buses made pickups and discharges were located one to seven blocks from the family residences, often separated by heavily traveled streets and busy railroads. There was testimony that buses were often late, requiring long waits at the pickup stations. No shelters were provided to protect waiting children from inclement weather. As no school lunches were provided the bused students carried lunch boxes, whereas students attending school in their own neighborhoods could enjoy warm lunches at home. Buses were often crowded, and children aboard were not properly supervised. None of these disadvantages were experienced by students who attended schools in their neighborhoods.

Oliver Brown was the fifth witness to be called by the plaintiffs. After routine preliminary inquiries, Mr. Brown testified that Linda Carol Brown, eight years of age, was his daughter; that the family lived in the Sumner School territory; that the Sumner School was about seven blocks from the family home, but that Linda attended Monroe School, about twenty-one blocks away. Mr. Brown stated that in order for her to catch the bus at the First and Quincy pickup point it was necessary for her to leave home at 7:40 A.M. and walk six blocks, passing through a railroad switchyard and crossing Kansas Avenue at a time when motor traffic was heaviest; that the school bus was often late, and on those occasions Linda often waited for long periods on the unsheltered street, exposed to cold, rain, and snow; and that she often arrived at the school before the doors were unlocked and was forced to wait outside the building.[20]

At the conclusion of Mr. Brown's testimony, Darlene Watson was called. Mrs. Watson, who lived across the street from the Brown residence, was white and the mother of a son who attended Sumner. She testified that her child, who walked to school, usually left home around 8:40 A.M., an hour later than Linda. After Mrs. Watson had testified, Judge Huxman, apparently impatient with this line of questioning, informed counsel that the court would judicially notice that the locations of the white and colored schools in Topeka required that some colored students travel farther to reach a colored school than would be necessary if they were permitted to attend white schools located closer to their homes.[21]

A few witnesses had special insights. Sadie Emmanuel sent her nine-year-old son to school on the city bus at her own expense because of the undue crowding and lack of supervision of children riding the school bus.[22] After one year in a black school, James Richardson, who lived near a white school, had withdrawn his son and enrolled him in Holy Name, a parochial school. His reason—"simply because I do not believe in segregation."[23] The children of Silas Fleming rode the city bus to school because the point at which the school bus would pick them up was almost as far from their home as the school. With leave of the court, witness Fleming explained why he was in the case: "But my point was not only that I and my children are craving light, the entire colored race is craving light, and the only way to reach the light is to start our children together in their infancy and they come up together."[24]

At the conclusion of the testimony of the plaintiff-witnesses, their case was carried forward by expert witnesses. Up to this point the claim of discrimination had focused on the hardships encountered by plaintiffs in travel to and from their distant schools. Mr. Goodell made frequent objections to the testimony of this group of witnesses on the ground that it was incompetent to show a violation of the Fourteenth Amendment. The apparent bases for his objections were that the location of a child's home was a matter over which the board had no control and that some white students, for whom the district provided no transportation, traveled even greater distances to attend school. His objections were overruled.

As the plaintiffs' case developed, the two major thrusts became clear. First, evidence was produced to show that actual inequality in access to schools, quality of buildings and physical equipment, academic programs, and other demonstrable facilities operated to deny black students equality of educational opportunity in the Topeka school district. Second, the plaintiffs contended for and sought to support a finding that racial segregation in public education was in itself, without reference to other conditions, an impermissible denial of equal protection of the law. Although a favorable ruling on the latter contention was the principal objective of the NAACP lawyers, the theory was accepted with some misgiving by their Topeka colleagues. In each of the cases that had preceded *Brown*, the Supreme Court had carefully avoided a determination that the separate-but-equal doctrine was constitutionally invalid. The Topeka lawyers wondered whether another refusal would operate to strengthen the precedent.

Regardless of the issues thought to be critical, the full development of the plaintiffs' case required the testimony of experts. The rules governing proof of facts distinguish between the ordinary or lay witness and the expert. Lay witnesses may speak only of what they know firsthand and may testify only as to facts. They may not give opinions, inferences, or conclusions. The *Brown* plaintiffs who testified were lay witnesses. By contrast, in cases where it may be helpful to the trier of fact, whether judge or jury, an expert witness may be called to assist in the analysis and interpretation of the evidence presented. The expert need not have the kind of firsthand knowledge required of lay witnesses. Because of his special expertise in the area of inquiry, the expert witness may testify as to his or her opinion, inference, and conclusions drawn from the other evidence.

Jack Greenberg had taken the lead in selecting and obtaining the testimony of the plaintiffs' experts. His first contact was with Dr. Hugh W. Speer, chairman of the Department of Education at the University of Kansas City, now the University of Missouri at Kansas City. Seven experts in the fields of education and behavioral science testified for the plaintiffs, and still others were on call. Their credentials were impressive. Collectively, the seven who appeared owned twenty academic degrees plus an incipient Ph.D. and represented more than a century of professional service.

Dr. Speer was the first expert to be called. At the request of the plaintiffs' attorneys, Dr. Speer had made an examination of Topeka's elementary schools, and his testimony reflected his findings and his general expertise in the field of public education. The transcript of Dr. Speer's testimony is long and detailed. He found no significant differences in quality and training of teachers or in class size between the black and white schools.

As preparation for a comparison of physical facilities, Dr. Speer and his staff had examined the board's files relating to all elementary schools and had visually inspected fourteen of the twenty-two buildings. Criteria used in the evaluation of each included site, nature of the structure, its plan, classrooms, service rooms, kindergartens, library books, supplies, safety features, and maintenance. Particular attention had been given to age and insured value. Topeka's twenty-two elementary schools had been built over a period of more than sixty years. Generally, the newer schools were more attractive, better designed and equipped, and had greater insured valuations than the older ones. The newest schools were often located in newer neighborhoods, which tended to be predominantly white. However, the oldest buildings in the system as well as the newest were attended by white students.

The gist of Dr. Speer's lengthy testimony comparing facilities was best stated by him in response to a question by Judge Huxman: "There is some inequality in physical facilities between the two groups in Topeka."[25] Mindful that some disparity was inevitable, Dr. Speer hardly made out a case of unconstitutional discrimination by his evaluation. Such variations as existed had no necessary relation to color or ethnicity. Their impact fell on some black and some white students alike. They were inescapable incidents of urban growth.

It was Dr. Speer's evaluation and comparison of the curricula of white and black schools that was critical to the instant case and significant in all similar cases. To make this comparison it was necessary to devise an ad hoc definition of curriculum. He testified:

> By curriculum we mean something more than the course of study. As commonly defined and accepted now "curriculum" means the total school experience of the child. [Education] is concerned with a child's total development, his personality, his personal and social adjustment. Therefore, it becomes the obligation of the school to provide the kind of an environment in which the child can learn knowledge and skills such as the three Rs and also social skills and social attitudes and appreciations and interests, and these considerations are all now part of the curriculum.[26]

Using this definition, Dr. Speer concluded that neither the Topeka curricula nor any school curriculum could be equal in a segregated system. Thus, the basic issue emerged.

Six other experts were called by the plaintiffs. All were examined by Greenberg or Carter and cross-examined by Goodell. Although the background, experience, and perspective of each was different from those of the others, all reached the conclusion that the legal segregation of black students in the public schools was a denial of equal educational opportunity.

The most telling of the expert testimony was that of Louisa Holt, a social psychologist who was then a member of the psychology faculty at the University of Kansas and whose prior experience included a staff position at the Menninger School of Psychiatry. Mrs. Holt was a resident of Topeka with children in the Topeka schools. When asked whether, in her opinion, enforced legal separation had an adverse effect on the personality development of the Negro child, she replied:

> The fact that it is enforced, that it is legal, I think has more importance than the mere fact of segregation by itself does because this gives legal and official sanction to a policy which inevitably is interpreted both by white people and by Negroes as denoting the

inferiority of the Negro group. Were it not for the sense that one
group is inferior to the other, there would be no basis, and I am
not granting that this is a rational basis, for such segregation. . . .
A sense of inferiority must always affect one's motivation for
learning since it affects the feeling one has of one's self as a person, as a personality or a self or an ego identity.[27]

These lines were later paraphrased and adopted by both Judge Huxman and Chief Justice Warren in writing for their respective courts.

Cross-examination of the expert witnesses seemed designed to
point up the speculative character of their testimony, to emphasize
that other conclusions were possible, to secure admissions of possibilities of error, and to recognize the existence of exceptions to the general assertions of the witnesses. The record of the cross-examination
does not show that any of the expert witnesses was seriously im-
peached.

When the plaintiffs had concluded, three witnesses testified for
the defense. Clarence G. Grimes, a school bus driver, testified that his
bus ran on time and that order was maintained among the student
passengers.[28] Thelma Mifflin, clerk of the board of education for nine
years, stated that a Negro student could attend any of the Negro
schools that he or she desired; that no distinction was made between
white and colored schools with respect to course of study, textbooks,
reference and other books supplied by the district, supplies and maintenance; that no transportation was furnished to white students; and
that the same criteria were used in fixing the salaries of white and colored teachers.[29] Dr. McFarland was the final witness for the defense.
His contribution appears to add little more than a few pages of transcript. An attempt by Mr. Goodell to show that the policy of the board
of education was consistent with the social customs and usages of the
community and that the administration had found no evidence that
the majority sentiment would desire a change did not impress the
court.[30] At the conclusion of Dr. McFarland's cross-examination, the
defense rested. The board of education called no expert witnesses,
nor did it otherwise attempt to rebut the plaintiffs' testimony as to the
psychological harm caused by segregation. As the board's attorneys
saw it, such testimony was irrelevant. *Plessy v. Ferguson*, they felt, required equality of physical facilities—no more. John W. Davis is re-

ported to have characterized the social scientists' testimony in the South Carolina case as "guff." Goodell and Brewster agreed.

The arguments of counsel were little more than restatements of the positions that had been apparent since the earliest stages of the trial. Mr. Carter, speaking for the plaintiffs, urged that the separate-but-equal doctrine was no longer a valid concept in public education. He also contended that the evidence showed that the Topeka schools for white and colored children were, in fact, unequal. Speaking for the defendants, Mr. Brewster argued that *Plessy v. Ferguson* had not been overruled but remained the law of the land; that the educational opportunities afforded to white and black students were substantially equal; and that the Topeka plan of classification of students for elementary school attendance on the basis of race was not unreasonable and, therefore, not unlawful. No argument was presented on behalf of the state of Kansas.

At the conclusion of the proceeding, Judge Huxman summed up. He commented:

> Now, the questions are comparatively simple to state and quite difficult to answer. There are only two questions in the case; one is, are the facilities, as I see them, are the facilities which are afforded by Topeka in its separate schools, comparable; that is one question and the other is, granting that they are, is segregation unconstitutional notwithstanding, in the light of the Fourteenth Amendment. As I get it, those are the two points in the case, is that right?[31]

Mr. Carter agreed. After fixing a schedule and agreeing upon a procedure for filing briefs, the court took the case unto its bosom and retired. The total trial time had been nine hours and twenty minutes.

THE DECISION

Within the month following the trial, briefs were filed by the parties. Briefs at this stage are simply the parties' arguments reduced to writing.

The plaintiffs argued that (1) racial segregation in public education is per se discriminatory and denies to individuals rights protected by the constitution; (2) the classification of elementary school students on the basis of race for the purpose of school attendance was an anomaly in Kansas law and had no reasonable basis; and (3) even if segregation was not unconstitutional per se, the inequalities, tangible and intangible, in the Topeka school system made it unconstitutional as applied.

The board's responsive arguments were hardly surprising. Their brief asserted that one, the structure and operation of the Topeka school system was authorized by a valid Kansas statute; two, the *Plessy v. Ferguson* doctrine of separate but equal had not been overturned and remained the controlling law; three, the evidence failed to show an unconstitutional discrimination against the plaintiffs; and four, the testimony of the behavioral scientist witnesses furnished no legal grounds to overrule *Plessy v. Ferguson*.

By an addendum to the board's brief the attorney general, on behalf of the state, joined in that portion dealing with the validity of the Kansas statute under attack.[32]

While *Brown* was being litigated in Kansas, constitutional questions regarding public school segregation were being raised in other courts. Of particular interest in Kansas was an almost simultaneous case in South Carolina in which black residents of Clarendon County in that state had sued, claiming inequality of facilities and the unconstitutionality of the South Carolina statute requiring segregation.[33] At the outset of the trial the attorney for the school district admitted that the educational facilities furnished to white and black students were not then substantially equal, but represented that an equalization program was under way. The board asked time to carry the plan forward. It denied that the South Carolina segregation law was unconstitutional. The Kansas court and attorneys were in close touch with their South Carolina counterparts.[34] On June 23, two days prior to the *Brown* trial, the South Carolina court by a two-to-one decision disposed of its case by (1) ordering that the district proceed to equalize its schools and to report within six months that such action had been taken, and (2) declining to hold the state's segregation statute unconstitutional.[35]

The interval between trial and decision is an occasion when lawyers speculate on probable outcomes. When more than one mind is to be involved in the determination—whether those of jurors or those of judges—the speculation inevitably involves counting heads. Which ones view the case as I do? Who is likely to be against me? Answers to these questions may lie in the determiner's general outlook, his philosophical approach to the law, his experience, and his demeanor and demonstrated attitude in the instant proceeding. In *Brown* both parties appeared to believe that Judge Huxman's sympathies ran to the plaintiffs. Writing to the attorney general of Virginia, General Fatzer commented on the opinion in the South Carolina case and added, "on this point it is my guess that two members of the three-judge federal court [in Kansas] will vote along the lines which Parker [of the South Carolina court] expressed in his opinion."[36] The two on which General Fatzer relied were Mellott and Hill. Years later Charles Scott spoke of the court's critical Finding of Fact No. 8. He said: "Mellott and Hill were quite able to prevent this, but they went along with him because Judge Huxman was a very strong minded person, and he had a great deal of influence upon that court. But this was basically our argument."[37]

On July 12, before any briefs had been received by the court, Judge Huxman, who had assumed responsibility for writing the court's opinion, had begun to work. He wrote to his colleagues on that date, saying, "The only controversial issue of any importance that there will be in the suggested findings of fact will be with respect to the effect of segregation itself."[38] With his letter, Judge Huxman submitted a proposed draft of a finding that legally enforced segregation affected the Negro child's motivation to learn and thus deprived him of some of the benefits he would receive in an integrated school.[39]

During the balance of July letters continued, and proposed drafts were circulated among the judges. From the beginning they were in substantial agreement, and there is no evidence that the briefs and suggested findings and conclusions of the parties had a significant impact on their thinking. Their views were apparently fixed by the time the trial ended, and there was no deviation from the course initially set. The opinion was entered on August 3. Most of its findings were self-evident and routine. The court found no material difference in physical facilities of the white and colored schools of Topeka. Teacher qualifications and quality of instruction were found to be comparable. The prescribed courses of study were identical. It was noted that transportation provided for colored students was not available to whites. Finally, and critically, the court announced its Finding of Fact No. 8, which, as finally written, was as follows:

Segregation of white and colored children in public schools has a detrimental effect upon the colored children. The impact is greater when it has the sanction of the law; for the policy of separating the races is usually interpreted as denoting the inferiority of the Negro group. A sense of inferiority affects the motivation of a child to learn. Segregation with the sanction of law, therefore, has a tendency to retard the educational and mental development of Negro children and to deprive them of some of the benefits they would receive in a racially integrated school system.[40]

Judge Huxman had listened to the testimony of witness Holt.

In spite of its finding the court was constrained by precedent. To the judges, *Plessy v. Ferguson* required equality only in the physical characteristics of buildings, equipment, the curricula, quality of instruction, and other tangible school services. Legal segregation in and of itself, without more, did not deny equal protection. *Plessy v. Ferguson* had not been overruled. Hence, judgment was entered for the defendants.

On August 4 *Brown v. Board of Education* for the first time made the front page of the *Topeka Daily Capital* under the headline, "Grade School Segregation Upheld: Ruling to Be Appealed"; in ten column inches the history of the case and the court's decision were summarized. The story also reported that Mr. Bledsoe had announced that the decision would be appealed.[41]

5

1952—Year of Indecision

Considerations of jurisdiction and venue required that Oliver and Linda Brown first present their grievance to the appropriate court in the place where the claimed wrong occurred—the United States District Court for the District of Kansas. Neither the judges of that court nor the parties to the lawsuit believed that a decision there adverse to the plaintiffs would be accepted by them. Their next move was to Washington, D.C., and the Supreme Court of the United States. Hence, it came as no surprise when the plaintiffs petitioned to appeal.[1]

In the ordinary federal case the appeal is to the court of appeals of the circuit in which the district court sits. On appeal the parties argue to a panel of three appellate judges who determine whether the trial court erred. In selected cases their decision may be reviewed by the Supreme Court. *Brown* was not an ordinary case. The plaintiffs were seeking to enjoin the enforcement of a state statute and a declaration that the statute was unconstitutional. A panel of three judges had heard the case in the first instance. In cases of this kind the law provides for a direct appeal to the Supreme Court.[2] Oliver and Linda Brown and their coappellants asked that the Supreme Court find that the trial court was in error (1) when it refused to enjoin the Topeka

Board of Education from maintaining racially segregated schools, (2) when it refused to find the Kansas statute authorizing segregation was unconstitutional, and (3) when it refused to enter judgment for the plaintiffs after finding that "plaintiffs suffered serious harm and detriment in being required to attend segregated elementary schools in the city of Topeka and were deprived thereby of the benefits they would have received in a racially integrated school system."[3] (Whether the third claim of error correctly states the court's finding is arguable.)

On November 9, a Topeka newspaper reported that a dinner marking the kickoff of a drive to raise funds to carry on the lawsuit had produced more than $1,200.[4] Thus, the plight of an eight-year-old black child who lived beside the railroad tracks in Topeka, Kansas, and who had been rejected by her neighborhood school became the concern of the nation's highest court and preempted the attention of Americans.

ON BEING RIGHT ON THE WRONG SIDE

As I read the relevant contemporary literature, it became apparent that the state's argument in support of its law would rest on judicial precedent and the history, traditions, and customs of Kansans. With few exceptions, the more articulate scholars who wrote in the fields of education and the behavioral sciences were against us. At the same time, to me it was clear that the state's position was supported by existing law. The doctrine of separate but equal still controlled; only by making new law could the Supreme Court sustain the contentions of Linda Brown and her friends. In my heart I found no objection to the change sought. If I had been a Kansas legislator or a member of the Topeka Board of Education, I should have been pleased to vote to repeal the segregation statute and repudiate the public school policy that it permitted. But I was not a legislator, nor was I an individual seeking to implement my personal moral standards. I was a lawyer committed to uphold the law and the adversary process. The appellants were represented by able counsel prepared to attack wherever they sensed vulnerability. As I saw it, the task of counsel for the state was to rebut that effort by bringing to the Court's attention all data and theories favorable to the state's position. Justice Oliver Wendell Holmes is reported to have said that the job of the judge is not to do justice but to play the game according to the rules.[5] The lawyer's task is to inform the court as to what his client believes the rules to be. Whatever the outcome, the lawyer who has been faithful to his responsibility will have made a useful contribution to the result.

The hostility of scholars to Kansas's position was compounded by the indifference of my professional colleagues. Most Kansas lawyers were uninterested in the problems of the Topeka Board of Education and its black constituents. My pursuit was a lonely one. The other side had the support of a far-flung network of scholars and practitioners in the areas of constitutional and civil rights law. Teamed with articulate, much published, and widely recognized experts in education, the social sciences, and philosophy, they were an impressive array of talent. At the trial seven expert witnesses had testified in support of the plaintiffs. None had appeared for the board of education. Aside from the parties, few Kansans were interested in Topeka's school problems. The only audible voices were those heard in the black communities and the ivory towers of academe. They were uniformly against us. It may have been my inexperience—perhaps a touch of paranoia—but I was lonesome.

Although lawyer indifference was the rule, there were a few exceptions. Three members of the Washburn University law faculty engaged in a spirited exchange of views in the pages of the *Journal of the Kansas Bar Association*. Professor Chester James Antieau, later a distinguished member of the law faculty at Georgetown, thought that the three-judge court erred grievously in its *Brown* decision. He argued that the court had misunderstood and misapplied the precedents it relied on, that its decision was inconsistent with its own Finding of Fact No. 8, that the decision was contrary to the Charter of the United Nations, and that "the decision is not only legally wrong and indefensible, but morally evil and sociologically and economically pernicious to the welfare of this nation."[6] In the following issue of the *Journal*, two of Professor Antieau's colleagues disagreed. Dean Schuyler W. Jackson, later a justice of the Kansas Supreme Court, argued that *Plessy v. Ferguson* and its successors stated the prevailing rule of law and were binding on the district court. Only the Supreme Court, he thought, was competent to overrule the precedents found in its earlier decisions.[7] Professor Melvin C. Poland, now a distinguished emeritus professor at Indiana-Indianapolis, agreed with Dean Jackson. Recognizing that sociological and moral considerations underlie most statutory and case law, Professor Poland rejected the suggestion that a lower federal court could, in the face of positive pronouncements to the contrary, support a decision adverse to precedent based upon an individualistic view of what is morally justifiable. He wrote: "The application of such a non-legal theological approach to the determination of legal questions, whether they be constitutional questions or other, would open the door for decisions based on the moral predilections of the particular judge, a highly undesirable if not intolerable result."[8]

Although the views of Dean Jackson and Professor Poland were refreshingly different from most that I had heard or seen, they were not particularly comforting to me as I surveyed our task. Whereas both were supportive of the decision of the three-judge district court, the thesis of each was that the lower federal courts were obliged to respect and to follow the precedents established by Supreme Court decisions. Neither suggested that the Supreme Court lacked power to overrule its earlier decisions and to announce new and different precedents. Neither argued that the district court judgment should be affirmed. Only I, an upstart assistant on the attorney general's staff, was seeking to make that case. Only I, as an advocate for the state of Kansas, faced the task of justifying and sustaining its laws.

DRESSING THE PART

The substantive aspects of the argument to be made for Kansas were not my exclusive concerns during those weeks of preparation. There were personal problems to be dealt with. Since I was not a member of the Supreme Court bar, to secure admission was my first objective. A call to the Court's clerk brought me the necessary application form and instructions for filling in the blank spaces. The form was simple, and the instructions were clear. In addition to the personal data required by the form, I was required to submit a certificate by the clerk of the Supreme Court of Kansas that I had been a member of the bar of that court for at least three years and was then in good standing. This was obtained routinely. Also required were the signatures of two sponsors who were members of the Supreme Court bar certifying that they knew me personally, that they were not related to me, that I was qualified for admission to the Supreme Court bar, and that my personal and professional character and standing were good. Governor Arn and General Fatzer signed the application as my sponsors. The completed form and supporting papers were mailed to the Supreme Court to await my appearance for admission.

The paperwork completed, I continued to study the rules and protocol that I, as a member of the Supreme Court bar, should know and respect. When to appear, where to sit, when to stand, how to address the court, and what to wear were all matters of concern. It was the problem of proper attire that caused me to pause. I was delighted to read that formal dress—cutaway jacket and striped trousers—was no longer required. Obviously, I, so recently a resident of Osage County, Kansas, was unlikely to own such garments. My delight subsided when I read in the next sentence that the acceptable alternative was a conservative business suit "in a dark color in keeping with the dignity of the Court." I had no dark suit. My best suit was tan gabardine and my second suit was pepper and salt tweed. These, plus a couple of sport jackets and some miscellaneous slacks, made up my wardrobe. I had nothing to wear to the Supreme Court.

Seeking a resolution to the problem, I made a visit to the Palace, then one of Topeka's leading men's clothiers, now only a memory of happier days. There I found an answer to my problem—a handsome, midnight-blue suit of worsted wool, a perfect fit. The double-breasted jacket was consistent with the vogue of the season and was pleasing to me, since I had read that Supreme Court decorum required that men in court wear either vests or buttoned jackets. I was assured by the salesman that a garment of that quality was a bargain at forty-five dollars.

Finding the blue suit only partially solved the problem. In 1951 the state of Kansas was hardly a lavish paymaster. With house payments, car payments, a wife, three children, and a household, I could ill afford a single unplanned-for expenditure of forty-five dollars. Hence this solution. With a five-dollar deposit the suit was removed from the display rack and laid away to be claimed and paid for later. To me this was an agreeable arrangement since I planned to be sworn in as a member of the Supreme Court bar wearing a crisp new suit. After a period of uncertainty, to be discussed later, I claimed and paid for the suit and wore it as I had planned. More than forty years later the blue suit, in good condition and an approximate fit, reposes in the Kansas Museum of History to remind viewers of the occasion of its wearing and the identity of its wearer. This is hardly the kind of immortality to which I aspired, but perhaps it beats oblivion.

SUMMER DOLDRUMS

Heat and resulting lethargy are features of most Kansas summers. In 1952 dog days set in early, sending temperatures beyond the hundred-degree mark and bringing hot winds from the southwest. Air conditioning was scarce forty years ago. Those who could afford the cost headed for the mountains of Colorado while the less affluent majority sweltered at home. In spite of the resulting slowdown in the affairs of Kansans, there was no cessation of activity in the attorney general's office. It was an election year and the attorney general faced opposition in the election. Politics that summer was the overriding concern of the general and his staff.

My own responsibility was compounded by a stepped up policy of law enforcement undertaken by the attorney general that summer. The law of Kansas then prohibited all forms of gambling.[9] Although two years earlier Kansas had amended its constitutional prohibition against the sale, possession, and transportation of intoxicating liquor, sales by the drink for consumption on the premises continued to be prohibited by statute.[10] Unhappily, some local prosecutors were not sympathetic with the law's limitations, and local enforcement policies were less than consistent with the law's expectations. In cases of local nonenforcement, the statutes expressly impose the duty to enforce upon the attorney general.[11] Dick Fatzer was determined to do his duty. The result was that I, as the assistant attorney general assigned to assist state and local law enforcement agencies, spent many summer hours collaborating in the investigation of claimed liquor and gambling offenses and the prosecution of offenders. For weeks *Brown v. Board of Education* yielded to politics and sin.

From the outset it had been our view that the state's participation in the appeal should be coordinated with that of the board of education. Because the board was the original defendant in the case and the state had intervened for the limited purpose of defending the constitutionality of the statute under attack, we had assumed that the board would appear as the primary appellee and the state would give it support on the constitutional issue. Accordingly, we determined that we would not prepare our brief and argument until we were advised of the board's plan of defense. The advice for which we waited was not forthcoming. As the weeks passed it became apparent that the members of the board disagreed as to the position that it should take. The new members elected in 1951—one half of the total membership—apparently declined to be bound by the posture of their predecessors. The services of Les Goodell and George Brewster, who had represented the board at the trial, were discontinued, and new counsel was engaged. The board's new attorney, Peter F. Caldwell, was a Washburn graduate who had practiced in Topeka for about twenty years. An able scholar, he enjoyed the respect of the Topeka bench and bar. He was a personal and political friend of newly elected board member Jacob Dickinson, who was emerging as the board's most visible and vocal antisegregationist. Since I was well and favorably acquainted with Mr. Caldwell, I looked forward to working with him in preparing for the arguments in the Supreme Court.

As midsummer approached, I sensed that Peter Caldwell shared my frustration at the board's unwillingness or inability to determine the position that it would take regarding the appeal. Early on it became apparent that a majority of the board did not wish to cooperate with or rely upon the attorney general and his staff—that they preferred to proceed independently without reference to the state's position. Dick Fatzer and Jacob Dickinson were not friends. Communications concerning the case were largely limited to my own telephone and face-to-face conversations with the board's attorney. Throughout the summer he reported that he had received no instruction to proceed. He was not free to disclose or discuss the conversations and disagreements that were occurring among members of the board, but from his comments and from the political scuttlebutt, I inferred, to my considerable dismay, that the board might be disposed to let the appeal go by default.

AUTUMN—THE SEASON OF OUR DISCONTENT

The indecision and inaction of the successful defendants in *Brown* was not duplicated in other places. Almost contemporaneously with *Brown*, segregation had been attacked in South Carolina, Virginia, Delaware, and the District of Columbia. In each instance an appeal

Peter F. Caldwell, attorney for the Topeka Board of Education during the post-trial proceedings in the *Brown* case. (Courtesy of the Kansas Judicial Council)

was taken or was expected to be taken by the disappointed party, to which the successful litigant would respond promptly. The South Carolina case, *Briggs v. Elliott*,[12] was begun earlier than *Brown*. It was decided two days before the *Brown* trial. Although the court found that the public schools maintained by the defendants for the Negro students in Clarendon County were in fact inferior to those attended by whites and ordered that the defendants begin to equalize the schools and report their progress in six months, it also upheld the separate-but-equal principle and denied the black students admission to the white schools. On an appeal the U.S. Supreme Court vacated the district court's judgment and remanded the case so that the district court might consider the defendant's progress report that had been filed after the appeal was taken.[13] On remand the district court found that substantial equality had been achieved, that satisfactory progress in rectifying the remaining inequalities was being made. On the issue of constitutionality the court adhered to the views expressed in its earlier opinion and denied an injunction abolishing segregation.[14] Again, the plaintiffs filed an appeal, which reached the Supreme Court *after* the *Brown* appeal had been docketed. The first *Briggs* appeal had been made earlier than the appeal in the Kansas case. Had it not been for the remand, the South Carolina appeal would have been first on the Supreme Court's docket, the aura of glory would have fallen on Harry Briggs, Jr., of Clarendon County, South Carolina, and the name of Linda Brown of Topeka might have been mentioned in a footnote to a Supreme Court opinion bearing the caption of *Briggs v. Elliott*.

Unlike Kansas, the state of South Carolina had not intervened and made a party in *Briggs*. But the state was by no means uninterested. In justifying his decision not to intervene, the attorney general of that state explained that he was apprehensive that his intervention might subject the entire state to the impact of a possible adverse order. He preferred that the court's jurisdiction in the case be limited to Clarendon County.[15]

At the trial of *Briggs*, the school officials were represented by two able South Carolina lawyers, S. Emory Rogers, of Summerton, and Robert McC. Figg, Jr., of Charleston. The governor of South Carolina was James F. Byrnes, one of the state's most honored citizens. After decades of service on the highest legislative, judicial, and executive levels of the national government, including a period on the Supreme

Court, he had returned to South Carolina and at the age of seventy-two had become the state's governor. Governor Byrnes was not anti-Negro. One of his early initiatives was to promote and secure the passage of a $75-million bond issue, to be paid by a 3 percent state sales tax, for the purpose of improving and equalizing the state's public schools. He regarded equal treatment of the races as an imperative responsibility of state government. At the same time, he was committed to preserving southern traditions and southern values. Racial separation and states' rights were important components of the southern way of life. Although the state was not formally a party to the lawsuit, it is clear that the successful defense of *Briggs v. Elliott* became a major concern of the governor.

Forty years earlier Governor Byrnes had served in Congress with John W. Davis of West Virginia. Davis's distinguished political and professional career had led him to become senior partner in Davis, Polk, Wardwell, Sunderland, and Kiendl, one of the great Wall Street law firms. Four decades after his death he is still spoken of as the greatest appellate advocate of the twentieth century. It was to his friend, Mr. Davis, that Governor Byrnes turned for assistance in the effort to repel the attack mounted against South Carolina and its public schools. Although then a resident of New York, Davis was essentially a southerner. He believed that the district court's decision in *Briggs* was legally correct. Governor Byrnes was his friend. Thus, against the advice of other friends, his professional associates, and his family, he became Supreme Court counsel for the Board of Trustees of School District No. 22, Clarendon County, South Carolina.[16] Few causes have ever been lost while enjoying such powerful and distinguished advocacy.

On March 11, 1952, J. Lindsay Almond, attorney general of Virginia, advised General Fatzer of his state's success in defending segregation before a three-judge federal court.[17] The case, brought on behalf of high school students attending segregated schools in Prince Edward County, had been decided on March 9 and had held that the state constitutional and statutory provisions relating to racial segregation in public schools were not per se unconstitutional.[18] As in South Carolina, school facilities for Negro students were found to be inferior to those for whites, and the district was ordered to improve its black schools. Unlike Kansas and South Carolina, Virginia had produced the testimony of experts who supported segregation. Educators, psychologists, and a child psychiatrist had given testimony favorable to Prince Edward County and its segregated schools. An appeal was expected, and preparations to defend the decision were under way.

In Topeka the *Brown* case remained in limbo. My admonition from General Fatzer was to sit on it—to do nothing until the board of education made its position known. Peter Caldwell continued to report that the board had made no decision. I laid the *Brown* file aside and carried on with my efforts to frustrate those who would sully the Kansas image by violating its laws. In a letter dated July 17 the clerk of the Supreme Court advised us that counsel should be in Washington on Tuesday, October 14, for argument of the case. A similar notice had gone to the attorneys in *Briggs*. The court had not yet noted jurisdiction in the Virginia case. When the notice of the setting came to my desk I referred it to General Fatzer with a request for instructions. My instructions were to wait. Although I spoke of the date set for the arguments in a telephone conversation with Peter Caldwell, the board later questioned whether it had been formally and properly notified of the setting. In any case its course was inaction.

Others, including numerous strangers to the litigation, did not share the Kansas reluctance to be heard. In each of the three cases in which appeals were pending, the appellant's briefs and supporting documents were filed in due time. Responses by the appellees were given high priority—except in Kansas. Around mid-summer we began to receive requests from organizations seeking to file briefs amicus curiae. Such briefs by nonparties could be filed only with the consent of the parties or when ordered by the court. I always responded affirmatively to such requests, feeling that the court should have the benefit of the thinking of anyone with serious views on the issues. Eventually amicus curiae briefs were filed on behalf of the American Jewish Congress, the American Civil Liberties Union, the American Federation of Teachers, the Japanese-American Citizens League, the American Ethical Union, the Unitarian Fellowship of Social Justice, the American Jewish Committee, the Anti-Defamation League of B'nai B'rith, the American Veterans' Committee, and the Congress of Industrial Organizations. All were filed with consent given by me on behalf of the state of Kansas. I later learned that the consent of the attorneys in the South Carolina and Virginia cases had been denied, and the amicus briefs were filed in the Kansas case only. My acquiescence had been critical. Without it the Supreme Court record would not have reflected the views of these organizations. The term "amicus curiae" means "friend of the court." As it turned out none were friends of Kansas and the Topeka Board of Education. All were against us. The most unkind cut of all occurred when the attorney general of the United States appeared with a brief suggesting that the separate-but-equal doctrine should be reexamined and overruled by the Supreme Court.[19]

The brief filed by the *Brown* appellants was a short document as appellate briefs go, containing only thirteen pages. The arguments were forthright and produced no surprises. First, the appellants contended that a statute that permits the classification of public school students on the basis of race and color alone is per se a violation of the equal protection clause of the Fourteenth Amendment. Second, it was argued that the district court's Finding of Fact No. 8, that segregation adversely affects the segregated child's ability to learn, was a finding of inequality requiring a judgment for the appellants, notwithstanding *Plessy v. Ferguson*. The brief was signed by Robert L. Carter, Thurgood Marshall, Spottswood W. Robinson III, and Charles S. Scott as counsel for appellants. Neither Marshall nor Robinson had actually appeared in Topeka. Marshall had tried the South Carolina case, and Robinson had been the principal trial counsel in the Virginia court. Their later careers attest to their stature as lawyers. Robert L. Carter is now a senior judge of the United States District Court for the Southern District of New York. Spottswood W. Robinson, now retired, served as chief judge of the federal court of appeals for the District of Columbia circuit. The achievements of the late Supreme Court Justice Thurgood Marshall are known to most Americans. Charles Scott, now deceased, had a useful career as a civil rights attorney and public official in Kansas. And there were others—the names of ten lawyers were shown "of counsel." They included, in addition to John Scott, one of the Topeka trial counsel, a later U.S. secretary of transportation, two who became federal judges, and others whose extraordinary professional accomplishments and public service brought honor to the bar of America. This was the array that I, who had joined the attorney general's staff to get some appellate experience, faced in my first foray into the appellate arena.

Later in the summer the appellants filed, as an appendix to their brief, a document entitled "The Effects of Segregation and the Consequences of Desegregation: A Social Science Statement." The gist of the statement was that segregation adversely affected the ability of the

segregated minority children to take advantage of the educational opportunities provided and that experience had shown no detrimental
effects of desegregation. Admitting that their conclusions were on the
"frontiers of scientific knowledge," thirty-two social scientists of national stature signed the statement. Among the names that I recognized were those of Dr. Kenneth B. Clark, whose testimony in the
South Carolina case had attracted widespread notice,[20] and Dr. Noel P.
Gist of the University of Missouri, who had been my teacher of sociol-
ogy at KU.[21]

THE BUCK STOPS WHERE?

On August 1, Attorney General Almond telephoned General Fatzer to request copies of the transcript of the Topeka trial. A copy was
mailed on the same day with a cover letter of more than casual interest. First, the General wrote, "I and one of the assistants of this office
plan to be present in the Supreme Court in October when this case is
called for hearing in defense of the state statute involved in this proceeding." I was the assistant referred to. Second, he reported that Les
Goodell had expressed doubt as to whether the Topeka Board of Education would defend the case. Finally, he responded favorably to General Almond's suggestion that Virginia move to consolidate the Virginia, South Carolina, and Kansas cases for argument and decision.[22]
In our situation, the prospect of company was indeed comforting.

On September 10 we received a letter from Governor Byrnes en-
closing a draft copy of the South Carolina brief prepared by Mr. Davis
(or a junior member of his firm). The governor hoped that Kansas,
South Carolina, and Virginia might take substantially the same position before the Supreme Court.[23] Fatzer replied on the same day. He
thanked Governor Byrnes and reported, "We are just now starting to
write the Kansas brief." Later on he wrote: "I would like to advise you
I understand that the Topeka board of education in the Kansas case is
not going to defend its position in the Supreme Court. This shall not
deter the position of the State of Kansas, as we shall defend in every
way the validity of our state statute."[24]

A letter from General Almond received on September 11 reported
that the Virginia case had been advanced and would be placed on the

docket for argument immediately following the Kansas and South Carolina cases, still set for October 14. He also requested to see a copy of the appellees' brief "at the earliest possible moment."[25]

During the remaining weeks of September there was no abatement in the Topeka dilemma. Although there were growing rumors that the board of education would not defend its position before the Supreme Court, my limited communication with Peter Caldwell brought only the response that no decision had been made. With no assurance as to what might occur, I began some desultory efforts in preparation for possible argument. I analyzed the appellants' brief, examined the authorities they cited, and began to organize the materials on which we would rely. Mainly, I was frustrated. I did not know what to do, and no one seemed able to tell me.

None was more troubled by the uncertainty and indecision of the board than Attorney General Dick Fatzer. Dick had often stated that racial segregation in the public schools of any Kansas community was morally, politically, and economically indefensible. As attorney general he had sought successfully to gain the support of the black community. Black leaders were his friends. From the beginning he had emphasized that he did not intervene in *Brown* to defend the racial policies of the Topeka Board of Education. He appeared only to defend the validity of a Kansas statute that was constitutional under all of the law that we then knew or could know. As days and weeks and months dragged on, he must have rued his eleventh-hour decision to intervene in the district court case. The attorney general had no statutory duty to appear, nor had he been ordered to do so by the governor, either branch of the legislature, or the court. At the trial the attorneys for the state had been passive participants. Looming large among the reasons that the attorney general was in the case was the urging of members of the board of education and their friends. The prospect of the board's abandoning the case, casting upon the state the entire burden of defending the appeal was, to say the least, displeasing.

Politics, too, was among the attorney general's concerns. Dick Fatzer had been the state's chief prosecutor for three years. In the performance of his duties he had been impartial, aggressive, and vigorous and had sometimes trodden on sensitive toes. He was aware that his policies had provoked controversy. In November 1952 he would face an opponent who was known as a competent lawyer and whose campaign was being well managed and financed. Although the black vote in the election would not exceed 5 percent of the total, Dick was reluctant to take a position that might alienate the black voters who had supported his past candidacies. Moreover, we who knew him were aware that Dick's political ambition looked beyond 1952. His predecessor, Ed Arn, had become governor. History, if given the opportunity, might repeat itself.

During the year that had elapsed since the district court's decision, Topekans had begun to awaken to the significance of the case. Other cases in other states and resulting national publicity told Topeka and Kansas that *Brown* had more than local dimensions. It was part of an offensive with far-flung implications. Whatever their former views, black Kansans were uniting in support of the attack on public school segregation. White Kansans, who had been largely indifferent, were beginning to ask why Kansas stood beside South Carolina and Virginia to defend a scheme based on an assumption of racial inequality. Some Topekans, I think, were merely embarrassed. Others who were more thoughtful looked for justification of the board's policy. Most found none. The stance of the state and the policy of the board were becoming politically unpopular. At the same time, they were wholly consistent with the law.

On Monday, October 6, an item in the *Topeka Daily Capital* informed its readers that the board of education would hold its regular monthly meeting that evening and that the agenda would include a discussion of the pending segregation case. The following morning a front page headline reported "Board Will Not Defend Racial Stand."[26] In the detailed account of the board's proceedings it appeared that the discussion began with an admonition from Mike Casey that the board had a duty to take some action. He then read from a prepared statement that the paper set out in full.[27] In part he said: "Apparently the board would like to be in the position of saying to the colored people, if the Supreme Court holds the statute unconstitutional, 'we have helped abolish segregation by not defending the suit.' While on the other hand they would say to the white people 'we are sorry, there is nothing we can do, the Supreme Court has held the statute unconstitutional and therefore segregation must be abolished.'" At the conclusion of his presentation Casey moved that "the board take action to abolish segregation immediately, and to employ colored teachers throughout the system the same as other teachers." Such action, he argued, would be consistent with the board's inaction. The motion died for want of a second.[28]

After the Casey motion failed Charles Bennett moved that the board's attorney be instructed to represent the board before the Supreme Court. Upon the motion of new board member Jacob Dickinson, the Bennett motion was tabled. Then the discussion turned to whether the attorney general would defend the statute. Mike Oberhelman, chairman of the board, said that ten days earlier Fatzer had assured him that "he personally would defend the state law." Other members of the board had heard otherwise. The reporter's account of the meeting continued: "The formality of the meeting was dropped while Oberhelman held a telephone conference with Fatzer. He reported upon return that Fatzer had changed his mind about defending the case and that he had apologized for not so notifying the board." Thus the story ended.

For weeks I had been conscious of the possibility that the board and the state might default, but it was only when I read the morning paper on October 7 that I learned that the decision had been made. I knew of Dick Fatzer's personal and political misgivings. I knew that during the preceding days he had talked at length with several of his black friends and with other political advisers. I also knew that the setting for argument was so close at hand that adequate preparation would have been impossible, although I assumed that we could request and obtain an enlargement of the time. To me the account of the meeting and its outcome was more disturbing than surprising. I felt strongly that as members of the bar representing an appellee before the Supreme Court of the United States we had a duty to make some response—either to defend the trial court's decision or to admit that it was wrong. I found it hard to reconcile our inaction with my notions of professional responsibility. Besides, I had a new blue suit on layaway at the Palace, with apparently no place to wear it.

There were no public postmeeting comments by members of the board of education. Dick Fatzer said only, "it's their [the board of education's] case."

IT'S NOT OVER TILL IT'S OVER

While Kansas and Topeka were searching their respective souls, things were happening elsewhere. On July 12 the expected appeal in the Virginia case reached the Supreme Court. In the local courts of the District of Columbia and Delaware the school segregation problems were coming to juristic heads. On October 8, two days after the Topeka Board of Education decided not to decide, the Court postponed the arguments in the Kansas and South Carolina cases, noted jurisdiction in the Virginia case, and set all for argument on December 8. The Court also took notice of the case then pending in the Court of Appeals for the District of Columbia and indicated that, if certiorari were applied for and granted in that case, it would be set for argument immediately following the arguments in the pending state appeals.[29]

On October 17 we received a letter, addressed to General Fatzer, from T. Justin Moore, of Richmond, advising us formally that Mr. Moore's law firm, along with Attorney General Almond, was counsel for the appellees in the Virginia case. He requested two copies of the Kansas brief (of which there was none in prospect) and told us that he understood that on the day set for argument the Kansas case would be called first, followed by South Carolina and Virginia, in that order. He suggested a conference of counsel for the appellees in Washington the evening before the arguments. Dick Fatzer was then deeply involved in his campaign for reelection, so the letter was referred to me. I did not reply to Mr. Moore immediately. I did not know what to say.

On October 29 there was a telephone call from Mr. Moore to me, person-to-person. He began by saying that rumors of a prospective default by Kansas had reached Virginia and South Carolina, that they were much concerned, and that Topeka board member Mike Casey had suggested that he, Mr. Moore, call me. Casey had told him that I was uncomfortable about Kansas's nonaction and that the attorney general often relied on my judgment. He urged that I counsel General Fatzer to reconsider his decision not to proceed and that I assure the general of the interest of the other states. Although I was flattered to be identified as one to whom the attorney general might look for advice, I was realistic enough to know that in this case my clout would be negligible. During the year that I had worked with him I had sensed that Dick respected my views on matters of law, but where the issue was one of policy with political overtones he usually looked elsewhere. I was not unwilling to talk with the general about another change of position, but I regarded the decision as his to make and mine to respect. I so advised Mr. Moore. In a follow-up letter written shortly after our conversation, Mr. Moore pointed out that the post-

ponement would give us time to get our brief in proper shape for filing and prepare our argument. His letter continued: "As you can appreciate, we feel, from the standpoint of the Virginia and South
Carolina cases, that it would be most unfortunate for your Kansas
case, which is the first case in this group to be called, to go by default.[30]

Mr. Moore had called me on Thursday. The following Tuesday
was election day. During the intervening days there was no time for
consideration of mundane office business. *Brown* and the state's position did not rank high among the weekend priorities. On Monday,
November 3, the morning paper reported that the board of education
would hold its regular monthly meeting that evening and would make
a final decision as to whether to be represented at the Supreme
Court's hearing of the *Brown* appeal. Although most assumed that the
board's action a month earlier had removed Topeka from the case, the
Bennett motion had, in fact, been tabled and awaited final action. At
the request of Mike Casey the matter had been placed on the November 3 agenda.

It must have been an exciting meeting. The front-page news story
was headlined "Board Kills Plan to Argue Segregation" and reported
a four-hour session of "fiery oratory and plain verbal slugging"—"by
far the most bitter words the present board has seen." Casey and
Dickinson were the chief antagonists. Casey argued that since the Topeka scheme of segregation had been created and maintained by the
board and sustained by the three-judge court, the board had a duty to
defend it when attacked. Dickinson urged, among other arguments,
that the board had no right to use taxpayers' money for the defense of
segregation; that blacks paid taxes and it was wrong that their tax
money should be used against them. Ed Rooney, Jake Dickinson's eloquent senior law partner, and McKinley Burnett and Bolivar Edgewa-
ter Watkins, NAACP leaders, also spoke at length in opposition to the
board's participation in the appeal. The debate ended. A vote was
taken. Dickinson, Conrad, and Oberhelman, all of whom were
elected in 1951, voted against the motion to participate. Bennett and
Casey voted in favor, and Mrs. Neiswanger abstained. The motion
failed. Topeka would not be represented in the Supreme Court.[31] The
following day Peter Caldwell wrote a letter to the clerk of the Supreme
Court advising the Court that the Topeka Board of Education would
neither file a brief nor be present for oral argument.

Nineteen fifty-two was a Republican year in Kansas. Fatzer was reelected with a comfortable majority, and his staff, which served at the attorney general's pleasure, began to relax. A few days after the election I spoke with him about *Brown* and told him of my conversation and correspondence with Mr. Moore. He was adamant. As he saw it, *Brown* was the board's case, for its school system was under attack. If the board was unwilling to defend its position, he saw no reason for the attorney general to assume that responsibility. I also inferred that he had made political commitments that he did not intend to repudiate. In any case he had no intention to resist the appeal. There were also other matters to claim the attorney general's attention. A grand jury sitting in Wyandotte County was investigating claims of corruption in the government of Kansas City. This and other affairs of state were assigned priorities higher than that of assisting the Topeka school system to avoid embarrassment.

While the state of Kansas and the Topeka school board were hoping the segregation case would go away, others seemed unwilling that it should do so. It was becoming evident that the Supreme Court was determined to settle the issue of school segregation once and finally. In addition to the three cases already docketed, two others in the judicial mill would be ripe for argument after Kansas, South Carolina, and Virginia had been heard. The District of Columbia case of *Bolling v. Sharpe* had been noted by the Court in its order of October 8. At the suggestion made there, certiorari was petitioned for and granted on November 10, and the case was put down for argument on December 8, along with the segregation cases already docketed.[32] On August 28 the Supreme Court of Delaware had upheld a chancellor's decision finding inequality of facilities in the cases of *Belton v. Gebhart* and *Beulah v. Gebhart*[33] and ordering the admission of black students to white schools. The attorney general of Delaware applied for certiorari on November 13, and the petition was granted on November 24.[34] Arguments were to be heard with the other cases on December 8, just two weeks later.

By November 24 I had become reconciled to a future without *Brown*, without a trip to Washington at taxpayer expense, and without admission to the Supreme Court bar. Before noon on that day, two telephone calls rekindled my excitement. At midmorning I had a call from H. Albert Young, attorney general of Delaware, who informed me that the Delaware case had been docketed and set for argument during the week of December 8, the fifth in the series of arguments to begin with *Brown*. He had been told of our reluctance to go forward, and he called to urge that we reconsider; he assured me of his hope that we might work together to make the strongest possible showing. Although General Young did not say so, I suspected that his call had been prompted by Mr. Moore, of Virginia. I later suspected that he might also have known of other action that the Court was about to take.

Within the hour that I spoke with General Young, I was called by Elon Torrence, a longtime friend, who was one of the Topeka reporters for the Associated Press (AP). His Washington bureau had just reported an order directed to the Kansas attorney general. While I listened, he read the order. The Court took notice that the case had been docketed and set for argument, that the clerk had been informed that there would be no brief filed or argument by the Topeka Board of Education, and that there had been no response or other action on behalf of the state of Kansas. The order continued: "Because of the national importance of the issue presented and because of its importance to the State of Kansas, we request that the State present its views at oral argument. If the State does not desire to appear we request the Attorney General to advise whether the State's default shall be construed as a concession of invalidity."[35] Kansas could no longer stay aloof. We were in the case regardless of our desire.

The action taken by the Court was unusual. The record shows no formal request by any party, nor was there any notice or hearing. So far as the record is concerned, the Court acted solely upon its own volition. I have long suspected, without evidence to support my suspicion, that the attorneys from South Carolina and Virginia, whose access to the Court was better than ours, might informally have called the Court's attention to the prospect of a Kansas default and suggested the Court's action. Whatever its background, the Court's desire was unmistakable.

When I received word of the Court's order, General Fatzer was in Kansas City working with the grand jury. I reached him by telephone and told him of the AP story. Except for an initial response of "Hell," he expressed no special chagrin or disappointment. After a short pause, he said that we would comply with the Supreme Court's request. He also said that he wanted to study the order further before making a public statement. Finally, he told me to begin to write a brief. Later in the day he spoke to the representatives of the press. It was reported that he said, "Of course if the court desires a statement from me on the matter, I would just have to say that I would assume the statute to be constitutional."[36] According to the same story, Mike Oberhelman, chairman of the board of education, said that the attorney general should defend the case, that the board was no longer involved since its facilities had been found to be equal. His statement overlooked the facts that the constitutionality of segregation was the issue and that the decision to segregate Topeka's schools had been made by its board of education, not by the attorney general of Kansas.

Thursday, November 27, was Thanksgiving Day. For my office colleagues the early days of the week were spent thinking about and planning for the holiday. My days were different. I had no plan, nor did I know what to expect. The morning paper of November 26 reported that Governor Arn had said that Kansas ought to file a brief.[37] When I arrived at the office, I was told that the chief justice wanted to talk with me. The then chief justice, W. W. Harvey, had just observed his eighty-third birthday. With thirty years of service on the Supreme Court of Kansas, he was widely honored as a person of integrity, learning, and wisdom. After inquiring about the status of the case, he told me gently but firmly that he thought the state should appear and defend the statute and that it was the attorney general's duty to do so. He also said that he would inform General Fatzer of his views when he had the opportunity.

Among other noteworthy events of that day before Thanksgiving was a call from Mr. Moore, of Richmond. The gist of his message was a proffer of assistance. He said that two of the young lawyers in his firm who had worked on the Virginia brief were willing to fly to Topeka immediately to assist me in briefing the Kansas defense. The offer was indeed tempting. There were only twelve days remaining before the case was to be called for argument. If I took into account the time that would be required for printing and mailing copies to our adversaries, I saw only a week available for necessary further research and for planning and writing the appellees' brief. I had learned that Mr. Moore's law firm was regarded as one of Virginia's finest, and I was certain that its members were competent lawyers. They had just gone through the process that I was commencing. I declined their offer with thanks because I did not think it appropriate for Kansas to rely on or to be too closely associated with Virginia and its counsel.

The Virginians were segregationists. They were defending a statewide policy that mandated segregated schools. Before the Supreme Court, Virginia's attorney general argued that desegregation would destroy the public schools of the state. In less august environments some of his fellow Virginians asserted that blood would flow in the streets of Richmond before black children would attend school with whites. Kansas had no sympathy for such views. Aware of my own limitations and troubled by the dimensions of the task, I thought it better to go it alone.

As I settled down to the now inevitable task of writing, I gave my attention to a few incidental chores. First, I canceled plans for Thanksgiving dinner with my parents in rural Osage County. Second, I obtained a key to the state law library, where I expected to spend the Thanksgiving holiday and weekend. Third, I spoke with the state printer and secured his promise to expedite the printing of the brief. Then, I went to work. To brief the law of the case was an easy task. The precedents, both federal and state, were on our side. I felt that the cases were forthright and their meaning clear and that only by a process of strained interpretation and specious reasoning could one argue otherwise. Yet I thought we would probably lose. To overrule *Plessy* and *Gong Lum* would require the Court to make new law, but, I thought, the time for new law might have come. History and the American social conscience had overtaken the law.

On Friday, November 28, Dick Fatzer returned to the office. As the first order of the day's business, we discussed the appeal. I reported on my activities earlier in the week and my proposals for the state's brief. He agreed that we were obliged to file something in defense of the constitutionality of the statute and instructed me to go ahead. Handing me the file that he had reviewed he said, "Take the damned thing and do your best." He then sent a telegram to the clerk of the Supreme Court advising him that a brief supporting the constitutionality of the statute was in preparation and that every effort would be made to have it completed, served on the adverse counsel, and filed before December 8. He thought that the Court's alternative suggestion, that he might concede the statute's unconstitutionality, was unfair. His response was:

> It is not within the prerogative of a public official in the executive department of the state government to concede the invalidity of

any act passed by the state legislature. All enactments of the legislative department of the state government are presumed to be constitutional until declared to be unconstitutional by a court of last resort. I assume that the Justices of the Supreme Court of the United States were aware of this fact when the order of November 24 was made.[38]

Copies of the telegram were distributed to representatives of the press when they made their afternoon call.

Also on the afternoon of November 28, Fatzer supplied the media reporters with copies of a letter he had addressed to Chairman of the Topeka Board of Education Mike Oberhelman earlier in the day. The letter requested the board "through its attorney, to join with the State of Kansas in the brief that is now being prepared and which will be filed in the Supreme Court of the United States, to present the views of your Board as to the constitutionality of the statute in question."[39] Although the meaning of the letter is not entirely clear, the general intended it to be a request that Pete Caldwell collaborate with me in writing the brief.

Mr. Oberhelman learned of the general's letter before he received it in the mail. Although the board's regular December meeting was scheduled for Monday evening, December 1, an earlier response from the board was hoped for. Each hour was becoming critical. Accordingly, the chairman attempted to call a special meeting for 8:30 A.M. on Monday morning. The board's rules of procedure provided for special meetings on two days' written notice to all members, unless waived by them. Oberhelman requested the special meeting by telephone. Because Jake Dickinson refused to waive the two-day-written-notice requirements, the special meeting was never called to order, and the request was considered eleven hours later at the regular meeting. After much discussion the board voted five to one to authorize Caldwell to assist in preparing the brief and, on behalf of the board of education, to join in its submission. The motion adopted provided expressly that the authorization to join in the brief in no way constituted an endorsement of segregation.[40] The dissenting vote was cast by Dr. Harold Conrad, one of the board's new members.

Meanwhile, the Topeka press began to show an interest in the proceedings. During the week of November 24 stories concerning the appeal were front-page news. The *Capital's Sunday Magazine* on November 30 featured the case in a full-page story, illustrated with pictures of some of the principals and describing the case as one to make history.[41] The author concluded that Brown was "by far the most important" of the pending segregation appeals since in it alone were the separate facilities in fact equal.

By the morning of December 2, when Pete Caldwell checked in with me, I had settled upon what I wanted to say and how best to say it. During the long Thanksgiving weekend I had been able to work steadily and with few interruptions. Four sixteen-hour days in the library had been productive. Data banks and computerized retrieval methods were then unknown, and legal research was mainly book research—the aspect of lawyering that I enjoy most. Briefing Kansas's case was fun. Precedent, history, and tradition were with us. I was not dismayed by the possibility—indeed, the probability—that in the year 1952 the Court might reject precedent and change the course of history. My duty was not to obtain a favorable judgment. I was a lawyer with the honor to represent my state before the Supreme Court of the United States and the duty to help to assure that the Court's judgment was a mature one, based on all relevant information. Hence, to think through the state's arguments and to formalize them in a printed document was a satisfying experience. The arrival of Pete Caldwell's talent was most helpful. I was no longer alone. He edited, critiqued, and, in some cases, redrafted my arguments. Also, he took the initiative in formulating an argument that the district court's Finding of Fact No. 8 did not warrant injunctive relief.

At the outset of our brief we tried to define the state's role as one of the appellees in the case. Pointing out that by our appearance we did not propose or advocate the policy of segregation of any racial group within the public school system, we wrote:

> We contend only that policy determinations are matters within the exclusive province of the legislature. We do not express an opinion as to whether the practice of having separate schools of equal facility for the white and colored races is economically expedient or sociologically desirable, or whether it is consistent with sound ethical or religious theory. We do not understand that these extra-legal questions are now before the Court. The only proposition that we desire to urge is that the Kansas statute which permits racial segregation in elementary public schools in

certain cities of the state does not violate the Fourteenth Amendment to the Constitution of the United States as that amendment has been interpreted and applied by this Court.[42]

Our argument in defense of the district court's judgment had two facets. The first argument was a general one designed to support the power of the legislature to authorize the operation of racially separate-but-equal public schools. The second argument was that, irrespective of the constitutionality of the statute, the appellants were not entitled to the injunction they sought because there had been no showing that any of the plaintiffs had actually and personally suffered harm by reason of their segregation.

In developing arguments on the constitutional issue, we traced the history of the statutes relating to public school segregation in Kansas and reviewed the decisions of the Kansas Supreme Court that had upheld and had spelled out the limitations in such laws. We then emphasized the Supreme Court's own decisions—*Plessy, Gong Lum*—and distinguished our case from the higher education cases, *Gaines, Sipuel, Sweatt,* and *Painter*. Augmenting our arguments based on tradition and precedent, we argued the wisdom of the Kansas statute permitting local determination. Looking beyond the record in *Brown*, we called the attention of the Court to Kansas cities where segregation had been or was being phased out—Wichita, Pittsburg, Lawrence—according to schedules compatible with local attitudes and needs. This evolutionary process, we argued, was consistent with the intent and purpose of the Constitution.

Our second argument may have been more legalistic than substantial, but courts often justify decisions by relying on legalisms. The appellants contended that the district court erred in refusing to grant the requested injunction after finding that they, the appellants, had suffered serious harm and detriment in being required to attend segregated schools and that they had been deprived of the benefits they would have enjoyed in an integrated school system. We argued that the appellants had overstated their case. They were relying on Finding of Fact No. 8. That finding was couched in broad and general language—"Segregation of white and colored children in public schools has a detrimental effect upon the colored children." There was no specific finding that any of the plaintiffs in *Brown* suffered actual harm or detriment or was personally deprived of any benefit he or she would have received in an integrated school. Such a showing, we argued, would be necessary to entitle the plaintiffs to an injunction. Mere membership in a class discriminated against is not enough. If the Supreme Court had wanted to decide for the Topeka Board of Education, this argument might have been persuasive, but it was becoming apparent that the justices had another decision in mind.

As we wrote the brief, we sent the copy to the printer piecemeal. As each section was completed, I hand-carried it to the shop (which was across the street from the Statehouse), and while there I read the galley proofs of earlier sections already set in type. Late Wednesday afternoon, December 3, the manuscript was complete, and the final pages were sent to the printing plant. Early Thursday morning I approved the galleys, and a few hours later, sixty copies of the completed forty-four page document were delivered. Twenty years later, historian Richard Kluger described the result of our effort as a "concise, correct and clearly competent brief."[43] Some contemporary comments were less kind. Board member Dickinson did not find the brief persuasive. He thought we had not sufficiently explained Finding of Fact No. 8, nor had we convinced him that the statute was constitutional. His colleague, Dr. Conrad, read the brief but declined to comment. He continued to think the board should not have joined with the attorney general.[44]

While immersed in the task of briefing, I had given little thought to the prospective oral argument. Based on my earlier understanding, I assumed that General Fatzer would make whatever argument that he deemed necessary. I hoped that I might accompany him, but by this time I had learned that to form and rely upon expectations was seldom profitable. I did not know what to expect. When General Fatzer and I first discussed the Supreme Court's order of November 24, he doubted that appearance and oral argument on behalf of Kansas was necessary. He thought that the brief should fully set out the Kansas position and the authorities that supported it. Oral argument would add nothing. He also felt that the presence of John W. Davis in the South Carolina case was assurance that all possible arguments would be made in support of the state's power to enact laws providing for segregated schools. Perhaps, he suggested, Kansas could in some fashion adopt Mr. Davis's argument as its own. From a practical standpoint these thoughts made sense. As we talked, it became clear he was unwilling to go to Washington. His personal convictions, his commitments to his friends in the black community, and his sensitivity to possible adverse political consequences combined to produce a reluctance to be too closely identified with the case. At the same time he was a conscientious public officer and lawyer and expected to do whatever duty and the Court required.

I saw our responsibility differently than he. The Supreme Court had said, "We request that the State present its views at oral argument. If the State does not desire to appear, we request the Attorney General to advise whether the State's default shall be construed as a concession of invalidity."[45] Since we were unable to concede invalidity, I thought we were obliged to appear. Also, I thought, although the cases were to be argued in sequence, they had not been consolidated. For the purposes of argument each was a separate case based on its own facts. Ours was scheduled to be heard first. Mr. Davis did not represent Kansas, nor had he shown a desire to do so. To my pedestrian understanding of appellate procedure, it would be awkward for Kansas to adopt prospectively an argument to be made by the lawyer for another party in another and later case. But Dick was the attorney general. I was one of the lawyers in the back room. I would respect his decision.

Several days passed while our entire effort and attention was directed at the completion of the brief. When I had read and approved the last galleys and the presses had been set in motion, I reported to General Fatzer. He wanted to talk to me about the case. He had decided that Kansas should be represented at the arguments before the Supreme Court. He then pointed out that the Wyandotte County Grand Jury was still in session and that residents of Kansas City were petitioning him to bring ouster proceedings against the mayor. Moreover, at the end of the week of December 8 the National Association of State Attorneys General would hold its annual meeting at Sea Island, Georgia, and General Fatzer expected to be elected president of the organization, an honor that he wanted to receive in person. He would not be able to go to Washington for the argument. Although other assistants in the office were senior to me, one was ill, and none was as familiar with the case as I. Coming to the point, he said, "I want you to go back there and do what you can with the damn thing." He was talking to me. It was Thursday, December 4. The case was set for argument on December 8.

When the news reporters stopped by that afternoon, the general gave them a prepared statement. In part, the general said, "After further study and consideration I am persuaded that I, as Attorney General, have a duty to see that there is oral argument presented in support of the validity of the Kansas statute under attack." He continued by saying that since the board of education had declined to have their attorney appear, he was sending me to make the argument. He made it plain that he felt the board of education was shirking its duty, although he acknowledged the valuable assistance that Pete Caldwell had given us.⁴⁶ The following day he wired the clerk of the Supreme Court:

> The State of Kansas will be present to orally represent appellees in the case of *Brown et al. v. Topeka Board of Education et al.*, on December 9, 1952, when this case comes on for hearing. Mr. Paul E. Wilson, Assistant Attorney General for Kansas will represent the State of Kansas and will make the oral presentation. Brief of the State of Kansas and the Topeka Board of Education will be filed by Mr. Wilson together with service upon counsel of record in Topeka, Kansas. Mr. Wilson has application pending for admission to the Supreme Court and will have to be admitted prior to appearance for the purpose of making oral argument.⁴⁷

From then on the case was mine (for a while).

The general's assignment "to go to Washington" and his blessing, "do what you can with the damn thing," provoked me to uncharacteristically prompt action. Calling the clerk's office, I ascertained that my preadmission paperwork was in order. Kansas's senior U.S. senator, Andrew F. Schoeppel, who was a lawyer and a member of the Supreme Court bar, would appear with me and move for my admission. The general's secretary made reservations for my transportation to and lodging in Washington. I wanted to go by train. I packed the relevant files and papers plus fifty copies of our brief in two bulging, heavy briefcases. Finally, I went to the Palace, paid for, and picked up my blue suit.

As a youngster I had sometimes daydreamed of standing before the Supreme Court, parrying the justices' thrusts and overwhelming the Court with logic. When I elected to become a Kansas country lawyer, I put aside my childish hopes and expectations. On December 4, 1952, I was placed in a position where I could dream again. But the process of getting there was somewhat different from that I had imagined.

6

In the Supreme Court

At the end of 1952, *Brown* had been on my mind for nearly a year. Indifference had been followed by the excitement of learning that I would have a part in the drama. Then had come periods of uncertainty, frustration, apprehensiveness, and, finally, high adventure. The last is the subject of this chapter.

EN ROUTE

When the eastbound Santa Fe Chief pulled out of Topeka just before noon on Saturday, December 6, I was aboard with my papers and fifty copies of the Brief for Appellees in *Brown v. Board of Education*. Forty copies of the brief were to be filed for use of the Court; two for our adversaries; one each for the attorneys representing the other involved states and the District of Columbia; one for my own use; and three for anyone who might desire them. I had grossly underestimated the public interest. Twenty-four hours after my arrival in Washington, more than twenty media reporters, law professors, students, and other interested citizens had requested copies of the document.

To the supersonic traveler of the 1990s the idea of a twenty-eight-hour train ride from Topeka to Washington may seem quaint. Forty years ago it was less strange. Train travel was then more accessible and more reliable than now. Commercial air travel was less routine, and I, a countryman, preferred to remain earthbound. I liked and still like to ride the trains. Few experiences give me greater pleasure than a laid-back view of America passing before a pullman car window. Trains help me make the best of being out of sync with my time, of perhaps living in the wrong century.

There was another reason why I chose to go to Washington by train. During the days before my departure I had been preoccupied with writing and supervising the printing of the brief, telephone conferences with the Court's clerk and attorneys who were to sit on my side of the table, checking train and hotel reservations, shaping up my wardrobe, and other miscellaneous but time-consuming logistics and legal details. The task of argument had been handed to me just a few hours before D-Day. I had had no time to think about what I might say to the Supreme Court and how I might say it. The train ride gave me twenty-eight uninterrupted hours, less sleeping time, to think. I reread the trial record, the appellants' brief, and the briefs of the numerous friends of the court—none of whom were friends of Kansas. Since I had written the state's brief, I was familiar with its contents and expected to use it as the basis for my argument. My effort to adapt it to oral presentation consisted of sketching an outline on the blank endpaper, making marginal notes, and underscoring the language I wanted to emphasize. This effort, to which I added a couple of rehearsals before the washroom mirror, was my preparation. Attorneys in the other cases, whose preparation had been more deliberate than mine, spoke from typed manuscripts, or outlines, or carefully arranged index cards. Perhaps that is why they were able to speak at greater length than I.

The Santa Fe carried me to Chicago, where I boarded a train of the Baltimore and Ohio. The route was lined with landmarks—places where historic events had occurred and notable persons had lived—that seemed relevant to my journey. Starting in Topeka, where in 1854 free-state settlers had proposed statehood for Kansas under a constitution that would exclude all blacks, we soon passed the village of Lecompton, the territorial capital of Kansas, where proslave partisans had written a constitution permitting slavery that was approved by Congress and signed by the president only to be rejected by the people of the territory. From Lecompton a few minutes brought us to Lawrence, founded and settled by New Englanders, the center of free-state, antislave sentiment and activity, and the target of proslave guerilla raiders, but which also had a history of school segregation. As we stopped in Kansas City, Missouri, I mused that Westport, only a few blocks from the Union Station, had been a major proslave port of entry to Kansas Territory and that numbers of its residents had voted in the first Kansas territorial elections and served in the first territorial legislature. For a few miles east of Kansas City the route followed in the fertile valley of the Missouri River, where slaves had been used extensively in the production of hemp, corn, and tobacco. Late in the afternoon, after passing through that part of Missouri still known as Little Dixie, we entered the free state of Illinois, the home state of Abraham Lincoln and of Stephen A. Douglas, the principal author of the bill that organized Kansas Territory and the protagonist of the doctrine of squatter sovereignty.

The first stop in Illinois was at Galesburg, site of the fifth Lincoln-Douglas debate of 1858, in which Abraham Lincoln had declared that perfect social and political equality between the white and black races was an impossibility.[1] It was long after dark when we reached Chicago, the city where Abraham Lincoln in 1860 had been first nominated as the Republican candidate for president. After my Chicago transfer I bedded down, sleeping across Indiana and Ohio, states whose emigrants, including my own pioneer ancestors, had helped to bolster the free-state population of early Kansas.

When I awoke on Sunday morning the train had stopped. Beyond an expanse of water, a cluster of tall buildings told me we were in a city. The porter said it was Pittsburgh. This was the Golden Triangle where the Allegheny and Monongahela Rivers join to form the Ohio. A century and a half earlier Pittsburgh was, for many, the gateway to the West. For me it was the gateway to the East. During most of that day the train passed through the wooded hills and fertile valleys of Pennsylvania while I remembered that a Pennsylvanian, James Buchanan, had been president of the United States during much of the time that Kansas had struggled to achieve statehood and that another Pennsylvanian, Andrew Reeder, had been the first governor of Kansas Territory. Around midafternoon we crossed the bridge at the junction of the Potomac and Shenandoah Rivers and were in Harper's Ferry, where a one-time sojourner in Kansas, bearing the quintessentially American name of John Brown, had earned immortality and a trip to the gallows. From Harper's Ferry we headed toward Washington paralleling for a while the former channel of the historic Chesapeake and Ohio canal. It was late afternoon. As the slanting rays of the early winter sun filtered through the trees of the adjacent forest, I must have subconsciously wished that the ride would never end. I knew that the next day would be different. It had been a good trip. It had given me the opportunity to rest, to collect and organize my thoughts about my assigned task, and to do a bit of thinking about America. I had even begun to entertain a vague belief that I might be involved in something that could add a dimension to history's seamless web.

ARRIVAL

It took a long time for the trainmen to maneuver the train into position for discharge of its passengers in Washington's Union Station. Darkness had fallen when I finally entered the terminal. The station was a bustling, noisy place through which thousands of travelers passed each day. As I waited to pick up my luggage, I bought a newspaper from a vendor who was canvassing the new arrivals. It was the *Washington Post* for December 7, 1952. I was immediately attracted by the front-page headline, "Legal Giants to Vie in Segregation Case."[2] That, I thought, is my case. I had hardly expected to be so described. Scanning the piece, I concluded that the editor who composed the headline had not had me in mind. Identified as the chief protagonists were John W. Davis, "one-time Democratic candidate for the presidency and a famed constitutional lawyer," and Thurgood Marshall, "the man who has directed the highly successful legal drive of the past dozen years to win equal rights for his race." They were the attorneys in the South Carolina case. The story continued by mentioning "other men of eminence" who would participate in the arguments. On the Davis side would be H. Albert Young, attorney general of Delaware, Milton D. Korman, of the District of Columbia corporation counsel's office; J. Lindsay Almond, attorney general of Virginia; T. Justin Moore, of Richmond; and "perhaps the Attorney General of Kansas." Names of the attorneys who would sit on Marshall's side of the table were then enumerated. I did not make the story. Either the reporter had not known of my intended appearance, or I was not a man "of eminence." I prefer to believe the former, but I cannot, in candor, deny the latter. The story concluded: "The issue before the Supreme Court this week has vast social and political as well as constitutional ramifications, whichever way it may be decided in the end. At least it will not be possible for either side to say that it suffered because it was not represented by first-class counsel."[3] I wondered whether the writer would be able to affirm his estimate at the week's end.

Leaving the great front entrance of the station, beyond the plaza and park with their fountains and statuary, I had a view of the domed Capitol of the United States. I was really in Washington. My hotel was a fifteen-minute cab ride from the station. At the suggestion of my Virginia associates, I had made a reservation at the Carlton, one of Washington's smaller but more distinguished hotels. Originally built in the 1920s and modeled after an Italian Renaissance palace, the Carlton is only two blocks from the White House. In the subdued elegance of its lobby one might encounter members of Congress, four-star generals, and even cabinet officers. It seemed an appropriate stopping place for John W. Davis and his entourage of Wall Street lawyers and the parties from South Carolina, Virginia, and Delaware. Upon checking in, I found that both Mr. Carter and Mr. Moore had called, each requesting that I call back as soon as I arrived. I assumed that Mr. Carter wanted to see our brief. Mr. Moore wanted to see me—to be assured that I was a real person and that I would stand up when the Kansas case was called.

Reaching my room, I made it my first order to unpack and spend a few minutes in relaxation while I listened to the evening news from a Washington radio station. The commentator spoke of the upcoming school segregation arguments in the Supreme Court. He mentioned the names of the attorneys who would be arguing before the Supreme Court, including Assistant Attorney General *Paul Williams* of Kansas. Returning Mr. Carter's call, I found that he and his associates were staying at the Statler, just across the street, and that he wanted to say hello and pick up a copy of our brief. Sensing that he was probably more interested in seeing the brief than in saying hello, I promised to deliver it shortly. Mr. Moore gave me the number of the

Virginia suite and said the attorneys on our side would meet there later in the evening.

For me the visit to the rendezvous of the enemy was memorable. Bob Carter met me at the door and invited me into a room filled with lawyers, many of whom were later to receive widespread recognition for professional and public service. Besides Carter and Charles Scott, I met Thurgood Marshall, Spottswood Robinson III, Oliver Hill, Jack Greenberg, James Nabrit, and others whose faces now blur in my memory but whose names have been recorded by historians. Although we met as adversaries, they were cordial, courteous, and agreeable men. Two of my first impressions remain vivid after the lapse of more than forty years. First, except for Greenberg, they were all black. His and mine were the only white faces in the room. I had never seen so many black lawyers in one place at one time, nor had I ever been racially in the minority. It gave me a strange feeling that I cannot describe but will always remember. Second, these black lawyers were different from the stereotype that I had in mind. In my rare contacts with black lawyers I thought them to be deferential rather than adversary, relying on favor rather than law. Even Elisha Scott played to the sympathy and emotions of judges and jurors. The lawyers I met at the Statler were confident. They sought only what they believed the law had given them. They looked me squarely in the eye and promised that they would win.

The later meeting with the attorneys who were to sit on my side of the table was good for my waning morale. In the spacious sitting room of the Virginians' suite in the Carlton, I met Mr. Moore, with whom I had become acquainted by telephone, Attorneys General Almond and Young, D.C.'s Milton Korman, and a dozen others who, after forty years, merge into a single pattern—young, well groomed, good looking, bright, self-confident, and articulate. Mr. Davis was not there. At seventy-nine, he was conserving his strength for his 140th Supreme Court argument, but South Carolina was represented by younger men from his firm and by Robert McC. Figg and S. E. Rogers, who had handled the case in the district court. For me it was a pleasant and exciting occasion. The men I met were attractive, sophisticated, civil, and clearly competent lawyers. Their accents charmed me. They appeared to accept me as a peer. Moreover, they, too, expected to win.

On arrival I learned that the arguments had been postponed until Tuesday, December 9. To me this news was a happy reprieve. One more day would help. After I had given copies of the Kansas brief to each of my associates, the meeting was largely a social event—a time for getting acquainted. I could sense that much of their interest was centered on me. They had wondered about the unknown lawyer from a place strange to most of them who would make the leadoff argument for their side. They inquired at length about Kansas and its black population, about its interracial relations, and about the public school system. After a few minutes they seemed to have been reassured that I would be present at the call of the docket, that I would respond for Kansas, and that I would neither concede the invalidity of the statute nor waive argument on the state's behalf. In an hour or so the group separated with the understanding that we would return for a more serious session on the following evening.

Shortly after my return to my room, my telephone rang. A masculine voice inquired if I was Mr. Wilson. I acknowledged my identity. Then the voice continued, "This is the Twentieth Century Escort Service. We heard that you might like some company this evening." Being neither imaginative nor quick-witted, I answered "No. You are mistaken." That call has haunted me for forty years. I assumed initially that it was intended for another guest at the hotel and that my room was rung by mistake. But what if it was not? Was someone trying to compromise me? Did I, fresh from Kansas, seem an appropriate target for a purveyor of an evening of pleasure? How might my life have been changed if I had said yes?

GETTING MY BEARINGS

When Monday morning came my number one chore was the delivery of the Kansas brief to the Supreme Court. Since it was a brisk yet sunny December day and I was anxious to learn about Washington, I decided to walk. Also, I was not sure that I trusted Washington cab drivers. The distance was greater than I thought and my briefcase heavier than I expected, but the trek was a good and satisfying experience. Leaving the hotel, I crossed Lafayette Square, past the White House, and headed down magnificent Pennsylvania Avenue. Along the Avenue I passed or glimpsed a few buildings that I recognized and many that I did not. On my left I saw the Willard Hotel, whose

Facade of the United States Supreme Court building, sometimes called the "marble palace." (Courtesy of the United States Supreme Court)

name has been part of our national history since the Civil War. A little way to the right I could see the National Archives, repository for much of America's past; huge buildings in the neighborhood housed the departments of Justice, Labor, Commerce, and Post Office and, with many other structures, provided places where thousands of government workers labored to keep America in business.

I had read that the Capitol sits on a hill, and because I approached it as a pedestrian visitor, I was ready to confirm that assertion. Breathing heavily, I reached the south (or was it the east?) steps where workmen were building a platform for the forthcoming inauguration of President-elect Eisenhower. I was close to my destination. Only a few hundred yards separated me from the gleaming white facade of the Supreme Court Building—sometimes called the Marble Palace. Massive fluted columns topped by ionic capitals support the pediment that (according to the tourists' guidebook) rises ninety-two feet above the ground and is faced with a sculptured frieze that, to me as a first time viewer, was more majestic than meaningful. Below the frieze I read the words "Equal Justice under Law." I suppose I was inspired, or should have been. Forty years later my reaction might be different. As a declared objective, the statement is eloquent and immaculate. As a statement of existing fact, I would take the words with a few ounces of salt. Fifty years at the bar have taught me that the law is no guarantor of equal justice, even in the Supreme Court.

Crossing the paved plaza and ascending the wide front steps, I found the massive front doors where eight bronze panels depict triumphs of mankind in developing a just society. Mr. Willey, the Supreme Court clerk, was expecting me. He was cordial, casual, and disarming. He accepted the brief without mentioning its lateness and reassured me that my admission papers were in order. He inquired if I had arranged for a sponsor to move for my admission, saying that he would be glad to call a lawyer from the solicitor general's office to appear with me if I desired. He then suggested that since the Court was in session, it might be helpful for me to spend some time in the courtroom as a spectator. I agreed, and Mr. Willey guided me across the pillared Grand Hall to the courtroom door.

As described in the literature, the Court Chamber is eighty-two by ninety-nine feet, with the coffered ceiling rising forty-four feet above the dark floor of African marble. Twenty-four massive columns of silver gray Italian marble line walls of ivory-veined marble mined in Spain. Gold leaf and red adorn the ceiling recesses. High on the four walls above the thirty-foot columns, four thirty-six-foot-long marble friezes depict the great classical and Christian lawgivers. The panel over the main entrance, the one faced by the justices while in session, arrays the powers of Evil, Corruption, Slander, Deceit, and Despotic Power against the forces of Good, Security, Harmony, Peace, Charity, and Defense of Virtue. Dominating the conflict is the winged female figure of Justice, flanked by Wisdom and Truth. The grandeur of the room is enhanced by its furnishings: "Tones of red in carpet and upholstery and heavy draperies, highly polished luster in solid Honduran mahogany, gleaming bronze lattice-work in gates to the side corridors."[4] Upon viewing the Chamber, one observer remembered a statement of Oscar Wilde's Lady Gwendolen Fairfax—"In matters of grave importance, style, not sincerity, is the vital thing." Whatever unspoken feelings may lie beneath their somber judicial robes, it cannot be gainsaid that the justices go in style.

As in all courtrooms, a bar separates the spectator section from the working area of the Chamber. The long mahogany bench rises against a backdrop of marble columns and heavy burgundy hangings. A large clock is suspended high above the bench to remind the sometimes too loquacious advocate that time marches on. Behind the bench, nine high-backed chairs are upholstered with dark leather but otherwise conform to no uniform pattern in style or shape. Each justice may bring to the bench the chair that he finds most comfortable. Just beyond the extreme right end of the bench the flag adds a touch of color to the white marble wall. The clerk's desk is at the left end of the bench, whereas the marshal's place is at the right. In front of and lower than the bench are the counsel tables. Squarely in the middle, facing the chief justice, is the lectern used by attorneys while addressing the Court. On the lectern are two lights—one white, which comes on when the speaker has only five minutes remaining; and the other red, which is the signal to stop. On each side of the lectern long tables parallel the bench and are used by attorneys waiting to be heard or otherwise interested in the case being presented. Back of the counsel tables are other chairs, usually occupied by attorneys waiting for their cases to be called. My students have often inquired, "What does it feel like to be in the Supreme Court?" I have no adequate answer. Feeling cannot be described in words—only felt.

The case being argued when I entered the Chamber was one involving a question of commercial law that, to me, was not very interesting. There were few spectators. From their general demeanor, I inferred that some of the justices shared my lack of interest. Some looked at the ceiling; some frowned; only a few seemed to be following the argument. I lingered in the Chamber mainly to identify the justices, none of whom I had seen before. I memorized the seating chart showing the position that each occupied when seated at the bench. The arrangement as determined by Court protocol places the chief justice in the middle of the panel with four associate justices on each side. The justice who is senior in point of service sits on the chief's immediate right as the Court faces out, and the justice who is second in seniority occupies the position on the chief's left. Thereafter, the justices are seated alternately right and left according to time spent on the court. The junior justice is always seated on the extreme left, or on the right as viewers see the bench. The array that I could expect to face, reading from my left to my right, was this:

Associate Justice Tom C. Clark, of Texas, age fifty-three, was appointed by President Truman in 1949. He was a former attorney general of the United States.

Associate Justice Robert H. Jackson of New York, age sixty, was

Members of the Supreme Court of the United States in 1954: *(front row, left to right)* Felix Frankfurter, Hugo L. Black, Earl Warren, Stanley F. Reed, and William O. Douglas; *(back row)* Tom C. Clark, Robert H. Jackson, Harold H. Burton, and Sherman Minton. (Courtesy of the United States Supreme Court)

former solicitor general and attorney general of the United States and chief prosecutor for the United States at the Nuremberg war crimes trials. He was appointed to the Court by President Roosevelt in 1941.

Associate Justice Felix Frankfurter, of Massachusetts, seventy, was appointed by Roosevelt in 1939. He was a former professor of law, Harvard University. Of the nine, I feared Justice Frankfurter most. He was reputed to be a relentless questioner of counsel who appeared before him and to be demonstrably impatient with responses he thought less than excellent. As I observed Justice Frankfurter, he was silent. Perhaps, I thought, he is planning an ambush for tomorrow.

Associate Justice Hugo L. Black of Alabama, age sixty-six, was appointed by President Roosevelt in 1937. He was a former United States Senator.

Chief Justice Frederick M. Vinson of Kentucky, age sixty-two, was appointed by President Truman in 1946. He was a former member of Congress, judge of the United States Court of Appeals for the District of Columbia Circuit, and secretary of the treasury.

Associate Justice Stanley F. Reed, of Kentucky, age sixty-six, was appointed by President Roosevelt in 1938. He was a former attorney general of Kentucky and solicitor general of the United States.

Associate Justice William O. Douglas of Connecticut, fifty-three, was appointed by Roosevelt in 1939. He was a former professor of law, Yale University, and chairman of the Securities and Exchange Commission. When appointed at the age of forty, Justice Douglas became the youngest person to sit on the Court during the twentieth century.

Associate Justice Harold H. Burton of Ohio, age sixty-four, was appointed by President Truman in 1949. A former United States senator, Justice Burton was the only Republican member of the Court.

Associate Justice Sherman H. Minton of Indiana, age sixty-two, was appointed by President Truman in 1949. He was a former United States senator and judge of the United States Court of Appeals for the District of Columbia Circuit. Justice Minton was the junior member of the Court. He sat at the left (my right) end of the bench.

When the Court rose for its noon recess I returned to my hotel, reassured by the hour in the Court Chamber. In contrast to the grandeur of their surroundings, the justices were remarkably relaxed and informal. They rocked and turned in their swivel chairs, whispered comments to each other, smiled when smiles were appropriate, and even looked bored when the arguments became boring. I began to realize that these were not demigods or supermen. They were members of the profession to which I belonged. They were human beings who shared my doubts, uncertainties, and misgivings along with their sense of duty. They were justices because they had politically bet on the right horses.

The next evening's meeting in the Virginia suite was a high spot in my Washington adventure. In addition to the lawyers present on the previous evening, I met John W. Davis. Tall, white-haired, and distinguished, he seemed to fit the role of the great lawyer. Forty years later I recall vividly his poise, civility, gentleness, and learning.

John W. Davis (left) and Thurgood Marshall, opposing counsel in *Briggs v. Elliott*, the South Carolina companion case to *Brown v. Board of Education*. Mr. Davis acted as sponsor for Paul Wilson's admission to the bar of the United States Supreme Court. (Courtesy of AP World Wide Photo, New York)

Mr. Davis, a legend among American lawyers, was a West Virginian by birth. His father was a lawyer and erstwhile member of Congress. After reading law in his father's office, young Davis entered the law school at Washington and Lee University, where he completed the prescribed course of study in one year. Returning to Clarksburg, he was associated with his father in the practice. His career as an advocate commenced before a West Virginia justice of the peace in a case involving the ownership of a turkey hen and her twenty-nine chicks. It ended fifty-seven years later in the Supreme Court of the United States, where he represented the Board of Trustees of School District No. 22, Clarendon County, South Carolina. In both instances he lost, but during the years that separated the two events he compiled a record of achievement that seldom has been paralleled in the annals of the American bar.

A decade and a half in West Virginia, less one year spent teaching law at his alma mater, brought Mr. Davis a substantial law practice, a seat in the state legislature, and the presidency of the West Virginia Bar Association. In 1910 he was elected to Congress, where his demonstrated understanding of the law and his talent for advocacy were soon recognized and led to his selection by President Wilson to be solicitor general of the United States. The solicitor general and his staff represent the government in cases before the Supreme Court. During his five-year tenure Davis personally argued sixty-seven cases, winning forty-eight of them and earning the respect of adversaries and justices alike.

When Mr. Davis left the solicitor general's office in 1918, he turned his talents to diplomacy, first as a post–World War I negotiator, and then as America's ambassador to the Court of St. James. In England he charmed royalty and commoner alike. King George V is said to have called him "the most perfect gentleman" the king had ever met. Back in the United States, after being mentioned as a possible Democratic nominee for president in 1920, he returned to law practice, this time on Wall Street. In 1922 he became president of the American Bar Association, serving one year. In 1924 he received the presidential nomination of the Democratic party, which was then in disarray. His decisive defeat by Calvin Coolidge prompted his return to practice as the senior member of the socially and politically correct law firm of Davis, Polk, Wardwell, Sutherland, and Kiendl. There, he wore the mantle of the ultimate Wall Street lawyer for more than thirty years.

As solicitor general, Mr. Davis had spoken in support of liberal positions taken by the Wilson administration. As a young lawyer he had represented Eugene V. Debs, the Socialist labor leader. Later, he had occasionally emerged from his Wall Street office to take civil libertarian stands on such issues as freedom of the press, religious freedom, and the rights of those who expressed conscientious objections to war. He represented J. Robert Oppenheimer in his fight for security clearance and expressed sympathy for Alger Hiss. His positions on race discrimination were mixed. As solicitor general, he had spoken for Negro voting rights. As a candidate for president, he had denounced the Ku Klux Klan. Yet he had remained aloof from the NAACP and declined to be identified with its causes when invited to do so. He was patronizing and tolerant in his relations with black individuals, but it is often asserted that he did not accept blacks as equals. It was as a representative of wealth and entrepreneurial enterprise that Mr. Davis had become rich and famous and had gained a reputation as a constitutional and corporation lawyer without peer in the American bar.

When I met Mr. Davis I knew little of his professional and personal achievements. I had a vague understanding that he was a distinguished and honored lawyer who had once run for president. I knew nothing of his politics and philosophy other than that he was a Democrat. It was his image that captured my respect and admiration—his bearing, his demeanor, his style. He had not been cast from common clay.

Mr. Davis had read my brief earlier in the day. He pronounced it "quite adequate." Then, for more than an hour he discussed the next day's argument with me. He told me what kind of questions I might expect from particular justices. He suggested the kinds of answers that would please the Court. He emphasized the importance of candor and cautioned against assertions that I could not support. Throughout the evening he gave no hint of impatience, condescension, or superiority. As the meeting broke up he graciously offered to move for my admission to the Supreme Court bar when we would appear the following day. Earlier I had spoken with Kansas's senior senator about performing this service, but aware that the name of my sponsor would appear on my Certificate of Admission, I made a hurried judgment that the name of John W. Davis of New York would add more luster to the document than that of my friend, Andrew F. Schoeppel of Ness City, Kansas, and I accepted his kind offer. The certificate, suitably framed, has hung on the wall of my study for more than forty years. I have often called the attention of visitors to the recital that my admission was moved by John W. Davis.

Much of the evening was spent speculating about the personal attitudes of the justices and their amenability to persuasion. All conceded that Black and Douglas would vote against us regardless of the strength of our arguments. On the other hand, most thought that the Kentuckians, Chief Justice Vinson and Justice Reed, would be friendly. Coming from a border state where historically the schools were segregated, neither was regarded as a social reformer. Justices Frankfurter, Jackson, and Burton would, they thought, be concerned about the stability of the law and would be reluctant to overrule long-standing precedents. Justices Clark and Minton were relatively new to the Court and their opinions too few to discern in them a consistent pattern of judicial thinking, although some thought that Clark would prefer to vote in favor of the states' positions, particularly if, in doing so, he would be aligned with the majority.

ARGUMENT

On Tuesday morning, December 9, that day's expected Supreme Court arguments were again front-page news in the Washington papers. In the story in the *Post* I was identified as the Kansas representative, and my name was spelled correctly. After reviewing the expected arguments in the several cases the story continued:

> Some observers feel that the hardest case to decide will be that of Kansas which filed its brief only yesterday, after a prod by the Court itself last month.
> In the three other state cases the lower courts have found as a fact that Negro schools are physically inferior. But in Kansas the court found equality of facilities, yet also found that segregation itself has "a detrimental effect on the colored children" and declared that segregation "has a tendency to retard the educational and mental development of Negro children and to deprive them of some of the benefits they would receive in a racially integrated school system."[5]

By high noon the Court Chamber was filled to its capacity. Officers of the Court, lawyers, litigants, members of their families, and spectators conversed in subdued voices while they awaited the opening of the session. In the Great Hall outside the courtroom several hundred people stood in lines, hopefully awaiting a place in the chamber or at least a glimpse of the Court. Then things began to happen. The marshal's gavel fell, the people in the chamber stood, and three justices emerged through each of three openings in the velvet backdrop as the marshal intoned, "The Honorable, the Chief Justice and the Associate Justices of the Supreme Court of the United States." While the justices moved to their places at the bench, the marshal continued, "Oyez! Oyez! Oyez! All persons having business before the Honorable, the Supreme Court of the United States, are admonished to draw near and give their attention, for the Court is now sitting. God save the United States and this Honorable Court." The marshal's gavel again rapped, and those in the courtroom resumed their seats. The Court was in session.

Admissions to the bar was the first item on the agenda. Mr. Davis was recognized and introduced me along with several other applicants who were members of his firm. Reading from a prepared script, he stated that he had examined the applications and supporting papers and was satisfied that each of us possessed the necessary qualifications for admission to the Supreme Court bar. Other applicants were presented by their sponsors. Then in the presence of the Court the clerk administered the oath collectively, binding each of us to "as an attorney and counsellor of this Court conduct [ourselves] uprightly and according to law" and to "support the Constitution of the United States."

After being sworn, we were welcomed by the chief justice to the fellowship of the bar and escorted by the clerk to an adjacent room where each signed the Register of Attorneys and paid the admission fee of twenty-five dollars. Thus, I became an attorney and counselor of the Supreme Court of the United States. Nowadays, a generation that prizes expediency above amenity has streamlined the procedure: one may be admitted in absentia by mail, and the rest is done by computers. When we returned to the Chamber, opinions in cases decided earlier were being announced. As the result in each was made public, the author of the Court's opinion read or summarized the decision. Other justices, particularly those who dissented, then had the opportunity to comment and express their views. The preliminary proceedings completed, the Court was ready to hear arguments in cases on the day's docket. It was 1:35 P.M. when the chief justice called "Case No. 8, Oliver Brown and Others versus the Board of Education of Topeka, Shawnee County, Kansas." The clerk responded "counsel are present." The attorneys had already taken places at the long counsel tables facing the bench. I sat on the immediate left (the Court's right) side of the lectern. Mr. Davis sat to my left and beyond him were counsel for Virginia, the District of Columbia, and Delaware. Next to the right (the Court's left) side of the lectern were Robert Carter and Charles Scott, with attorneys in the other cases seated in the order in which they would speak.[6]

Since the burden of making the first argument falls upon the appellant, Mr. Carter spoke first. This gave me a brief reprieve and an opportunity to observe the justices at close range. In response to a smile and recognition by the chief justice, Robert Carter arose and moved to the lectern. He was a good lawyer. Young, tall, and slender, he was self-confident and articulate. He knew his case. He had been in the Supreme Court before. The first several minutes of his presentation were spent in reviewing the proceedings in the district court and defining the issues to be determined in the appeal. At this early stage he made it clear that the challenge in *Brown* was aimed at segregation per se. He declared:

> Here we abandon any claim, in pressing our attack on the unconstitutionality of this statute—We abandon any claim—of any constitutional inequality which comes from anything *other than the act of segregation itself* [emphasis added].
>
> In short, the sole basis for our appeal here on the constitutionality of the statute of Kansas is that it empowers the maintenance and operation of racially segregated schools.[7]

At the hour of two, Mr. Carter was interrupted by the chief justice, who announced that lunch time had arrived.

As Mr. Carter resumed his argument after the recess, the justices became more active participants in the dialogue. Justice Reed wondered whether there was evidence to support the trial court's Finding of Fact No. 8 that segregation had a detrimental effect on colored children that affected their motivation to learn and whether the finding went to ability to learn or "merely the emotional reactions."[8] In response to questions by Justice Burton and the chief justice, Carter argued that because education involved more than tangible physical facilities, *Plessy*, a case involving transportation facilities, was not applicable and that the controlling precedents should be the higher education cases—*Gaines, Sipuel,* and *Sweatt*—whose rationales applied with equal force to elementary schools; nor did he find a precedent in *Gong Lum,* since in that case Gong Lum had not denied the state's power to enforce racial classifications in its elementary schools—a question *never* squarely presented to the Supreme Court in any of the earlier cases.

At that point Justice Frankfurter became interested. He pointed out that *Gong Lum* was a unanimous opinion of a Court that included such civil libertarians as Holmes, Brandeis, and Stone and according to its own terms rested on the assumption that the issue had been settled by a large body of adjudication going back to "what might fairly have been called an abolitionist state," the commonwealth of Massachusetts.[9] Carter's attempted answers were hardly persuasive, and Justice Frankfurter continued: "The more specific question I would like to put to you is this: Do we not have to face the fact that what you are challenging is something that was written into the public law and adjudications of courts, including this Court, by a large body of decisions and, therefore, the question arises whether, and under what circumstances, this Court should now upset so long a course of decisions?"[10] Later on Justice Frankfurter pointed out that the court was for the first time considering segregation "unembarrassed by physical inequalities" and commented:

> A long course of legislation by the states, and a long course of utterances by this Court and other courts in dealing with the subject, from the point of view of relevance as to whether a thing is or is not within the prohibition of the Fourteenth Amendment, is from my point of view almost as impressive as a single decision. . . . I do think we have to face in this case the fact that we are dealing with a long-established historical practice by the states, and the assumption of the exercise of power which not only was written on the statute books, but has been confirmed and adjudicated by state courts, as well as by the expressions of this Court.[11]

The comments reached sympathetic ears on our side of the table. Mr. Davis passed me a note saying I should bear down on Justice Frankfurter's point. This, to him, was the jugular vein. Justice Frankfurter continued to probe. Noting that the Kansas statute was not a legislative aberration but was representative of the law of many states, he inquired, "What is the root of this legislation?—Why was there such legislation—Was there anything in life to which this legislation responds?"[12] After urging that there was no rational basis for the classification, no reason sufficient in law, Mr. Carter asked to reserve the balance of his time for rebuttal and left the lectern.

My time had come. The chief justice nodded in my direction and said, "General Wilson." I rose, stood behind the lectern, and, somewhat to my surprise, heard my voice saying, "May it please the Court . . ." Quickly, I tried to emphasize that I appeared only for the state of Kansas and only to defend the constitutionality of a statute passed by the Kansas legislature. I did not represent and carried no brief for the Topeka Board of Education. I then sought to explain the state's tardy appearance by pointing out that the attorney general had regarded the case as local in nature and not of statewide concern, that the Topeka Board of Education was the original defendant and had borne the burden of defense in the trial court, and we felt that the state's participation in the appeal should be governed by the board's decision not to appear. I emphasized that we had never at any time entertained any doubt about the constitutionality of our statute. The chief justice seemed to understand. He said: "General Wilson, may I state to you that we were informed that the Board of Education would not be represented here in argument, and would not file a brief, and it being a very important question, and this case having facets that other cases did not, we wanted to hear from the State of Kansas. . . . We did not want the State of Kansas and its viewpoint to be silent."[13]

With this reassurance, I had a clear duty—to inform the Court of the viewpoint of the state of Kansas.

Richard Kluger read the transcript of the arguments twenty years after the fact. He found my presentation to be "a perfectly able but somewhat simplistic argument for the state of Kansas."[14] I do not quarrel with the historian's evaluation. I regarded *Brown* as a simple case. The law was, to me, clear and was on our side. The factual justification for the law was more difficult. Hence, I chose to limit my argument to the law. Moreover, in the twenty-odd years that had elapsed between the argument and Kluger's comment, the law governing interracial equality and discrimination had grown vastly more complex. What seemed simplistic in 1972 might have been less so twenty years earlier.

Since my purpose was to inform the Court, I outlined the statutory scheme of public schools in Kansas, emphasizing that racially segregated elementary schools were permitted, not required, in only a few communities and that in those communities the local policy was for local determination. Also emphasizing the finding of no substantial inequality among the Topeka schools, I suggested that "it is our theory that this case resolves itself simply to this: whether the 'separate but equal' doctrine is still the law, and whether it is to be followed in this case by this Court." At this point, questions from the bench required that I depart from my planned argument. Justice Frankfurter wanted to know how many blacks lived in Kansas (about 73,000 or 4 percent of the total population) and where they lived (more than two-thirds in the twelve cities of the first class). Justice Black asked where Indians went to school (they attended white schools). Justice Frankfurter returned to the act to inquire about the possible consequences of reversal. What problems did I foresee? What further action by the Supreme Court might be needed to carry out the decree? I replied: "In perfect candor, I must say to the Court that the consequences would probably not be serious."

"As I pointed out, our Negro population is small. We do have in our Negro schools Negro teachers, Negro administrators, that would necessarily be assimilated in the school system at large. That might produce some administrative difficulties. I can imagine no serious difficulty beyond that."[15]

Justice Reed asked whether efforts had been made to repeal the statute being challenged in this case. (I knew of none.)

Justice Jackson's turn was next. Of the nine members of the Court, I think I admired Jackson most. He was handsome and dignified, yet relaxed and disarming. He had a human quality not readily discernible in some of his colleagues. I was not uncomfortable when he questioned me. It went like this:

JUSTICE JACKSON: Mr. Attorney General, you emphasized the four percent, and the smallness of the population. Would that affect your problem if there were heavier concentrations?
MR. WILSON: It is most difficult for me to answer that question. It might. I am not acquainted with the situation where there is a heavier concentration, in other words.
JUSTICE JACKSON: I mean, your statute adapts itself to different localities. What are the variables that the statute was designed to take care of, if any, if you know, at this late date?[16]

My response, although unartfully expressed, was intended to convey my belief that considerations of demography, economics, history, and tradition all had an impact on the local decision. In some cities the black population was too small for separate schools to be economically feasible. The first settlers in some communities were from the South and the border states where segregation was a way of life. In other places the New England antislavery sentiment had been strong and less friendly to any discrimination based on race. In Topeka, one of the original free-state towns, the impact of the Exodus had exacerbated racial tensions and contributed to the continuance of segregation. These considerations along with other factors that were uniquely local combined to produce variations in local attitudes. Justice Reed asked what city in Kansas had the largest concentration of Negro residents by percentage. My answer was Kansas City, but my estimate of 10 percent was too low. Twenty percent would have been more accurate.

After disposing of these unplanned for and incidental inquiries, I continued with my prepared argument. Emphasizing the opinions of the Kansas Supreme Court on which Kansans had relied, I stressed *Reynolds v. Board of Education of Topeka*,[17] where, in 1903, the court had faced squarely and found in favor of the constitutionality of the Kansas statute under attack. I continued:

> It is our position that the principle announced in the *Plessy* case and the specific rule announced in the *Gong Lum* case are absolutely controlling here.
>
> We think it is sheer sophistry to attempt to distinguish those cases from the case that is here presented, and we think the question before this Court is simply this: Is the *Plessy* case and the *Gong Lum* case and the "separate but equal" doctrine still the law of this land?
>
> We think if you decide in favor of these appellants, the Court will necessarily overrule the doctrines expressed in those cases and, at the same time, will say that the legislatures of the seventeen or twenty-one states, that the Congress of the United States, that dozens of appellate courts have been wrong for a period of more than seventy-five years, when they have believed and have manifested a belief that facilities equal though separate were within the meaning of the Fourteenth Amendment.

The assertion that a reversal would imply that the earlier decisions were wrong aroused objection:

> JUSTICE BURTON: Don't you recognize it as possible that within seventy-five years the social and economic conditions and the

personal relations of the nation may have changed so that what may have been a valid interpretation of them seventy-five years ago would not be a valid interpretation of them constitutionally today?

MR. WILSON: We recognize that as a possibility. We do not believe that this record discloses any such change.

JUSTICE BURTON: But that might be a difference between saying that these courts of appeals and state supreme courts have been wrong for seventy-five years.

MR. WILSON: Yes, sir. We concede that this Court can overrule the Gong Lum doctrine, the Plessy doctrine, but nevertheless until those cases are overruled they are the best guide we have.

JUSTICE FRANKFURTER: As I understood my brother Burton's question or as I got the implication of his question, it was not that the Court would have to overrule those cases; the Court would simply have to recognize that laws are kinetic, and some new things have happened, not deeming those decisions wrong, but bringing into play new situations toward a new decision. I do not know whether he would disown me, but that is what I got out of it.

MR. WILSON: We agree with that proposition. But I repeat, we do not think that there is anything in the record here that would justify such a conclusion.[18]

When asked a similar question, John W. Davis had a better answer. He said, "My answer to that is that changed conditions may affect policy, but changed conditions cannot broaden the terminology of the Constitution. The thought is an administrative or a political one, and not a judicial one."[19]

The final segment of my presentation was directed at the trial court's Finding of Fact No. 8, which I feared might be our Achilles heel. If the finding were to be accepted as true, if segregation of white and black children does, in fact, have a detrimental effect on the black children, it if retards their educational and mental development and deprives them of benefits they would receive in a racially integrated school system, then it becomes difficult to argue that separate schools are or can be equal. My task, therefore, was to persuade the Supreme Court that the finding was not material to the issues before the trial court. First, I argued, the testimony of the social scientists on which the finding was based was not material under the *Plessy* rule. Relying on its understanding of the limited issue before the court, the board of education had produced no testimony to rebut the plaintiff's expert witnesses. The court had not had the opportunity to consider both sides of the issue. Hence, I urged, the finding was suspect. Second, I argued that in finding that the objective, demonstrable facilities were substantially equal, the court had found compliance with the law; that psychological and emotional reactions are unpredictable and not measurable and not subject to the board's control. Third, I contended that within the framework of the case before the court, Finding of Fact No. 8 was legally insignificant and immaterial and that the finding of equality in tangible facilities met the *Plessy–Gong Lum* test. Finally, I pointed out that none of the defendants had shown, nor had it been found, that he or she had suffered actual or threatened injury as a result of the board's policies. The most that had been shown was that they belonged to a class that might have been better off in integrated schools. This, I thought, did not entitle them to injunctive relief.[20]

During the last several minutes of my argument the justices asked no questions. They appeared to listen but I suspected that their interest was waning. I had said all that I could honestly say on behalf of Kansas. I doubted that more words would add quality to my argument. To continue would be to invite questions that I might not be able to answer. Although I had used hardly half of my allotted hour, I decided it was time to stop. I sat down. The task that I had anticipated with dread and distress had not been unpleasant.

Mr. Carter's rebuttal was brief and consisted mainly of colloquy with Justice Black. He zeroed in on Finding of Fact No. 8 and urged that the finding required that the trial court's judgment in favor of the board be set aside. Justice Black doubted that the Supreme Court's decision should rest on a single finding in a particular case. What if the trial court had made a contrary finding? What if another court in another district made a different finding? "If you are going to go on the findings, then you would have different rulings with respect to the places to which this applies, is that true?" Faced with these questions from the justice who had been assumed to be among those most friendly to his case, Carter seemed hurriedly to back away from the finding. To urge that it alone would justify reversal seemed no longer feasible.[21] Reasserting the unconstitutionality of segregation per se, he concluded his argument. He had spoken for about forty minutes. *Brown v. Board of Education* was at repose in the bosom of the Court.

Candor requires me to say that, in the view of the press and the people, *Brown* and the Wilson-Carter arguments were only the preliminaries leading up to more dramatic events. I counter by suggesting that the *Brown* role was important to the later proceedings. We had defined in its simplest terms the issue the Court was to decide—whether laws requiring or permitting racial segregation in education, uncluttered by considerations of inequality, violate the constitutional guarantee of equal protection of the laws. On the pragmatic side, I am sure that those who were to follow Bob Carter and me to the lectern benefited by observing our performances. They heard our presentations, saw the justices' reactions, listened to the Court's questions and our responses and, by reason of that, were, perhaps, a little better prepared when their turns came.

At 3:15 P.M. the chief justice called "Case No. 101, Harry Briggs, Jr., et al. against Roger W. Elliott, chairman, J. D. Carson, et al., member of Board of Trustees of School District No. 22, Clarendon County, South Carolina, et al." As John W. Davis moved into the chair that I had vacated, Thurgood Marshall approached the lectern and began to speak. The main event was under way. A dispassionate analyst would find little in the speeches that was new and different. The ideas were ones that I had heard, read, or thought of before, but the force and eloquence with which they were expressed gave them new vigor and meaning. The contrasting personalities of the adversaries added drama to the debate. Each seemed to be an eminently suitable protagonist of the view that he urged. Mr. Davis, the near octogenarian, was a patrician. His voice was mellow yet strong, his sentences clear and complete, his diction exquisite. The justices listened to his argument with almost deferential respect. Only twice was he interrupted by questions from the bench. He spoke to support an understanding of the Constitution that he believed was rational and just and consistent with traditional American values. His challenger, Thurgood Marshall, was, at forty-five, in the prime years of a brilliant career in advocacy. The descendant of slaves and son of a country club steward, he was the product of Baltimore's segregated public school system and of the law school at Washington's then all-Negro Howard University. It is part of the Marshall folklore that as a law student he regularly cut classes to attend Supreme Court sessions whenever John W. Davis was appearing there. He was more laid-back than dignified, his speech was more forceful than elegant, and he was more concerned with issues of social justice than with history and precedent. He thought America could do better. Much of his argument emerged in impromptu responses to questions from the bench.

After Davis and Marshall had spoken, I felt that whatever would follow would be superfluous. They had said it all. I was satisfied that I had been witness to something special, something that historians would write about for a long time. In the Davis involvement I sensed an element of poignancy—one of the century's greatest advocates employing his wit and eloquence to support a cause that had already been lost, not to Thurgood Marshall and his associates, but to history and the maturing American social conscience.

Counsel in the Virginia case followed South Carolina to the podium. Spottswood W. Robinson III, of Richmond, represented the appellants and made the first presentation to the Court. Mr. Robinson, who had earned the highest academic honors at the Howard University School of Law, was then in his mid-thirties and an experienced civil rights lawyer. His argument was orderly and thoughtful. Two of the commonwealth's legal luminaries spoke for the school board of Prince Edward County. The leadoff man was T. Justin Moore, Esq., a senior partner in the Richmond law firm said to be Virginia's finest. During the uncertain months preceding the argument Mr. Moore had provided the liaison between Kansas and Virginia and the other interested states. Although he was primarily a corporation lawyer, he also functioned as chief counsel for the Prince Edward County Board of Education. Mr. Moore seemed peculiarly suited to the role in which he was cast—a traditional southern gentleman defending a traditional southern institution. With Mr. Moore was Virginia's white-maned Attorney General J. Lindsay Almond, Jr., a former congressman and a prospective governor of the commonwealth.

In addition to the arguments made in the earlier cases, Mr. Moore urged that unlike those in the Kansas and South Carolina cases, the record in the Virginia case showed that the evidence of psychological detriment to the segregated minority children had been neutralized by evidence that mere segregation produced no such effect and that the trial court had declined to find that such detriment had been proven. He argued that an order to integrate would seriously disrupt the commonwealth's system of public schools. He also emphasized that Virginia had undertaken a massive building program designed to equalize Virginia's public schools. As I reflect on Mr. Moore's presentation, two immaterial incidents of the speech stand out. First, I was intrigued by his pronunciation of the word *Negro*. He called it "nigra" and made it sound almost like "nigger." Second, General Almond, who sat beside me, thought Mr. Moore talked too long. He whispered bitter complaints as Moore's remarks extended into the time that had been reserved for the general. Finally, his time came. The attorney general was an orator. His speech was delivered with fire and flourish, but I do not recall what he said. The case was concluded with a rebuttal by Mr. Robinson focused on the intent of Virginia's segregation laws and the power of the Court to outlaw segregation without implementing legislation by Congress. The Virginia case ended at 3:30 P.M. on the second day of arguments. As the District of Columbia case was being called, I left the Supreme Court Chamber. I expected to catch a train for Kansas in the late afternoon and would miss the arguments in the D.C. and Delaware cases.

RETURN TO KANSAS

I was glad when my train left the station in the early evening of December 10. I had been in Washington for three days, and I was anxious to get back to Kansas. I would be riding the same train over the same route that I had followed in reaching Washington; only the direction and the time were reversed. On this trip I would travel in daylight along those parts of the route that had been dark before. Again I would have twenty-eight uninterrupted hours of my own, but my thoughts would be different. Instead of anticipation and anxiety, my mood would be one of retrospection and resignation. What would be had been.

At one point in his distinguished public career Justice Jackson had served as solicitor general of the United States, and in that role had appeared many times before the Court of which he was later a member. Referring to that experience, he wrote, "I made three arguments of every case. First came the one that I had planned—as I thought, logical, coherent, complete. Second was the one actually presented—interrupted, incoherent, disjointed, disappointing. The third was the utterly devastating argument that I thought of after going to bed that night."[22] As I reflected on my performance, I appreciated what Justice Jackson had said. My presentation to the Supreme Court had shown little of the learning and logic that I had planned. My after-the-fact analysis left me with a slight emptiness as I reviewed the things I did not say or could have said differently. I wished I could have had a second chance. However, I was not unhappy or dissatisfied. I had managed to say all that could be said honestly in support of the Kansas law, and I had said it as well as I could under the circumstances. The Court could take the case for decision with full information on the merits of both sides. During my presentation I had been questioned by five justices. All of their questions had helped me to develop my argument. None seemed intended to embarrass or harass me. The arguments had been fully and widely reported by both the Washington papers and the national news media. The stories had been fair. I cannot deny that I was pleased when my name, spelled correctly, appeared on page one of the *New York Times*.

On Friday, six days after my departure for Washington, I was back at my desk in the Statehouse. Pending matters needed my attention. In Topeka the news media had given *Brown v. Board of Education* much less attention than in Washington, New York, and other parts of the country. Few Kansans were conscious of the significance of the case, nor could they foresee its impact on history. I immediately settled in to the task of preparing for the forthcoming session of the legislature, which would convene early in January, and to pursuit of the mundane but persistent problems of crime and corruption. My Washington adventure seemed ended—but there were occasional reminders. In a letter addressed to me by Attorney General Almond of Virginia he wrote: "You made a profound contribution in the presentation which you made on behalf of the State of Kansas. I probably heard more than you the splendid appraisal in commendation of the able and scholarly manner in which you argued your case. Some days ago I wrote to General Fatzer in this connection."[23] I was pleased but was also mindful that General Almond was a politician and that the statements of politicians are sometimes more pleasing than sincere. Months later, after the case had been decided adversely, a friend wrote to General Fatzer in a letter addressed to *him* and referring to a conversation she had had with Justice Clark. She wrote:

> We had a pleasant chat with Clark during which he complimented *you* highly on *your* argument in the school segregation cases—said *you* really straightened him out on the history of segregation in the schools.
>
>   I don't think such compliments from a Justice of the Supreme Court should be taken lightly, and I thought you would like to know what people were saying about *you*.[24]

General Fatzer accepted the compliment graciously. Of course, I was pleased to learn that Justice Clark had found the argument helpful. I would have been even more pleased if he had known to whom he had listened.

7

1953—Second Time Around

The process of deciding cases in the Supreme Court is one to which the public has no access. Although the arguments are heard in open court and decisions are announced orally from the bench, the deliberations that occur between the argument and decision stages are cloaked with secrecy. When the justices are in conference, no other person is present in the conference room, nor is there any public disclosure of the discussions and proceedings. No record is kept, but the notes made by individual justices often find their way into various public archives. Hence, when the Court took *Brown* and its counterparts at the end of argument in the Delaware case on December 11, 1952, it was assumed that in due time a decision would be announced and that until that time the parties and their counsel would be in waiting.

POLITICS AS USUAL

Monday, January 12, was inauguration day. Dick Fatzer, Ed Arn, and eleven other Statehouse incumbents were sworn to commence new terms to which they had been elected the preceding November.

The historian of *Brown* may find the commencement of the new national administration more relevant than the Topeka affair. On January 20, Dwight D. Eisenhower became president of the United States.

Although the new president had declared his personal disapproval of segregation and had moved to eliminate discrimination in those areas where his authority was clearly established,[1] he apparently preferred a neutral stance on the constitutional issue raised in *Brown*. His significant contributions to the issue before the Supreme Court were the appointments of Herbert Brownell as attorney general and Earl Warren to be chief justice of the United States. Brownell, a New York lawyer with Nebraska antecedents, believed that segregation was unconstitutional. It was he who framed and secured the president's unenthusiastic approval of the Department of Justice position that the Fourteenth Amendment prohibited legally segregated schools. Warren wrote the opinion that resolved the issue and secured the unanimous approval of his fellow justices.

On January 13 the thirty-eighth biennial session of the Kansas legislature convened. It was a session that was not distinguished by statesmanship. Had it not been for their preoccupation with politics, the legislators might have given some attention to Kansas's segregated schools. As I think back and search the journals of that session, I find no mention of the problems posed by *Brown*. I do not purport to know what their silence may have meant. Some legislators may have thought it appropriate to do nothing while awaiting the Court's decision on the constitutional issue. Most, I suspect, were indifferent. Apparently, none was inclined to reevaluate legislatively the state's historic position. As *Brown* had drawn into question a policy of state government affecting many Kansans, a more sensitive body might have reviewed the policy and considered adjustments that an evolving society required. Had there been more legislative concern in 1953, *Brown* might not have been pending in 1993. I had argued before the Supreme Court that state educational policy ought to be determined by the state legislature. As in earlier sessions, the Kansas legislature of 1953 did little to validate my argument.

The Topeka Board of Education was not able to enjoy the luxury of indifference that the Kansas legislature found agreeable. For all boards maintaining segregated schools there were immediate problems. An April 6 news headline announced "Negro Teacher Purge to Begin in Kansas."[2] The story reported that in nine cities of Kansas,

7,521 black students attended segregated schools where classes were taught by 237 black teachers. There were no black teachers in mixed or white schools, and school officials assumed that most white parents would be unwilling for their children to attend classes taught by Negro teachers. It was also believed that the Supreme Court would probably find segregation to be unconstitutional and would require that students be assigned to schools on some basis other than color. The result would be fewer all-black classrooms. The boards asked, "What are we to do with the excess of black teachers?"

In Topeka's four segregated elementary schools there were twenty-seven teachers and 729 students—all black. At a special meeting on March 12, the board of education had decided that to reduce the number of black teachers to that required for predominantly black schools the contracts of six Negro teachers would not be renewed. The story reporting the decision indicated that the matter would be considered again at the regular board meeting to be held on the evening of April 6 and that "fireworks" were likely to "explode."[3] The next morning's headline read "Firing Negro Teachers to be Contested."[4] The issue of the validity of the firings arose when the minutes of the March 12 special meeting were read for approval. Board member Casey objected, saying that the special meeting was illegal because he had not been given the required two-day written notice and that he refused to waive the notice.[5] In the debate that ensued Casey and Jacob Dickinson were described as "arch antagonists," with Casey contending that he had been denied the opportunity to vote against the firings of the six Negro teachers. Finally, the minutes were approved, but the prospect of further contest loomed.

April 7, 1953, has another significance in the *Brown* story. It was election day in Topeka, and three positions, half the membership, on the board of education were to be filled. Mrs. Neiswanger had chosen not to seek reelection, but both Mike Casey and Charles Bennett were candidates to succeed themselves. When the votes were in, both had been defeated. The newly elected members of the board were Dr. Richard Greer, a physician, Charles J. Sheetz, an engineer, and Mrs. Ernest Shiner, wife of a Topeka businessman. Their preelection statements and campaign advertisements do not indicate that segregation was a controlling issue in the election. However, the defeated incumbents had been members since 1941 and had served for twelve years on the board that sanctioned the status quo. The newly elected members would take office in the August following their election. Then, all who had been on the board when Oliver Brown filed his lawsuit would have been succeeded, and a new group of officials would determine Topeka's school policy. Although the personnel and politics of the board were new, its members reflected no ethnic or demographic change. Each was white, and all lived in good neighborhoods west of Kansas Avenue.

BACK TO BROWN

As spring 1953 drew to an end with no decision or other communication from the court, we began to suspect that the justices were having difficulty in reaching a consensus. Later writings of authors with better access to sources of information than I have confirmed our suspicion.[6] Although the Court constituted a collegial body, it was public knowledge that there were deep philosophical differences and serious personality clashes among the justices. Opinions of the Court in important cases were seldom unanimous. Upon the basis of his extensive investigation, Richard Kluger believed that as the Court approached the end of the term, the justices were seriously divided on the issue raised in *Brown*. Four justices—Black, Burton, Douglas, and Minton—were ready to overrule *Plessy v. Ferguson* and reverse the judgment of the district court. One justice, Reed, would have affirmed the district court, and two more, Vinson and Clark, seemed likely to vote for affirmance. Frankfurter and Jackson were apparently troubled. Had the cases been without precedent, both would have found segregation unconstitutional. Indeed, Frankfurter stated his willingness to reverse the District of Columbia court and to find that racial segregation in public education in the District violated Fifth Amendment due process of law. The state cases, they found, were more difficult. A mass of judicial precedent and state legislative action had relied upon and was consistent with the *Plessy* rule that Fourteenth Amendment equal protection was satisfied by separate-but-equal facilities. To find otherwise would be to repudiate more than a half-century of judicial and legislative experience. How to hold for the appellants and maintain the integrity of stare decisis was the problem that gave the justices pause. Frankfurter, apparently the intellectual leader of the Court, felt it imperative that the decision be unanimous. Nothing less than a consensus could settle an issue so volatile and so far reaching. As the end of the term approached with no prospect of unanimity, the justices agreed with Frankfurter that more time was essential and more information would be helpful. As reflected in their order, many of their concerns were focused on (1) the original intent of those who framed and ratified the Fourteenth Amendment; and (2) the impact of desegregation on segregated school systems and ways of minimizing its adverse effects.[7]

In view of our remoteness from Washington, of the Supreme Court's policy of confidentiality of intra-Court discourse and communication, and of the low priority assigned to *Brown* in the Kansas Attorney General's Office, we did not know and had neither the means nor inclination to learn of the happenings that others have discovered or inferred to have taken place in the Court's conference room after the cases were submitted. From the conclusion of the December 9, 1952, argument we waited until June 8, 1953. On that date I was called by George Mack, the Statehouse reporter for the *Capital*, who told me that the wire services had reported that the Supreme Court had just ordered that *Brown* and its companion cases be restored to the docket for reargument commencing on Monday, October 12. A day later we received a copy of the Court's order. In each of the five cases the Court requested that on reargument attention be focused on specific questions summarized as follows. (1) Did or did not the Congress that proposed and the state legislatures that ratified the Fourteenth Amendment understand and intend that it would prohibit segregated public schools? (2) Assuming question one is answered in the negative, was it understood that (a) future Congresses might abolish segregation or (b) the courts might construe the amendment to have abolished segregation of its own force? (3) Did the courts have power in construing the amendment to abolish segregation? (4) Assuming segregation to be unconstitutional, (a) must immediate desegregation be ordered or (b) might a gradual adjustment be permitted? and (5) Assuming gradual adjustment to be allowed, (a) must the Supreme Court formulate decrees containing detailed directions to school boards? (b) what issues should the decrees reach? (c) should a special master be appointed to hear evidence and recommend terms of such decrees? or (d) should the cases be referred back to the district courts with instructions to frame appropriate decrees? The attorney general of the United States was requested to participate in further proceedings if he so desired.[8] Contrary to our hopes and expectations, *Brown* had not gone away.

TO THE DRAWING BOARD AGAIN

Although the order for reargument was a surprise to me, it was also encouraging. If the intent of those who wrote and ratified the amendment was to be critical in the Court's decision, I felt that we could make a persuasive argument in support of our position. My research had convinced me that public school segregation was not an important consideration in the adoption of the amendment. The Congress that proposed and the legislatures that ratified the amendment were motivated by an intent to strike down the post–Civil War black codes that denied substantial rights to and imposed heavy burdens upon the newly emancipated black citizens. The right to education in public facilities had not then been defined, nor was segregation then deemed a denial of a right of citizenship.

Other Topekans expressed surprise similar to my own, although they may have drawn different inferences from the request. The president of the local NAACP was dismayed by the prospect of further delay. Board President Oberhelman and Superintendent Godwin thought the board might wish to go ahead with its own desegregation plan if the decision were to be delayed unduly. Godwin's most immediate concern was what to do about the six Negro teachers who were still awaiting contracts. Peter Caldwell did not know what the Topeka board would do, but he opined that if it should abandon its policy of segregation and integrate its elementary schools, the *Brown* case would probably become moot and be dismissed by the Supreme Court.[9]

Another decision announced by the court on June 8 was taken by some as evidence of the justices' thinking about civil rights cases. In *District of Columbia v. John R. Thompson Co., Inc.*[10] the defendant was prosecuted for refusal to serve members of the Negro race in its restaurant in violation of a penal act, long forgotten and unenforced, passed by the Legislative Assembly of the District of Columbia, a body that had been abolished by Congress in 1874. For more than six decades it had been assumed that the act had been repealed by implication, but without dissent the Supreme Court resurrected the act, reversed the District of Columbia court, and sustained the prosecution. Although the legal issues in *Thompson* were quite different from those in *Brown* and had no utility as precedent, the opinion gave little comfort to our side.

This time, unlike the last, there was no indecision or equivocation as to the state's position. Kansas was in the case and would respond to the Court's order—if the Court would hear us. Although Dick Fatzer, as attorney general, retained his interest and ultimate control of the position to be taken by the state, he made it clear that the case was mine for the purposes of briefing and oral argument. I was pleased. I had enjoyed my earlier experience in the Supreme Court, and I was anxious to return.

With the arguments set four months later, there would be time for a more deliberate preparation and more mature thinking than before. In an effort to get in step with the attorneys representing the other states I promptly wrote to Mr. Moore.[11] I mentioned our uncertainty about the position that the Topeka board would take. To that date there had been no official expression by the board, and I thought it likely that segregation would continue another year. I also considered the effect of a board decision to desegregate upon the pending case. I wrote: "Should segregation be abandoned in Topeka, I assume our case will be moot. . . . I am not sure just what our status would be."

Mr. Moore's reply to my letter is dated June 12. "We would consider it to be a most unfortunate circumstance if your school board proceeded with integration of its schools without awaiting the final decision of the court. Certainly you appreciate the importance, indeed, the practical necessity of your continuing in the case, having participated in the former hearing, unless circumstances change so that your position becomes absolutely moot."[12] An early conference with representatives of the Davis firm was expected, and Mr. Moore hoped that I would attend (I did not). On June 19, I advised Mr. Moore that it appeared that the Topeka Board of Education would not disturb the status quo until the pending case was finally disposed of by a definitive ruling by the Supreme Court.[13]

I was out of the office during the latter part of June. Returning in early July, I learned that our Dixieland counterparts had been busy. A letter from Mr. Moore enclosed a memorandum of the planning session with Mr. Davis and members of his firm.[14] General strategy had been agreed upon and responsibility for research allocated among the attorneys involved. A letter from General Almond enclosed a copy of a letter and questionnaire that he had addressed to each of the thirty-seven states that comprised the Union when the Fourteenth Amendment was adopted.[15] Also, there was a letter from Governor Byrnes addressed to Governor Arn requesting information similar to that called for in General Almond's questionnaire.[16] Apparently, the governor of South Carolina had jumped the gun a bit. The letters had been acknowledged by General Fatzer and placed on my desk for further responses.

Mr. Moore's memorandum summarizing the New York meeting reported that it had been held on June 16.[17] The questions in the Supreme Court's order of June 8 were gone over, one by one, a consensus developed as to appropriate responses, and responsibility for investigation and research was assigned. Not unexpectedly, Virginia and South Carolina assumed a major responsibility for investigating and preparing responses to those questions that were common to all of the cases—the understanding of the Congress that framed the Fourteenth Amendment and the power of the Supreme Court to order desegregation. To determine the intent of the thirty state legislatures that ratified the amendment would require a state-by-state investigation. The attorney general of Virginia would, by letter and questionnaire, request the attorney general of each ratifying state to examine the ratification process in his state and the state's understanding of the amendment's impact on public school segregation. This research would require looking at records of legislative debates, contemporaneous legislation, state court findings, and other relevant expressions of intent. General Almond would address the initial inquiry to all states, and each of the other attorneys involved were assigned groups of states for follow-up communication to assure prompt responses. In addition to reporting for Kansas, I was asked to prod, if necessary, the attorneys general of seven other midwestern states. All information obtained from the states was sent to General Almond's office, where it was analyzed, compiled, and made available to each of the other states and the District of Columbia.[18]

In addition to its questions relating to original intent, the Court had asked for argument on the power of the Court to order desegregation, whether such an order would require immediate integration or could be implemented gradually, and whether the Supreme Court should formulate detailed plans for desegregation or leave that task to the district courts in the concerned states. Since there was agreement upon the arguments to be made on these issues, the discussion among the conferees was brief. They agreed that if the Supreme Court found that it had the power to abolish segregated public schools and did so order, they saw the problems of desegregation in each state as discrete and best handled by the local district courts, who should be empowered to permit gradual adjustment, having due regard to local conditions. As I read Mr. Moore's summary of the meeting, I sensed a feeling by the participants that the discussion of a desegregation plan was not only premature, but superfluous. They thought that they would win the case.

The willingness, indeed, the eagerness of Virginia and South Carolina to assist and cooperate with Kansas both pleased and troubled me. I was anxious to maintain the separate identity of *Brown*. Although circumstance had placed Kansas beside jurisdictions with histories of slavery and pervasive segregation, Kansas was not one of them. The basic issue in all of the cases was the same, but, I thought, our motivation and objectives were different. To what extent could we cooperate with South Carolina and Virginia and keep our separateness? In this incipient dilemma, practical considerations prevailed. We had a duty to respond as fully as we could to the questions put by the Supreme Court. South Carolina and Virginia were ready and willing to commit whatever personnel, money, and other resources that might be needed to answer those questions. The libraries and other facilities for legal research in Washington and New York were patently superior to those in Topeka, Kansas. Hence, it was helpful to me to exchange information and engage in discourse with counsel for the other states whose laws were under attack. At the same time, we made our own interpretation and evaluation of the data made available, and it was the attorney general and I who determined the position Kansas would take.

A short time after the June 8 order, Peter Caldwell informed me that the board of education would not join with the attorney general in preparing and filing the brief on reargument. It had no desire to be heard on the Fourteenth Amendment issue, but would file a separate brief responding to the Court's questions regarding the content of the decree to be entered if its segregated schools were found unconstitutional. It would ask for time to make a gradual transition.

Although I was hardly surprised at the board's decision to go it alone, I was disappointed that I would not be working with Peter Caldwell. In the few days that we had been associated in the preparation of the earlier brief he had made important contributions. I regretted that I could no longer have his help. I had learned that the Davis firm and the Moore firm had each assigned two lawyers to work full-time on the cases and that local counsel in South Carolina and the Virginia attorney general's office were giving the cases the highest priority. Also, the attorney general of the United States, whom the Court had invited to participate amicus curiae had a corps of lawyers involved in research and in compiling data to be used in preparing a brief and argument. The Kansas case was only one of several matters sharing my divided time. I thought the state's commitment should be greater if our analyses and evaluation were to be truly independent ones. At my request General Fatzer authorized me to seek help outside the office. I spoke with several Topeka lawyers who I thought might be helpful, but all were either too busy or unwilling to give up planned summer vacations. Since the University of Kansas harbored scholars who spoke and wrote learnedly about constitutional law, I made inquiry at the law school and the political science department there. Neither was able to help. Their people were already fully committed to other projects. I also inferred a lack of enthusiasm for our side. I had more success at the Washburn University School of Law, where Professor James Ahrens, an able and respected scholar, provided important help in preparing responses to the questions relating to the understanding of the framers of the amendment and the limitations on judicial power to order desegregation. Also, in the later stages of our preparation, Charles C. McCarter, a bright young Washburn graduate, joined the attorney general's staff. He was able to devote a considerable amount of time to the task of research, and his contribution to the Kansas brief was significant. Together, we put together a document that, I felt, reflected credit on Kansas.

In its order of June 8, the Supreme Court invited the attorney general of the United States to take part in the oral argument and to file a brief if he so desired. Former Attorney General McGranery had filed a thirty-two-page brief prior to the first argument but had made no oral presentation. In January 1953 McGranery was succeeded by Brownell. Brownell's views on segregation were unequivocal. His representative had appeared in the *Thompson* case to urge desegregation of the restaurants in the District of Columbia. He believed that segregation by race in the public schools was unconstitutional and that *Plessy* should be overruled. President Eisenhower, for whom Brownell worked, was more inclined to caution. The depth of his misgiving and reasons for his reluctance have been interpreted differently by writers whose sources of information are better than mine.[19] Obviously, at my desk in Topeka I could have no insights or understanding of the philosophical and political concerns that were vexing the Department of Justice and the Office of the President in Washington. Moreover, I had no great amount of interest. I assumed they would be against us.

On July 27, more than six weeks after the Court's order, we received a letter from General Brownell requesting that we, along with the other parties concerned, consent to a postponement of the argument, then set for October 12. His reason was that there would not be sufficient time for his staff to complete the necessary research and prepare the government's brief before the October setting.[20] Kansas was glad to consent. Any postponement of what had begun to look like doomsday was to be desired. The other states agreed to the postponement, although reservations were expressed. Mr. Moore pointed out that delay was already causing embarrassment to Virginia school authorities, and because an adverse decision would have a serious impact on the state's ongoing school construction program, it was highly important that a final disposition be had as soon as practicable.[21] On August 4, the Court made an order reassigning the cases for argument on Monday, December 7. Eight more weeks. With ample time, with the issues framed by the Court's questions, and with the assurance of needed help, I felt comfortable. Things were falling into place.

AUTUMN VAGARIES

My assumption of early August that the case had reached a point of stability was premature. The next sixty days demonstrated how wrong I was.

On August 4, the three members of the board of education who had been successful at the April election took their positions. Mike

Casey was retired, along with Martin and Mrs. Neiswanger. At their first meeting the board was reorganized, with Jake Dickinson as president. Peter Caldwell was again retained as the board's attorney. The news reports of the meeting did not indicate that there had been any discussion of the *Brown* case or of the board's segregation policy. Caldwell later advised me that he did not know what action, if any, the board might take.

The next regular meeting of the board occurred on September 5. The following morning a four-column headline in the *Topeka Daily Capital* proclaimed "School Board Votes End to Topeka Segregation."[22] The story beneath the headline reported that near the end of a long meeting, Dickinson, without prior announcement, moved, "Be it resolved that it is the policy of the Topeka Board of Education to terminate maintenance of segregation in the elementary grades as rapidly as practicable." Conrad moved to amend by providing that no action be taken until fall 1954; the motion failed. The vote on the Dickinson resolution passed by a majority of five to one. Only Oberhelman voted no, explaining that he viewed the motion as ill timed. Notwithstanding the announced new policy, the board proceeded to approve a contract for bus transportation of Negro students to segregated schools during the 1953–1954 year.[23]

Other unrelated but contemporary developments in the community were indicative of the rising concerns of Topekans for the racial policies of their local government. It was reported that the board of county commissioners would study a petition to permit Negroes to swim in Lake Shawnee, a county-owned and -operated facility. The same article mentioned that a suit to open the Gage Park swimming pool to blacks was pending in the Supreme Court.[24]

On September 8 the first step in a plan to end segregation was presented to the board. Two elementary schools were to be integrated immediately. The second step would be announced in December or January. Both schools slated for immediate integration were located in affluent white neighborhoods. Superintendent Godwin thought that about fifteen black students might be affected. The plan permitted those black students who had attended segregated schools to continue in those schools if they preferred to do so. Apparently, some of the black students chose to attend their former schools, since it was later reported that only ten blacks were enrolled in the two schools that had been desegregated.[25]

The board's announced intention to desegregate its schools was made without consultation with or knowledge of the attorney general. The possible impact of the action on Kansas in the Supreme Court litigation was apparently a matter that the board did not consider. As I review the history of the litigation I cannot avoid a feeling that the board's action fell short of that which might be expected from a responsible agency of government. At the outset the board was the principal defendant. Its schools were under attack. At the trial level the state had intervened to be heard on a single, limited issue of law, and its role had been passive. The state had assumed an active part in the appellate proceedings only after the board's default and at the Supreme Court's specific request. Changes in the board's membership had not altered its institutional responsibility to the Court and to the other parties to the case. Board members were aware of the time and effort spent by members of the attorney general's staff in preparation for the second round of arguments. Whether by design or by chance, the board's action of September served further to embarrass the state, already troubled by its role. The issue of mootness now loomed before us.

It is basic jurisprudence that courts decide only actual, existing controversies—cases in which the decision will have some impact on the status, rights, or conduct of the parties. Issues that have become academic or dead will not be adjudicated. An exception may be recognized where the issue is a recurring one and is likely to be raised again in a dispute between the same parties. My initial thought, which I continue to entertain, was that the case was not moot. The board's resolution had not abolished segregation in the Topeka schools. It was a declaration of intent to do so "as soon as practicable." Insofar as I could learn, only one child who was a plaintiff in the pending case was affected by the board's action. For most black children in Topeka the board continued to maintain segregated schools and did not concede that it had no lawful right to do so. As a matter of law, the then existing board or a later board might have decided to change the declared policy and reinstitute segregation. The board did not and could not concede the constitutional invalidity of the state statute under attack. We thought that a dismissal on the ground of mootness would preclude a final determination of that issue. We felt strongly that the best interests of Kansas and its cities of the first class required that the question be resolved.

During the days following the board's action the other parties, the press, and the curious often inquired about our intended course of action. A letter from the Department of Justice pointed up the aspect that we thought critical. The writer inquired, "Could you please advise when this reported order of the Topeka Board of Education is to become effective, and how soon it will apply to the colored complainants in the *Brown* case?"[26] I could not advise the writer. The board's resolution called for desegregation only "as soon as practicable."

If the resolution of the Topeka board had been to desegregate all of its elementary schools immediately and to integrate at once, a suggestion of mootness might have been proper. Even though some issues would remain unsettled, a decision would have had no actual impact on any party to the controversy. Similarly, I reasoned, if the appellants were to move for dismissal on the ground of mootness, we probably could not have resisted successfully. Implicit in such a motion, I thought, would be the admission that the appellants had received the relief that they sought. Impelled by these thoughts, I wrote to Robert Carter, from whom I had not heard. After calling his attention to the action of the Topeka board (quite unnecessarily, I am sure), I continued:

> It has been our position that the action is in no wise abated by the policy declaration and other action of the Topeka Board of Education, and that the case will be argued in December along with the other similar cases now before the Court.
>
> In view of the fact that the Topeka Board of Education still maintains a policy of segregation with respect to substantially all of the Negro population of Topeka, under authority of the statute, it is our view that the pending action cannot be considered as moot.
>
> You will recall our experience prior to the other arguments, at which time the Court indicated its desire to have all of the cases fully presented. With that experience in mind, and with the understanding that the case is not moot, we are preparing the brief and will argue that matter fully when it again appears on the docket.[27]

My files do not show nor do I remember that Mr. Carter replied directly to my letter. On November 6, Mr. Moore, of Virginia, called me to express his concern at a report from Thurgood Marshall that Kansas was thinking of abandoning the appeal since the case no longer presented a justiciable issue. My assurance that we did not regard the case as moot and were about to complete our brief seemed to mitigate his anxiety. Since none of the concerned parties had excepted to our position on the mootness issue, we thought that the matter was settled and that the question would not again be raised. As I was to learn later, at least one of the justices of the Supreme Court had a different view.

After-the-fact critics have occasionally suggested that *Brown* was effectively terminated by the resolution of the Topeka board and that the appeal should have been dismissed. The inference that our continued resistance to the appeal was an abuse of the judicial process has troubled me, but forty years later I have no misgiving about the course that we pursued. I have tried to imagine consequences that might have followed *Brown*'s dismissal at this stage. These are some of my thoughts, legal and otherwise.

First, the dismissal of *Brown* would not have terminated or shortened the litigation before the Supreme Court. Cases from three other states and the District of Columbia remained on the Court's docket. Those cases were neither moot nor likely to become moot.

Second, a dismissal would have left the issue of the constitutionality of the Kansas statute undetermined. Granting that the broad language used by the Court in striking down the separate-but-equal doctrine would have precluded a defense of the Kansas law, in the fall of 1953 I thought a specific and final determination of the statute's validity would be helpful to all parties.

Third, the appellants apparently had no inclination to raise the question of mootness. The case was before the court on their appeal, and it was they who could best judge whether the Topeka board had met their demands. In my view, their disposition to pursue the appeal obliged us to respond.

Fourth, only the Kansas case presented squarely the issue of the validity of the separate-but-equal doctrine. Only in Kansas had there been a finding that the segregated facilities were substantially equal. But for Kansas, the Court could have found for the black plaintiffs without overruling *Plessy*.

Fifth, if the Kansas case had been dismissed, presumably it would have been removed from the Supreme Court's docket. *Briggs v.*

Elliott, the South Carolina case, was next in order. It, not *Brown*, would probably have supplied the title of the Supreme Court's consolidated opinion. Topeka would have been spared the ignominious characterization as a Jim Crow town, the plaintiffs would have been denied the spotlight's warm glow, and I probably would not be writing this story. Of course, the case was not dismissed, and we continued to prepare for the showdown.

On September 8, 1953, Fred M. Vinson, chief justice of the United States, died. An appointee of President Truman, he had headed the Court since 1946. Although his appointment to the Court was preceded by a long and distinguished career in public service, historians have not regarded him as a strong and effective chief justice. However, his death caused deep concern among my southern associates. The chief justice was a Kentuckian and had shown no evidence of an agenda for social reform. The attorneys for Virginia and South Carolina had counted his vote as one favorable to their position. Dismayed at his departure, they anxiously awaited the naming of his successor.

The death of Chief Justice Vinson gave President Eisenhower the opportunity to make his first Supreme Court appointment. Speculation as to possible appointees was rife. The president canvassed many possibilities. Among those considered was John W. Davis, for whom President Eisenhower had great admiration. Mr. Davis, at the age of eighty, was hardly a feasible candidate. After several weeks of mulling over the merits and demerits of many suggested appointees, the president named Governor Earl Warren of California to succeed Chief Justice Vinson. Although his appointment was not yet confirmed, the new chief was on hand to preside at the opening of the Court's October 1953 term.

My knowledge of the new chief justice had come from the newspapers and other sources of public information. He was sixty-two years of age, a former California district attorney and attorney general, and had served as governor of that state for more than ten years. He was a popular governor and had been reelected as the nominee of both the Republican and Democratic parties. In 1948, he had been the Republican nominee for vice-president and in 1952 had sought his party's nomination for the presidency. Known to be a moderate Republican, as governor he had promoted political and social reforms in state government. As I try to remember, I experienced no particular reaction to the news of his appointment, nor did it occur to me that the change in the Court's leadership would have a special impact on *Brown*. Indeed, I thought that the new chief justice, whose entire public career had been in state government, might be sympathetic to an argument in support of the state's right to manage its internal affairs.

My southern associates were less complacent than I. In a telephone conversation shortly after the appointment, Mr. Moore spoke of his disappointment. He had reviewed the Warren record in California and he found nothing that would give comfort to the advocates of separate-but-equal schools. He saw the Warren appointment as more evidence of the determination of the Eisenhower administration to abolish every form of segregation. I suspect I was less disturbed than Mr. Moore because the Kansas stake in the outcome of the case was much less than that of Virginia. Also, I was more naive than he. At that stage in my intellectual development, I had a vague conception of the law as consisting of fixed, impersonal principles, subject to discovery by proper analysis, regardless of the predisposition of the analyst. I had read, but had not fully understood, Mr. Justice Holmes's assertion that "even the prejudices which judges share with their fellow men have had a good deal more to do than the syllogism in determining the rules by which men should be governed."[28] Fifty years of living with the law have compelled me, reluctantly and regretfully, to concur.

BRIEFING FOR REARGUMENT

The briefs filed before the first arguments were concise and directed to the main point in issue. It would appear that all counsel had seen the question as one that, at its outset, was not complex—whether the Court would and should adhere to a well-understood interpretation of the Fourteenth Amendment—and did not require extensive investigation. The request for additional but limited argument signaled a relaxation of the earlier self-imposed restraint. Mr. Davis, in his exquisite style, put it thus:

At the previous hearing of this case I think all counsel on both sides of the controversy, and in every case, realizing that it was an act of mercy and, perhaps, even of piety, not to increase the reading matter that comes to this Court, briefed the case in rather concise fashion. An effort was apparent, and I am sure I shared it, to condense the controversy to the smallest compass it would bear.

Now, for a rough guess I should think the motion for reargument has contributed somewhere between 1,500 and 2,000 pages to the possible entertainment, if not the illumination, of the Court. But I trust the Court will not hold counsel responsible for that proliferation.[29]

In preparation for reargument, the appellants, our opponents, filed a brief of 235 pages. The attorney general of the United States, as amicus curiae, submitted a brief of 188 pages accompanied by an appendix of 393 pages. Other parties produced documents that were of comparable length. We found that we could answer the Court's questions in fewer pages than most of our fellow litigants and filed a more modest document, containing both the argument and the appendix, consisting of 96 pages. The separate brief of the Topeka Board of Education was only 7 pages long.

The Fourteenth Amendment was proposed and submitted to the legislatures of the several states by the first session of the Thirty-ninth Congress on July 16, 1866. A proclamation declaring the amendment ratified was issued on July 28, 1868. By that time thirty states, including Kansas, had ratified the proposal. Section one of the amendment provided:

All persons born or naturalized in the United States, and subject to the jurisdiction thereof, are citizens of the United States and of the State wherein they reside. No State shall make or enforce any law which shall abridge the privileges or immunities of citizens of the United States; nor shall any State deprive any person of life, liberty, or property, without due process of law; *nor deny to any person within its jurisdiction the equal protection of the laws.* (emphasis added)

The *Brown* issue arose under the last clause of the amendment. Section 5 is also relevant to the Court's questions. It provides: "The Congress shall have power to enforce, by appropriate legislation, the provisions of this Article."

Our investigation of the intended impact of the Fourteenth

Amendment proceeded along these lines. First, we examined the journals and other records of the Congress that proposed the amendment and the state legislatures that ratified it to determine if members of those bodies had expressed an understanding that the amendment would preclude segregated schools. Second, we examined contemporaneous legislation to determine if other enactments might provide insight to the legislative understanding of the impact of the Fourteenth Amendment upon racial segregation. Third, we searched concurrent and subsequent administrative and judicial declarations and actions to find whether other agencies of government had recognized such a legislative intent. The questions relating to the powers of the Court to order desegregation required analysis of the language of the amendment and an examination of the extent of and limitations on judicial power. To cope with these questions, in the precomputer era, required many hours in the library perusing statutes, legislative journals, cases, and treatises.

As our research progressed and our thinking matured, we began to formulate our answers to the Court's questions. Our answers are summarized hereafter. Perhaps it should be noted that our adversaries, using the same data, reached quite different conclusions. Forty years later neither of us has been told who was right. The *Brown* result was reached by a route that made original intent irrelevant. Our conclusions, to which I still ascribe merit, were as follows.

The Intent of the Framers

When we examined the records of debates in the congressional session that proposed the Fourteenth Amendment, we found them barren of comment on the amendment's impact upon segregation in the public schools. To us, the reasons for this dearth of expressed concern for school segregation were clear. First, public education had not yet been recognized as a major function of government. Indeed, in some of the ratifying states, systems of public schools had not been established. There was no recognized constitutional right to education at public expense. Second, the Republican congressmen who conceived and enacted the Reconstruction legislation of 1866, of which the Fourteenth Amendment was a part, were concerned with far graver forms of discrimination than that incident to the relatively refined concept of separate-but-equal educational facilities. They were mindful of the welfare of a people that had been forcibly rescued from slavery and were still subject to the extraordinary burdens and disabilities imposed by Black Codes passed by their late masters. These laws enacted by legislatures in former slave states prohibited the recently emancipated slaves from making contracts; from suing; from giving evidence; from buying, inheriting, holding, or selling property; from moving from place to place; and imposed other burdens designed to perpetuate the blacks in a condition of serfdom. As we viewed it, it was against these kinds of intrusions upon the basic rights of life, liberty, and property that the Fourteenth Amendment was intended to operate.

The most persuasive evidence of congressional understanding was, we thought, found in the contemporaneous congressional policies in the District of Columbia. Congress had exclusive power to legislate for the District. The Thirty-seventh and Thirty-eighth Congresses, in 1862 and 1864, established segregated public school systems in the District.[30] The Thirty-ninth Congress, at the very time that the Fourteenth Amendment was being debated, passed laws to implement and expedite the segregated system of public schools.[31] Proposals specifically designed to end segregation in the District failed to pass in both the Forty-first and Forty-second Congresses.[32] We found it unlikely that Congress would have disregarded a limitation that it intended to impose on the states.

On the basis of our investigation and analysis, we argued that the Congress that proposed the Fourteenth Amendment did not understand or contemplate that the amendment would abolish segregation in the public schools. The appellants took a contrary view. They argued that it was understood and contemplated that the amendment would abolish all forms of state-imposed racial distinctions, necessarily including racial segregation in public education. The attorney general of the United States found that while the legislative history "does not conclusively establish" that the Congress that proposed the Fourteenth Amendment specifically understood that it would abolish racial segregation in the public schools, there is evidence that the intent of the amendment was to forbid all distinctions based on race or color. The results of the days of research and reams of printed argument were, perhaps, best summed up by Mr. Davis when he addressed the Court.

Now, Your Honors then are presented with this: We say there is no warrant for the assertion that the Fourteenth Amendment dealt with the school question. The appellants say that from the debates in Congress it is perfectly evident that the Congress wanted to deal with the school question, and the Attorney General, as a friend of the Court, says he does not know which is correct. So Your Honors are afforded the reasonable field for selection.[33]

The Understanding of the Ratifying States

At the time of ratification there were thirty-seven component states in the Union, of which thirty had ratified by the date of promulgation.[34] To generalize concerning the understanding of the ratifying legislatures is a task that defies accomplishment. Included in the group was Massachusetts, the pre–Civil War abolitionist sanctuary; South Carolina, a slave state where secession had begun; Minnesota, with a Negro population of one-fifth of 1 percent; and Mississippi, where black residents were 53 percent of the total. The ratifying states included the eleven that had made up the former Confederacy. Of these eleven states, only Tennessee ratified the amendment when it was first submitted. Each of the other ten had initially rejected the amendment, and their later ratification was accomplished by Reconstruction legislatures. Since ratification was a condition of the seating of their representatives in Congress, it is not unreasonable to infer that ratification by those states was motivated by a desire to regain their representation and provides no insight as to their understanding of the amendment's impact on public school segregation. A state-by-state survey revealed that at the time of ratification, segregated schools existed in twenty-four of the thirty-seven states of the Union and that in ten of those states, laws authorizing or requiring segregation were passed by the same legislatures that ratified the Fourteenth Amendment.

When we focused our attention on Kansas, we found that the Fourteenth Amendment was recommended for passage on January 8, 1867, by Governor Samuel J. Crawford, who stated that while the amendment was not fully what he might desire, it had received the approval of the electors at the preceding general election.[35] Without reference to committee and apparently without debate, the resolution for ratification of the amendment was adopted by both houses of the legislature, and ratification was completed on January 18, 1867.[36] It is significant that at the time the amendment was ratified, segregation was authorized by the statutes of Kansas in all elementary schools of the state.[37] Indeed, the legislature that ratified the Fourteenth Amendment almost simultaneously enacted legislation specifically authorizing segregation in cities of the second class.[38] Later legislation provides no evidence that the legislature believed that its power to authorize segregated schools had been diminished.

These findings led us to conclude that in neither Kansas nor a majority of the states that ratified the Fourteenth Amendment was there an understanding that the amendment's effect would be to abolish segregation in the public schools. The appellants evaluated the historical data differently. They concluded that it was the clear understanding of both the proponents and the opponents of ratification that the amendment would remove all racial distinctions from existing and prospective state laws, including those pertaining to public education. The attorney general of the United States found the state materials too sparse and the specific references to education too few to justify any definite conclusion that the state legislatures that ratified the Fourteenth Amendment understood that it either prohibited or permitted separate schools.

The Intended Future Impact of the Amendment

Our responses to the questions concerning the postamendment powers of Congress and the courts assumed that our earlier argument was sound. If neither the Congress that proposed the Fourteenth Amendment nor the states that ratified it had intended that it would prohibit segregation in public education, then neither the Congress nor the courts could at a later time enlarge its scope to include matters that lay beyond it at the time of its adoption. The argument here was the familiar but often disregarded one that the federal union is a government of delegated powers, that it can thus neither grant nor secure to any citizen any right or privilege not expressly or by necessary implication placed within its grant of jurisdiction, and that all powers of government not lodged by the people in the United States therefore remain in the states. Thus, we contended, to empower the Congress or the federal courts to abolish segregation in state-supported public schools would require that the Constitution be further amended. Furthermore, we argued, if it should be determined that the amendment authorized the use of federal power to end segregated schools, then the power could be exercised only by Congress. This conclusion seemed the clear intent of Section 5.

Predictably, both the appellants and the government disagreed with us.

As I write this memoir, forty years after the fact, I am aware that, to many of my colleagues at the bar, the arguments that we made may seem quaint, simplistic, and unsound. With due respect for these who disagree, I am still of the view that our position was one that merited the Court's consideration. It is said that great cases, like hard cases, make bad law. *Brown* was a great case.

The Decree: How? When? Where?

The final questions submitted by the Court assumed that segregation would be found unconstitutional. The Court then inquired whether integration must be ordered forthwith or if a gradual transition might be permitted, and by what court or other tribunal should the process of desegregation be supervised. These questions were dealt with by the Topeka Board of Education in its separate brief. Hence, our treatment was summary, but generally, we were in agreement with the board's positions. We did not believe that the reversal of the district court's judgment would necessarily require admission of Negro children forthwith to schools of their choice. We thought that the Court in the exercise of its equity powers could permit an effective gradual adjustment. We argued that the necessity for safeguarding the integrity of the school system at large should be reconciled with the need to effect constitutional guarantees. An order that might currently disrupt the orderly conduct of the Topeka public school system would not, we thought, be a proper exercise of equity jurisdiction. We also suggested that the Supreme Court should not formulate a detailed decree but should simply reverse and remand to the district court with instructions to frame an appropriate decree.

The appellants found no basis or justification for postponement of the effective date of a decree abolishing segregation or for an order allowing gradual integration. They did, however, recognize the possibility of delays caused by needed administrative and program adjustments but suggested that these be handled on a case-by-case basis on application of the school officials concerned. The views of the Department of Justice on questions four and five of the Court's order appear to agree with the position taken by the Topeka board.

The Kansas *Brief on Reargument* was completed, printed, served on our adversaries, and filed in accordance with the rules of the Supreme Court. With ample time, sufficient resources, and a fascinating subject, I had found the task to be an agreeable one. Although I had little optimism about the probable outcome of the case, I regard the fall of 1953 as one of my most rewarding seasons. To be able to spend uninterrupted days and weeks learning about America, its people, and their ways is a satisfaction that I have seldom enjoyed. I have no sense of what, if anything, my effort contributed to the case and its outcome. As I reviewed the work of others who were involved in the cases as parties and amici, I was confronted with an array of six-by-nine-inch documents standing vertically on eight full inches of shelf space. Our brief was a mere five-eighths of an inch thick. The briefs of those who opposed us bore the signatures of dozens of the most distinguished civil rights advocates of my generation, including two prospective Supreme Court justices, Thurgood Marshall and Arthur J. Goldberg, who was on the CIO amicus brief. The Kansas brief was signed only by Harold R. Fatzer, attorney general, and Paul E. Wilson, assistant attorney general of Kansas.

Dick Fatzer was apparently pleased with the effort. He sent copies to several of his attorney general friends. Among the acknowledgments was one from Attorney General Harry McMullan of North Carolina. He wrote:

> I believe that your brief will, perhaps, be more convincing than any one which has been filed in this case. . . . I do not see how anyone could read your brief and fail to agree that the Congress which proposed the Fourteenth Amendment, and all of the States having a sufficient Negro population to cause them to provide separate schools, did not consider that the Fourteenth Amendment would do away with segregation. I can't quite understand why Attorney General Brownell, in his brief, could not read this clear record of direct and circumstantial historical facts in support of this proposition.[39]

Unfortunately, the attorney general of North Carolina had no vote on the Supreme Court. An unexpected approval came from the Supreme Court reporter for the *New York Times*. He wrote to request a copy of the brief, adding, "Incidentally, I thought it was a good brief. I read it in the Supreme Court press room."[40] This, from the *Times*, was more than I could have hoped for.

8

Judgment Day

Repeat performances tend to be anticlimactic. Thus, recollections of my second journey to Washington are less vivid than those of the earlier adventure. I did not travel alone as before, but I enjoyed the company of my wife and our five-month-old son. Again we traveled by train. En route I felt little of the excitement and anxiety that I had experienced a year earlier when I had traveled over the same route with the same objective. This time I had the confidence that comes from experience. I knew—or thought I knew—what to expect, and I looked forward to the encounter. I had thought through and re-hearsed the arguments that I proposed to make and had reduced my intended statement to writing. The typed, twenty-page manuscript, carried in a loose-leaf binder, was indexed and tabbed for prompt reference. I felt secure and ready.

The afternoon after our arrival a strategy session was held in the suite of the Virginia group. The concerns of my southern associates focused on the new chief justice. What would he want to hear, and how was he likely to vote? Earl Warren had written no opinions, and a paper trail from which his thinking might be inferred was virtually nonexistent. The proponents of separate but equal were counting on the votes of Frankfurter, Jackson, Reed, and probably Clark. They conceded Black and Douglas to the opposition. They were optimistic that they could find at least one sympathetic voice among Burton, Minton, and the new chief.

The second round of arguments did not enjoy the media notice that had been given to the 1952 debates. On December 7 a story announced that the Supreme Court would hear arguments in the school segregation cases that afternoon. After identifying the jurisdictions involved, the piece reviewed the history of the cases and the issues that they raised. Scant attention was given to the "legal giants" who would vie for the Court's favor. The reporter did not expect an early decision. He wrote: "As the arguments stand to-day the history of the cases makes one thing apparent. The Court is in no mood and has no intention of rendering a quick decision upon an issue so complicated and fraught with so many implications."[1] He thought it unlikely that the case would be decided before spring.

REARGUMENT

The lapse of a year had produced few changes in the Supreme Court scenario. The courtroom procedure and protocol were as before. Again, the hearing chamber was filled to capacity while hopeful hundreds stood outside the door, buoyed by the remote prospect of seeing or hearing part of the proceedings. Seated at the counsel table were all of the attorneys who had argued in the earlier round, with one important addition. J. Lee Rankin, assistant attorney general, was there to present the views of the United States Department of Justice. The bench faced by counsel differed from the 1952 Court in one significant respect. The new chief justice, Earl Warren, sat in the position that a year earlier had been occupied by the late Chief Justice Vinson.

The order in which the cases were to be called had been changed since the earlier arguments. The South Carolina and Virginia cases were consolidated and assigned to the first position on the calendar, followed by Mr. Rankin, and then the Kansas, District of Columbia, and Delaware cases. I do not know whether the reshuffling was done by the Court on its own volition or at the suggestion of parties. Since the circumstances and law involved in the South Carolina and Virginia cases were so similar, their consolidation seemed quite appropriate. Their assignment to the leadoff position may have been occasioned by the expectation that the strongest arguments would be made and the issues most vigorously contested in those cases. Moreover, the uncertain posture of the Kansas case created by the action of the Topeka board hardly justified its retaining the number-one slot. Whatever the reasons for the rearrangement, I was entirely acquiescent. I was not troubled by the prospect that my speech might be buried in the oratorical avalanche to be launched by my colleagues. Four hours were allocated for argument of the consolidated South Carolina-Virginia case, one hour for Mr. Rankin, and one hour for each side in the Kansas, D.C., and Delaware cases. Thus, at 1:50 P.M. on December 7, 1953, the justices settled in for eleven hours of eloquence.

The consolidation of the cases from South Carolina and Virginia had enabled counsel in those cases to integrate their presentations into a single, coherent argument. Mr. Robinson spoke first for the appellants. At the beginning of his statement he informed the Court that he would limit his remarks to the issue of the congressional and state legislative understanding of the impact of the equal protection clause on segregated schools and that Mr. Marshall would follow with a discussion of the judicial power to order desegregation. Mr. Robinson's argument was scholarly and thorough. He concluded that the intent and purpose of the Fourteenth Amendment was to accomplish the complete legal equality of all persons, regardless of race, and to prohibit all state-imposed caste and class systems based upon race. He further concluded that segregation in the public schools on the basis of race is necessarily embraced within the prohibitions of the amendment. About halfway through his presentation, Mr. Robinson was interrupted with a series of questions by Justice Frankfurter concerning the weight to be given to statements by individual legislators. Later on, Justice Reed inquired about the role of Congress in enforcing the amendment. Except for these two diversions, Mr. Robinson was permitted to present the argument as he had planned.[2]

Thurgood Marshall was next at the lectern. Prior to the first arguments, I had been hardly aware of the existence of Mr. Marshall and had known nothing of his effort and leadership in the black civil rights cases. After that first encounter, I had undertaken to inform myself about the man and his exploits. I learned that he was one of the great advocates of my time and had played the leading role in the successful attacks on discrimination in higher education in the years preceding *Brown*. I found that he was accorded the highest respect by his professional colleagues, including those who had opposed him. Although I sat on the other side of the table, I looked forward to his performance with some eagerness. I was a little disappointed. Things did not seem to go well for him. Announcing that he proposed to show the Court's past and continuing recognition of the intended broad scope of the Fourteenth Amendment by reviewing the relevant Supreme Court decisions, he was interrupted by Justice Jackson, who suggested that the Court was not really interested in that line of argument. The justice commented, "I do not believe the Court was troubled about its own cases. It has done a great deal of reading of those cases."[3] Thus deflated, Marshall's argument seemed to become less coherent and effective. In the colloquies that followed, in which Jackson was joined by Frankfurter, the chief justice, and Reed, it appeared that the Court was most interested in a discussion of whether it was empowered by the terms of the Fourteenth Amendment to abolish segregation in public education, particularly in the absence of legislation by Congress. As I listened to the exchanges, and as I have reviewed the transcript, I had the feeling that in this early part of his presentation, Mr. Marshall did not come to grips with the issue to the justices' satisfaction. His argument was far reaching but seemed beside and beyond the point. Apparently sensing his failure to establish a satisfactory rapport with the Court, Mr. Marshall terminated his remarks and requested leave to save the balance of his time for rebuttal.[4]

The first argument in defense of the school districts in the consolidated cases was made by Mr. Davis. I suspect that whoever conceived the scheme of rearrangement of the cases for argument was mindful of that prospect. A year earlier, I had been the first to argue for the states and, except for the reshuffling, *Brown* and Kansas and I would have again enjoyed first billing. Under the rearranged order of argument, Kansas yielded its number-one position to South Carolina, and instead of my uncertain discourse, the Court was first informed of the states' positions by the venerable and honored Mr. Davis, of whom Richard Kluger wrote, "No one else in the cases came near matching him for bite, eloquence or wit."[5] During the course of more than fifty-four years that I have spent in and around courthouses, I have witnessed many dozens, probably hundreds of advocates in action and have listened to their words. None has approached the literary and forensic stature, the scholarship and the logic, of the speech made by John W. Davis in the Supreme Court in the waning hours of that day near the end of 1953. For me, forty years have not dimmed its luster. One scholar has described the speech thus: "Davis' argument was carefully organized, and his urbaneness and splendid rhetoric is shown again and again in the record. When one adds what all observers call the magic of his voice, the total effect was almost—almost—irresistible."[6] The same essayist also comments, "If he lost the School Segregation case, it was only because in 1954 no lawyer could have won it."[7]

With few interruptions by the justices, Mr. Davis analyzed the contemporaneous intent and understanding of the legislators who proposed and ratified the Fourteenth Amendment. Recognizing that diverse views were entertained during the debates that occurred in the drafting and adoption process, he concluded that "the overwhelming preponderance of the evidence demonstrates that the Congress which submitted, and the state legislatures which ratified, the Fourteenth Amendment did not contemplate and did not understand that it would abolish segregation in public schools."[8] To remove all doubt of the congressional understanding, he referred to acts sanctioning segregated schools in the District of Columbia passed by Congress immediately before, immediately after, and during the period of discussion of the Fourteenth Amendment. He found the evidence equally persuasive that it was the intent of a majority of the ratifying states not to enter the field of public education.

Finding nothing in the amendment to authorize the later abolition of segregation by Congress or the courts, he turned to the principle of stare decisis. He declared: "But be that doctrine what it may, somewhere, sometime to every principle comes a moment of repose when it has been so often announced, so confidently relied upon, so long continued that it passes the limits of judicial discretion and disturbance."[9]

As to the kind of a decree the Court might enter if it should decide that the South Carolina statute was unconstitutional, a decision "not to be expected and that God forbid," Mr. Davis thought that in the exercise of its equity powers, the Court might permit a gradual transition to integrated schools. He further argued that the process of adjustment should be undertaken and controlled by the appropriate state officials without federal judicial interference. Neither the Supreme Court nor the district court, he asserted, could act as a glorified board of education nor sit in the chairs of the legislature of South Carolina and mold its educational system. The state establishes its schools, pays the needed funds, and has the sole power to educate its citizens. Hence, it should have the power to devise any alternative that the Supreme Court might require. Finally, he reminded the Court of the state's good-faith, but tardy, efforts to provide equal educational opportunity for students of all races in a traditional segregated setting. With visible emotion (Thurgood Marshall said with tears on his cheeks), he told the Court:

> Let me say this for the State of South Carolina. It does not come here, as Thad Stevens[10] would have wished, in sack cloth and ashes. It believes that its legislation is not offensive to the Constitution of the United States.
>
> It is confident of its good faith and intention to produce equality for all of its children of whatever race or color. It is convinced that the happiness, the progress and the welfare of these children is best promoted in segregated schools, and it thinks it a thousand pities that by this controversy there should be urged the return to an experiment which gives no more promise of success today than when it was written into their Constitution during what I call the tragic era.
>
> I am reminded—and I hope it won't be treated as a reflection on anybody—of Aesop's fable of the dog and the meat: The dog, with a fine piece of meat in his mouth, crossed a bridge and saw the shadow in the stream and plunged for it and lost both substance and shadow.
>
> Here is equal education, not promised, not prophesied, but present. Shall it be thrown away on some fancied question of racial prestige?
>
> It is not my part to offer advice to the appellants and their supporters or sympathizers, and certainly not to the learned counsel. No doubt they think what they propose is best, and I do not challenge their sincerity in any particular period but I entreat them to remember the age-old motto that the best is often the enemy of the good.[11]

As Mr. Davis left the lectern, a respectful silence prevailed. He had said all that could be said for the values that his client cherished, and no one within the knowledge and experience of those present could have said it better. As I have read and reread his speech, my first impressions have been reinforced. Still, however splendidly stated, two allusions in his otherwise immaculate peroration cause me some discomfort. The first is his reference to the risk posed to equal education by "some fancied question of racial prestige." During all of his self-conscious years, John W. Davis had enjoyed the respect, prestige, and even the adulation of those who constituted his human environment. I wonder if he, having known only the highest regard of his fellows, was able properly to evaluate the importance of prestige to a member of a race whose history had been one of rejection, degradation, and enslavement and to whom equality was promised but not accomplished by the basic tenets of his or her society. The second ground for my misgiving went to his concluding words, "The best is often the enemy of the good." I do not and cannot doubt that in the real world, society confers greater benefits on some of its members than on others. It is equally free from doubt that a gained advantage may be lost in an effort to secure an even greater gain, as illustrated by the fable of the dog and his shadow. But I think the illustration is not apt when applied to benefits conferred by law. There can be no gradations in the equality guaranteed by the Fourteenth Amendment. Here, the good ought not to be arrayed against the best. If the illustration is to suggest that the educational opportunities that the law grants to some citizens are good while others may enjoy the best, and that good implies a lesser degree of excellence than best, then I get little help from the argument.

Mr. Moore was to complete the South Carolina-Virginia argument. He was recognized, took his position at the lectern to speak, and was getting well under way when, at 4:30, the Court adjourned for the day, leaving Mr. Moore and his uncompleted argument in a state of suspense, to be resumed at noon on the following day.

Much of the Moore argument was a rerun of the history already examined by Mr. Davis. He emphasized the special problems caused by the large black population of Prince Edward County and other areas of the South and pointed to Virginia's accelerated building program designed to provide equality of opportunity for all of Virginia's children, whether black or white. He also contended, as in the earlier argument, that when faced with conflicting evidence, the trial court had declined to find demonstrable adverse effects resulting from segregation. After using most of Virginia's time, Mr. Moore yielded to Attorney General Almond. General Almond was an orator in the best southern tradition. He made a spirited statement of Virginia's case. I cannot say whether his eloquence added to the Court's understanding.

Time remained for the appellants' rebuttal argument to be made by Thurgood Marshall. The overnight recess had given Mr. Marshall the opportunity to reflect on the strategy of attack. In his opening argument on the afternoon before, he had attempted not too successfully to rely on an interpretation of evidence of historical intent and an analysis of judicial precedent. This time he took a different, more effective, approach. He came on like a locomotive. He did not speak in the exquisite phrases of John W. Davis nor in the garnished rhetoric of Lindsay Almond. His was the vernacular of the marketplace. His appeal was to nine rational and compassionate human beings who collectively constituted the highest court in the land. Segregation, he asserted, is wrong; it is irrational and a lingering vestige of slavery and the Black Codes that the authors of the Fourteenth Amendment sought to bar. He argued: "Those same kids in Virginia and South Carolina—and I have seen them do it—they play in the streets together, they play on their farms together, they go down the road together, they separate to go to school, they come out of school and play ball together."[12] Finally, he came to the heart of his argument:

> We charge that [the challenged state laws] are Black Codes. They obviously are Black Codes if you read them. They haven't denied that they're Black Codes, so if the court wants to very narrowly decide this case, they can decide it on that point. . . .
>
> The only way that this Court can decide this case in opposition to our position, . . . is to find that for some reason Negroes are inferior to all other human beings."[13]

Later that afternoon, my wife, who has difficulty in accepting the notion that courtroom rivalries can be put aside at the courthouse door, was surprised to observe Thurgood Marshall being congratulated by Mrs. Robert McC. Figg, whose husband had occupied the chair next to Mr. Davis during the South Carolina argument. Mrs. Figg had found the Marshall presentation one of the most effective arguments to which she had ever listened.

In an adjudicative system more concerned with efficiency and less committed to the right of all parties to be heard, the arguments would have ended when Mr. Marshall left the podium. Except for the unique question raised in the District of Columbia case, whether in the context of school segregation the requirements of due process differ from those of equal protection, nothing remained to be said. Still, seven hours remained for the rehashing of arguments already heard. The chief justice smiled as he recognized the assistant attorney general who would speak for the government. Mr. Rankin came not as a partisan with an axe to grind, but as a friend of the court. The position of the friend of the court is that of a participant in litigation who has no substantial stake in the immediate case. At the same time, the amicus is seldom an uninterested bystander but usually has a strong interest in the outcome and enters the case to suggest a rationale consistent with its views. Mr. Rankin's presence strengthened the hand of our adversaries.

The brief and accompanying appendix filed by the Department of Justice prior to the arguments generally supported the NAACP position. Mr. Rankin's argument was an echo of the government's brief. However, the brief had not unequivocally asserted that state laws requiring or permitting segregation were unconstitutional.

Mr. Justice Douglas was concerned, and as Mr. Rankin's argument developed, it became clear that the justice was not satisfied with the government's tentative position on the issue of constitutionality. Seeking to clarify an earlier question, he asked point-blank whether the Department of Justice had taken a position on the issue of constitutionality. Mr. Rankin's reply erased any doubt as to his department's position: "It is the position of the Department of Justice that segregation in public schools cannot be maintained under the Fourteenth Amendment, and we adhere to the views expressed in the original brief of the Department in that regard."[14] When Mr. Rankin concluded his presentation and resumed his seat at the counsel table there were no gestures of approval from those who sat on my side. The Topeka case was to be heard next.

Robert Carter, who again led off for the appellants, had spoken precisely eighty-one words when Justice Frankfurter interrupted with the inquiry, "Is your case moot, Mr. Carter?"[15] Carter thought the case was not moot because most of the Topeka school system was still segregated, there had been no indication of when the process of integration would be completed, and the constitutionality of the statute was still undetermined. Justice Frankfurter was not satisfied. He continued to press the issue of mootness and was joined by Justices Jackson and Reed. With evident uncertainty and frustration, Carter suggested that he yield his time to the state "and see what the state has to say about this." The chief justice then spoke to me. I shall always remember his words: "Mr. Wilson, will you please address yourself to the question of whether it is moot or not?" I was dismayed. Suddenly, the argument that I had so carefully prepared became irrelevant. Whether I should have been prepared to argue the issue of mootness may be a proper question. The fact was that I had come before the Court prepared only to argue for the constitutionality of a Kansas statute. Yet, my standing to be heard was dependent on the existence of a bona fide controversy between Mr. Carter's clients and the Topeka Board. Mr. Carter thought a controversy existed. I agreed, but I was not authorized to speak for the board—indeed, the board had made it clear that it did not want to be represented by the attorney general. These thoughts troubled me as I moved to the lectern. What should or could I say?

I began by pointing out that only one of the plaintiff children had been admitted to an integrated school. All of the others were required to attend schools that remained segregated. Justice Frankfurter then took charge and, employing his Socratic skills to my considerable discomfort, undertook to test my knowledge of the law of mootness. He was not impressed with my argument that the Topeka announcement had no legal significance; that the board might change its mind and reverse the declared policy; and that the constitutionality of the Kansas statute remained an issue that ought to be determined.

Minutes passed—it seemed like hours—before Justice Jackson tried to change the subject. He inquired whether I would add anything to that already covered by Mr. Davis and "Judge" Moore. My response was:

My conclusions, my interpretations, are substantially those that Mr. Davis and "Judge" Moore have presented to this Court.

MR. MOORE: That is "Mr. Moore," I would just like to correct that.

MR. WILSON: I am not sure whether it is proper to apologize under the circumstances or not. (Laughter)[16]

This spontaneous and not very thoughtful comment may have been the high point in my argument. It was specially reported in a framed item entitled "Lawyer's Jest Unbends High Court" in the next morning's *New York Herald Tribune*. Fearing a reprimand for contempt, I was relieved when the chief justice smiled and directed me to proceed.

Thinking the question of mootness had been set aside, I turned my attention to a discussion of the merits, soon to learn some of the justices were not yet satisfied on the mootness issue. This time Justice Black joined Justice Frankfurter in questioning whether a bona fide controversy existed. More questions brought more responses, all apparently unpersuasive. Finally, the chief justice silenced his colleagues by saying, "I think when both parties to the action feel that there is a controversy, and [we have] invited the Attorney General to be here and answer these questions, I, for one, would like to hear the argument."[17]

I shall always think fondly of Chief Justice Warren. Had it not been for his firm intercession, I might have suffered the humiliation of being figuratively tossed out of the Supreme Court. My distinguished associates were observing my performance. My wife was in the courtroom. My friends in Topeka were watching the papers for news from the Supreme Court. By virtue of the Chief's indulgence, the headline in the next morning's *Kansas City Times* read "Kansas Case In," with the subheading "Warren to State's Rescue." The story, which bore an AP dateline of December 8, reported in part:

The attorneys in the Kansas case, which originated in Topeka, had a tough time getting their arguments under way.

Justice Frankfurter and other justices bombarded Wilson and another lawyer, Robert L. Carter of New York, with questions as to whether the case was no longer a live issue. . . .

The lawyers did not get their arguments under way until Chief Justice Warren said he would like to hear the arguments;

this cut off further questioning as to whether the Kansas case was moot.[18]

Justice Frankfurter's understanding of the law may have been right, but the chief justice clearly was more sensitive to matters affecting the human ego.

Although the chief justice had given me the signal to discuss the issues, I soon sensed that most of the justices did not regard my argument as vital. Hence, I did not present the argument that I had planned. I abbreviated, summarized, and passed over points that were relevant, but not critical. No questions were asked from the bench. As I spoke, it became increasingly clear that my position at the lectern was at the indulgence of the Court. After using only a little more than half of my allotted hour, I sat down with a vague feeling of emptiness and frustration. Things had not gone as well as I expected. My carefully prepared speech was still largely unspoken. Mr. Carter's rebuttal was brief. He agreed with me that the case was not moot. He thought that I had offered no new arguments on the merits and chose not to burden the record further.

After my less than triumphant retreat, the District of Columbia and Delaware cases remained to be heard. In each instance the justices, led by Justice Frankfurter, continued their pestiferous ways. In the D.C. case, Justice Frankfurter questioned whether Milton Korman of the corporation counsel's office actually represented the board of education as it was constituted in December 1953. Only after he had documented his status as the board's representative was Mr. Korman permitted to pursue his argument on the merits, but not without frequent interruptions.[19] In the Delaware case the plaintiffs had prevailed in the state courts on the ground that the physical and educational facilities maintained for Negro children were inferior. There was no finding that the Delaware segregation law was unconstitutional. The state appealed, but the plaintiffs did not cross-appeal. Hence, the justices challenged the right of the attorneys to argue the constitutional issue.[20]

By the time the arguments were concluded, I felt that the justices no longer viewed the Kansas, D.C., and Delaware cases as very important. Earlier, the Court had shown a disposition to seek and consider as many points of view as possible. It had, in Justice Frankfurter's words, "cajoled" an appearance by the state of Kansas. It had taken special steps to accelerate the D.C. and Delaware appeals. A year later all of these parties were before the Court, each prepared to present its views on specific questions asked by the Court; yet it appeared that the justices were not interested in hearing them. Collateral issues—mootness, authority to appear, whether review had been properly sought—were interjected, with the result that argument on the merits was discouraged or limited. Assuming that there had been a change in the Court's attitude and interest, I suspect that it may have resulted from the Court's growing realization that the time had come when history and society demanded a rethinking of the constitutionality of segregation per se—can racial separation in public education ever be squared with the Fourteenth Amendment? With this as the issue to be determined, the conditions that existed and what people thought in Kansas and the District of Columbia and Delaware became less important.

After the initial go-around, in which Mr. Davis and Thurgood Marshall were the chief protagonists, the arguments were largely cumulative. By the time the Kansas case was reached, I suspected that Justice Frankfurter and his colleagues may have felt that they had heard enough. They may have begun to believe that history and precedent and oratory were not likely to supply an answer to the basic problem before them. The question was what is right and just in twentieth-century America—whether a democratic society, in conferring its benefits, can rightfully discriminate among its members on the basis of complexion and ethnic origin. The answer would not be found in books of law and history nor in the sophisticated arguments of learned men, but in the collective conscience of Americans. Theirs were the voices that spoke with the greater weight.

RETURN TO KANSAS

At 2:40 on Wednesday afternoon, Attorney General Young arose and respectfully informed the Court that Delaware would offer no argument in rebuttal. Thus, the drama in Washington ended. The Kansas news media had reported the Supreme Court arguments with little emphasis or comment. The national wire service releases had been carried in most of the daily newspapers circulated in the state; although in Topeka larger headlines and local embellishment were featured, Kansas columnists and editorial writers took little note of what was happening in Washington. Except for members of boards of education and employees of school districts where segregation was practiced, most nonblack Kansans had little interest in the case, and few were able to appreciate its significance.

When I left Washington, I had no expectation of an early decision. The experience of the previous year and the apparent complexity of the problems to be resolved in some of the companion states had prepared me for months of delay. I felt no surprise or anxiety as months passed and the end of the term loomed with no word from the Court. The more mundane and parochial concerns of Kansas government in an election year demanded as much attention as I could give. Moreover, I had by this time accepted the probability that we would not—and should not—win. I did not then, and do not now, concede that our position was inconsistent with the law as we then understood it. I recognized, however, that the time was at hand when the public conscience required that new law be made and that the Court's decision would probably involve considerations beyond history and tradition and judicial precedent.

Scholars and producers of documentary films have undertaken to reconstruct the intra-Court negotiations and compromises that occurred following the December 1953 arguments.[21] Halfway across the continent, in Topeka, we had little comprehension of what might be occurring behind the closed doors of the inner chamber of the Supreme Court's marble palace. We could only bide our time and await the Court's pleasure. The answer came at 12:52 P.M. on May 17, 1954.

WE CANNOT TURN THE CLOCK BACK

Both Attorney General Fatzer and I were at our desks that Monday in early summer when shortly after noon, Kansas time, the phones began ringing. The first call was from Elon Torrence of the AP, who reported that his wires were carrying a story that the chief justice was then delivering an opinion that would strike down public school segregation as a violation of the Fourteenth Amendment. Within a few minutes there were calls from the *New York Times*, the *Washington Post*, and other out-of-state newspapers. Before midafternoon the entire corps of statehouse reporters, including representatives of the national wire services, the Topeka, Kansas City, and Wichita newspapers, and Topeka and Kansas City radio stations, assembled in the attorney general's office to discuss the case with Dick Fatzer and me. They sought our comments. Because we had not had the opportunity to read the opinion nor had we been officially advised of the holding, our comments were guarded, but we expressed no chagrin. A banner headline on page one of the afternoon paper proclaimed "School Segregation Banned."[22] The next morning's *Capital* reported that General Fatzer had again emphasized that his office "had never argued the validity of segregation—only the state's right to regulate their own schools by state legislation." Expressing confidence in the good faith and cooperation of Kansas school administrators, Fatzer pledged that his office would see that the ruling was complied with to the fullest degree.[23] The story continued: "Paul Wilson, Assistant Attorney General who argued the case before the Supreme Court said: 'Segregation in Kansas schools can be ended in two years without any great problem except the assimilation of Negro teachers.'"[24]

Again I was wrong. The black teachers have long been assimilated, apparently without serious problems. And forty years later the problems of ending segregation in Topeka's schools still perplex the court and the parties.

When interviewed later the same day, Governor Arn said, "The long litigated question has now been decided and is the law for all states of the nation and the Kansas education procedure will have to ultimately be adjusted to comply with it."[25] Other Topekans expressed satisfaction with the ruling. President Dickinson of the board of education praised the opinion as in "the finest spirit of the law and true democracy." M. L. Burnett, Topeka branch NAACP president said, "Thank God for the Supreme Court" and announced a celebration to be held at Monroe School that evening. Oliver Brown, whose name will ever loom large in the history of civil rights law, was "wonderfully happy about the decision," seeing it as a great step forward to better race relations. His only expressed concern was for the black teachers and their integration into the school system.[26] The virtually unanimous approval of the decision reinforced my already formed judgment that in the Kansas context, the *Brown* litigation was unnecessary and might have been avoided if earlier generations of

The *Brown* decision is announced in Topeka's afternoon newspaper, May 17, 1954. (Courtesy of the Kansas State Historical Society)

legislators and members of boards of education had been more sensitive to their world and less lethargic in their responses.

Tuesday's mail brought us a printed copy of the Court's opinion and our first opportunity to examine the holding and the thinking that produced it. With no great surprise or dismay I learned that my argument had failed to persuade a single justice. The views expressed and the analyses propounded by counsel on my side of the table were apparently taken as invalid or immaterial. The decision was against us, and the opinion contained little to assuage the indignity of our defeat. The four state cases were decided in a consolidated opinion written by the chief justice, who also wrote the opinion in the District of Columbia case. Both were unanimous decisions.

After reviewing the history of the several cases and the issues presented for determination, the chief justice had considered in a somewhat summary fashion the history of the Fourteenth Amendment and the understanding and intent of those who proposed and ratified it. He found little evidence of its intended effect on public education. Turning to the judicial construction, he questioned whether *Plessy v. Ferguson* was consistent with earlier Fourteenth Amendment cases and noted a recent erosion of the separate-but-equal doctrine and the concomitant enlargement of the role of public education in America. He then appeared to suggest that history and precedent are not very important in the determination of justice in a contemporary social setting. He wrote:

> In approaching this problem, we cannot turn the clock back to 1868 when the Amendment was adopted, or even to 1896 when *Plessy v. Ferguson* was written. We must consider public education in the light of its full development and its present place in American life throughout the nation. . . .
> We come then to the question presented: Does segregation of children in public schools solely on the basis of race, even though the physical facilities and other "tangible" factors may be equal, deprive the children of the minority group of equal educational opportunities? We believe it does.[27]

As it continued, the Court set out the full text of Finding of Fact No. 8 in the Kansas case, noting that this finding is "amply supported by modern authority." With this finding as its point of departure the Court concluded that "in the field of public education the doctrine of 'separate but equal' has no place. Separate facilities are inherently unequal."[28]

With the substantive issue settled, the Court was not yet prepared to formulate a decree for the implementation of the decision. Accordingly, the cases were again restored to the docket for further reargument on the manner in which compliance would be accomplished in each of the states before the Court. The attorney general of the United States was again invited to participate, and the Court announced that the attorneys general of all states whose laws required or permitted segregated schools would be permitted, on their requests, to file briefs and to participate in the further reargument.

REACTIONS

Outside of Kansas the reaction to the opinion was varied.[29] Among the jurisdictions that were parties to the litigation, Delaware and the District of Columbia had, like Kansas, anticipated the decision and had begun to plan for its implementation. Neither foresaw difficulty in making the transition. Governor Byrnes of South Carolina expressed shock and disappointment but delayed a decision on further action until he had had the opportunity to study the opinion and consult with legislative and other state leaders. Meanwhile, he counseled South Carolinians to exercise restraint and keep the peace. In Virginia, the chief officer of the state's school system promised no defiance (a promise not later honored), whereas the governor was noncommittal, saying that he intended to call a conference of state and local officers to weigh the effects of the ruling. He also suggested the possibility of a special session of the legislature.

Seventeen other states either required or permitted some or all of their school districts to maintain racially segregated schools. Although these states were not parties, their laws and policies were affected by *Brown*'s broad declaration of unconstitutionality. Among the states of this group, reported reactions of leaders in government and education were diverse, ranging from acceptance, with differing degrees of enthusiasm, to outright defiance, some urging the dismantling of their public school systems. It was from states that had been among the members of the late Confederacy that the most strident protests and direst threats were heard. Quite apart from the emotion-charged concerns for southern traditions and southern social values, all were apprehensive about the transition process, particularly the probable cost and the impact of integration upon the professional lives of Negro teachers and school administrators. It was foreseen that the adjustments required by the decision would require the construction of new buildings, the improvement of existing facilities, and changes in curriculum and personnel that might require the expenditure of millions of dollars from public treasuries that were already impoverished. It was also expected that white southern parents would not permit their children to attend classes taught by black teachers. Hence, it was believed that the demise of separate black schools would end the careers of many black educators and deny to other blacks the opportunity to enter the profession. These pragmatic considerations troubled all southerners, including those that did not object to the Court's concept of equality. Kansans foresaw few problems of adjustment. Their concerns were when and how the transition was to be accomplished, and their apprehensions were minimal.

Because of the widespread interest in the case and its foreseeable impact on American education and social policy, it was inevitable that it would be given the closest scrutiny, not only by attorneys involved in the cases or who might be involved in similar cases, but by scholars, journalists, and others interested in the social environment. Their comments went not only to the result of the opinion but to the quality of its argument and the craftsmanship of the writer. From my simplistic perspective, I found little fault with the opinion. It was unanimous. It was short. It was written in clear and direct words and phrases, unburdened by legalistic jargon and cumulative citations and understandable to lawyer and lay person alike. After reading the opinion, I had no doubt as to the Court's meaning and the status of our position. We had lost.

As one of the many lawyers who had invested weeks in the investigation and analysis of the original understanding and later application of the Fourteenth Amendment, I had thought that this part of our argument would be given more consideration than the summary declaration, "We cannot turn the clock back." However, as I now reflect, I am inclined to agree that a discussion of the views and judgments of earlier times was hardly necessary. Implicit in history is the concept of change. If there were no change, there would be no history. The history of the law teaches us that where social issues are at stake, the test of the validity of legislative acts and judicial decisions is their relevance to the environments and the times that produced them. *Brown* arose in a different America than the one that existed when the Civil War ended or when *Plessy v. Ferguson* was decided. Although I viewed it as my duty that I inform the Court of what I believed to be the Kansas understanding of the purpose and scope of the equal protection guarantee, I do not take exception to the Court's decision to focus its attention on "public education in the light of its full development and present place in American life."

James Reston, one of America's most distinguished journalists, writing in the *New York Times*, described the segregation opinion as a "sociological decision," founded on the "hearts and minds" of Americans, rather than upon law. He declared: "In ruling out racial segregation in the nation's public schools, it [the Supreme Court] rejected history, philosophy and custom as the major basis for its decision and accepted instead Justice Benjamin N. Cardozo's test of contemporary social justice."[30] Justice Cardozo, an eloquent judicial writer, had more than thirty years earlier formulated his test in words quoted in Mr. Reston's column:

> Finally, when the social needs demand one settlement rather than another, there are times when we must bend symmetry, ignore history and sacrifice custom in the pursuit of other ends.
>
> From history and philosophy and custom, we pass to the force which is in our day and generation the greatest of them all, the power of social justice which finds its outlet in the method of sociology.
>
> The final cause of the law is the welfare of society.[31]

If Justice Cardozo had been speaking for the Supreme Court in 1954, he might have spoken more eloquently than Chief Justice Warren, but I suspect his conclusion would have been the same.

In a milieu where economy in the use of words is seldom honored, the *Brown* opinion is refreshingly brief. The four state cases were disposed of in a consolidated opinion of 10 printed pages. The separate District of Columbia opinion, also written by the chief justice, is 2 pages long.[32] Nearly a century earlier another chief justice, Roger Brooke Taney, had written 55 pages to deny Dred Scott's appeal,[33] whereas each of his eight associates had filed a separate concurring or dissenting opinion, which, taken together, were of the aggregate length of 254 pages. The Court that in 1857 required more than 300 pages of text to argue and justify the denial of one black man's citizenship was able, in 1954, in 12 printed pages to require the admission of 11 million black children to full participation in America's public schools. Perhaps it is easier to do right than to justify wrong.

In the weeks following the decision, Topeka continued to move forward with its previously announced plans to integrate the schools within its jurisdiction. In other Kansas cities affected by the decision, desegregation programs were either under way or being planned. Black residents were satisfied with the ruling. Religious leaders were pleased. Social activists were jubilant and vocal. State officials and other political leaders expressed their warm approval, particularly in those places where there were significant numbers of black voters. Rural Kansans and those living in small towns where the "Negro problem" was unknown were largely indifferent, and whatever their inclinations, they said nothing. As I reflected on the comments of my fellow Kansans, it became clear to me that the constituency that I had represented before the Supreme Court was not disturbed by my failure to succeed.

Honesty requires that I admit to mixed emotions in the wake of the decision. Circumstances neither contrived nor controlled by me had cast me in the role of an advocate opposing a result that I believed was foreseeable and just and proper. In fulfilling my role, I was a competitor in an adversary proceeding. I had spent weeks, perhaps months, preparing to compete effectively. No serious competitor enjoys the experience of losing. I lost. It was not only just and proper that I lose, but it was inevitable. Still, losing is no fun. A few days after the decision, General Fatzer, who had assigned the case to me and whose name appeared above mine on the brief, wrote to the chief justice congratulating him on the Court's opinion and expressing his personal pleasure at the outcome of the case. He wrote: "The court's opinion in this case reaffirms the faith of many citizens in the constitution, and in the forthright and courageous manner this was decided. If the decision had been otherwise, I feel it would have been a great victory for communistic ideologies in this country, and throughout the world."[34]

As I continued to fret about justice, duty in no-win situations, and the fickle finger of fate, a balm for my bruised morale appeared from an unexpected source. Bob Carter, my NAACP adversary, wrote me a letter. Among his comments and suggestions concerning further proceedings in the case, he wrote: "We are certain that your refusal to approach this matter other than in a purely lawyer-like examination of constitutional power, unfreighted with emotion and demagoguery, helped to embolden the court to make its courageous and statesmanlike declaration of May 17. However poorly stated, this is meant as a tribute to your honesty and integrity as a member of the bar and an official of the state of Kansas."[35]

9

Brown II

Nearly eleven months were to elapse before the Supreme Court again sat to hear argument in the *Brown* litigation. The decision of May 17, 1954, determined only that segregated public schools were unconstitutional. It provided no guidelines to be observed by officials responsible for bringing schools then segregated into compliance with the decision. Because of their widespread impact and the variety of local conditions in which they would apply, the framing of suitable decrees would involve problems that were both varied and complex. Thus, the cases were restored to the docket for further reargument directed at ways and means of implementing the decisions in each of the concerned states. No time was set for the hearing of such further arguments. For a long time our *Brown* file was inactive.

THE STATE'S ROLE?

Although further proceedings were required, it was my view that the state was not and should not be further involved. The issues not yet determined related only to when and how Topeka would complete the desegregation of its elementary schools. That was a controversy between the parents and children who had taken their claim to court and the Topeka Board of Education. The attorney general had intervened for the sole purpose of defending the constitutionality of the statute under attack. That issue had been determined. There was no possible appeal. John W. Davis, who bowed out of the case after the May 17 opinion, is reported to have written to his associate, "We have met the enemy and we are theirs."[1] That, I thought, should be the position of Kansas. Our part of the case seemed closed.

The attorney general thought differently than I, and we remained active in the case, not only because he was the attorney general, but because he was probably right. As he saw it, Kansas was still a party and he, as the state's chief legal officer, had a duty to respond to the Court's request for further assistance. He felt we could be helpful to Kansas and to the Court, which then sought input from diverse sources. It had invited participation by the attorney general of the United States and had suggested that requests to appear amici curiae by attorneys general of other affected states would be honored. Kansas, the general thought, should be heard. Also, the case was no longer a political hot potato. As before, I was given responsibility for research, collecting data, and writing the brief. Unlike the earlier occasions when the case was to be called for argument, both Dick and I would go to Washington this time, he to make the oral presentation and I to carry the papers.

Although the case continued to be adversary in form, we no longer considered our position to be adverse to the contentions of the black Topekans. We accepted the Supreme Court's decision on the merits, and our only postdecision interest was to assist the Court in developing a desegregation program that would be agreeable to black Kansans and, at the same time, would avoid or minimize the risk of disruption of the public school systems affected.

DEFIANCE IN DIXIE

During the weeks following May 17, special meetings of the governors and attorneys general of the concerned states were called to explore possible courses of legal action to preserve segregated schools. Neither Governor Arn nor General Fatzer attended these meetings. Dick Fatzer had many personal friends among the southern attorneys general. As a former president of their national association, he enjoyed their respect. He consistently urged restraint. Speaking to the Southern Regional Conference of Attorneys General at their San Antonio meeting in April 1954, he anticipated the May 17 decision and counseled moderation and responsible legal action to conform.[2] He was particularly concerned that too much resistance by state officials would result in increased federal control of education. I cannot say whether his counsel had a significant impact on his southern counterparts. I suspect that most of them reacted as the attorney general of North Carolina, who wrote:

> I sincerely believe that if you were Attorney General of Georgia or Attorney General of Mississippi or any other southern state that had a high percentage of Negro population, your views and attitude towards what we shall now do about the court's decision would not be different from that entertained by the Attorneys General of these states. . . . You are confronted with an utterly different problem from that which we are now up against in North Carolina and what our friends in Virginia and South Carolina have to contend with.[3]

In 1954 Eugene Cook, attorney general of Georgia, succeeded Dick Fatzer as president of the national association. The annual meeting of the group was planned to be held in Biloxi, Mississippi, late in the year. The focus of the meeting was to be directed at the relationship between the state and federal governments. It was a matter of long-standing tradition that the attorney general of the United States be invited to address the annual meeting. Although urged to do so, General Cook refused to extend the usual invitation to Herbert Brownell. In justification he declared his "firm opinion that Mr. Brownell's frequent, ill-advised and sometimes ruthless political conduct has done irreparable damage to our efforts to promote better Federal-State relations."[4] Characterizing the segregation cases as "suits by a private corporation [the NAACP] and embracing a vicious attack on the integrity of seventeen Sovereign States," he asserted that Brownell's intervention had deeply offended most of the attorneys general of the southern states.[5] He also stated that he had been informed that a Brownell appearance at the meeting would be offensive to the attorney general and the people of Mississippi. Enclosed with Cook's letter, which was circulated to all state attorneys general, was a memorandum calling it to their attention that the NAACP was opposing his reelection as attorney general of Georgia and that the election would be a referendum on Georgia's determination to circumvent the *Brown* decision.[6]

Many of his fellow attorneys general were dismayed by Cook's position. From Don Eastvold, attorney general of Washington and president of the Western Association of Attorneys General, came a strong denunciation of Cook's demonstrated lack of respect for the Supreme Court and the attorney general of the United States, and a demand that he resign as the national association's president.[7] General Cook did not resign. He was reelected as attorney general of Georgia. The meeting was held, not in Biloxi, but in White Sulphur Springs, West Virginia, and Attorney General Brownell spoke at the annual banquet.

REACTION IN KANSAS

Kansans, too, were speaking their minds about the May 17 decision. Almost without exception those who commented agreed with the Supreme Court's opinion. There were few accolades for the attorney general or his assistant who had presented the apparent Kansas view to the Supreme Court. At a panel discussion in my church, I was referred to as a lawyer who, with the opportunity to be a Lincoln, had behaved like a Douglas. I did not fully understand the comparison, but I am sure it was not intended as a compliment. One of my professional mentors deplored my efforts to "embalm the Constitution."

When the Republican State Convention assembled in Topeka in August to draft the party's 1954 platform, it declared: "We hail the recent historic decision of the Supreme Court of the United States as upholding the traditional position of the Republican party that there can be no second class citizens under our American form of government." However laudable the expressed sentiment, I was reminded that during all but six of the first ninety-three years of statehood the Republican party had controlled the state legislature and that a Republican had held the governorship in all but fourteen years of the state's history.

Most of the constituent mail was critical. A letter written on the letterhead of a western Kansas newspaper chided the attorney general for making Kansas "the associate of half a dozen backward states in the unenviable and false position of favoring segregation," saying that the writer had never seen an explanation or excuse for why the attorney general "horned in on this case to start with." He continued, "You know—or should now—that you [*sic*] action was contrary to the sentiment of a vast majority of the people of Kansas and exposed the state to unjustifiable ridicule."[8] Although this writer was more caustic than most, I cannot recall any comment, written or oral, made after the *Brown* decision by a Kansan who acknowledged that he or she had favored segregated public schools or approved of the position taken by the attorney general's office.

I have no reason to doubt nor do I question the genuineness of the awakening of the Kansas social conscience following *Brown*, but I think it is also appropriate to mention that these same Kansans had for many years elected the legislators and members of boards of education that provided for and supported separate schools; that these elected officials had the power to abolish segregation and would have done so if their constituents had so demanded. Many of these Kansans had sent their children to segregated schools without protest; they had patronized places of public accommodation and entertainment that denied service to Negroes; and they had spent their off-duty hours on the golf courses and in the game rooms of lily-white country clubs. In many cases I suspected that their post-*Brown* chagrin was less a reflection of their concern that segregation had existed in Kansas than a resentment at having their attitudes and actions subjected to public view and discussion. They were less righteous than embarrassed.

SUMMER IN KANSAS—1954

Summer passed with no date set for the further reargument in *Brown* and lingering uncertainty as to the state's role in the case. I did some desultory research, assembled data on desegregation progress in Kansas cities other than Topeka, and was occasionally in touch with other attorneys in the case. Otherwise, I marked time.

After the May 17 opinion, I wrote to Mr. Carter and mentioned our uncertainty as to whether the state was still in court, but assured him of our continuing willingness to be helpful. I also called his attention to the progress toward integration being made in Topeka and suggested that the case was fast becoming moot. I wondered if a request for dismissal on the ground of mootness would be proper.[9] In his reply he suggested that he would prefer a consent decree in which a plan for desegregation of the Topeka schools might be agreed upon by the parties and incorporated into a judgment.[10] He suggested a meeting of the attorneys involved at which the terms of a consent decree could be discussed and agreed upon. To me his proposal seemed reasonable, but since the decision was one for the board, I referred the letter to Peter Caldwell.[11]

There were occasional letters of inquiry from Mr. Moore, the Department of Justice, and state attorneys general who were preparing to appear for their states. Six states had sought permission to appear amici curiae.

When the Topeka schools opened in September 1954 fourteen elementary schools had been integrated. Included in this number were the two that had been desegregated in September 1953 and two where integration was partial. Four schools remained segregated and black whereas enrollments in five other schools were limited to whites only. The preterm estimate was that 123 Negro children would attend mixed schools and 714 would remain segregated. The board promised further steps in the integration process as "rapidly as practicable."[12]

In 1954 the statute that was struck down in the *Brown* decision applied to eleven Kansas cities in addition to Topeka, ranging in population from just over 10,000 to nearly 170,000.[13] Negro populations varied from about 2.3% to 20.6% of the totals. Each city had its own history and traditions and its unique blend of ethnic and cultural diversities. Although all of them accepted the mandate for desegregation, each sought to develop its own plan and schedule for compliance. It was our intention to tell the Supreme Court that Kansas communities were competent to handle their desegregation programs with minimal federal judicial supervision. Accordingly, in late summer 1954, we surveyed the entire group to determine the responses already made to the May 17 decision. The data assembled were included in our supplemental brief.

We found no resentment toward the decision nor any reluctance to comply. The only concern consistently expressed was the reassignment of black teachers. One eligible district had never segregated its schools.[14] Two had completed desegregation in 1952.[15] Two others, one of which was only partially segregated, ordered an end to their separate schools immediately after the May 17 decision.[16] Another resolved to desegregate at the end of the 1954–1955 school year.[17] Four others had formally adopted plans or announced policies to gradually desegregate commencing in September 1954.[18] The estimated times of completion ranged from one year to "five to fifteen" years. No formal action had been taken in only one district,[19] but it was estimated that the transition there could be accomplished in not more than two years. In this latter district, it was reported that the only objection to desegregation had come from black parents.

The approaching end of summer did little to clarify the role of the Kansas attorney general. Again the Topeka Board of Education would go it alone, filing its separate responses to the Court's questions and electing not to be represented at oral argument. Although the board's offices were only a block from the Statehouse grounds, communication between the board and the attorney general was minimal. There was a clear lack of cordiality between the two. Had there been greater rapport, my task would have been easier.

Early in September, Mr. Carter wrote me a follow-up to his earlier letter concerning the possibility of a consent decree.[20] He had written to Mr. Caldwell but had received no reply, and through Charles Scott he had heard that the board was not disposed to discuss the matter. More weeks passed. Finally on October 14 Dick Fatzer wrote to Peter Caldwell urging that a conference be held to attempt to frame a decree to be entered as soon as possible. The general wrote:

I would like to have the State of Kansas on record as complying with the Court's decision holding unconstitutional our Kansas permissive statute which permits segregation in certain of our public schools. . . .

It is my view that if the State of Kansas and your Board of Education can agree with the attorney for the appellant on some

sensible decree whereby the Board of Education can give reasonable assurance of compliance with the Court's opinion and this
office can secure similar commitments from other Boards of Education, it would be to the best interests of our state and your
school board, as well as having a quieting effect on racial unrest
throughout the nation.[21]

Ten days later Mr. Caldwell responded by letter. He stated that
the board had decided that in view of the position already taken,
"there was no point in having a conference with the attorneys for the
NAACP to attempt to arrive at an agreed journal entry."[22] Thus, my
season of delay came to an end. The preparation of the *Brief on Further Reargument* moved to the top of my list of priorities.

PREPARING FOR FURTHER REARGUMENT

When the Supreme Court convened for its October 1954 term, it
set the school segregation cases for argument in the week commencing December 6. When advised of the December setting, we decided
that November 15 should be the deadline date for having our brief
ready for filing.

Briefing for the third round of arguments was easy. The constitutionality of segregation was no longer an issue. We sought only to report and comment on the Kansas effort to end segregation. We believed that Kansans and their communities had demonstrated and
were demonstrating the capacity and will to make the required adjustments without specific instructions or close supervision by the
courts. This was the view that we hoped the Supreme Court would
adopt.

Traditionally, we argued, Kansas was committed to the principle
that all citizens are equal before the law. The single exception that allowed limited racial segregation in the public schools of a few communities was an anachronism, justified only by local tradition and experience. Segregation had never existed in Kansas as a matter of *state*
policy. Indeed, racial discrimination generally had long been expressly prohibited by law. The segregated schools that had existed reflected local preference. Termination would require no change in
state policy. No provision of the Kansas Constitution was affected by

the *Brown* decision. State legislation would not be required to provide for or implement desegregation. The discontinuance of segregated schools would require no alteration of any existing policy of the Department of Public Instruction or any other administrative agency of the state. No cultural problem nor disruption of an established way of life could be foreseen. Thus, we concluded that at the *state* level there were no barriers, legal or otherwise, to the immediate termination of those segregated public school systems that existed in Kansas.

Since I concluded that no state interest remained at issue, I again wondered what was the attorney general's role? on whose behalf did he speak? and what might he appropriately say? General Fatzer believed that we should respond fully to all of the Court's questions concerning the desegregation process. Kansas remained a party to the lawsuit. Although Topeka had declined to be represented by the attorney general, eight other Kansas cities had racially segregated schools. The officials of those districts had expressed the intention to comply with whatever standards the Supreme Court found the Constitution to require, and they would rely upon the attorney general for advice as to procedures for compliance.

Because the questions were specific, we attempted to respond with equal specificity. The entire *Supplemental Brief* was only twenty-three pages long, with half its pages given to reporting on the current progress of desegregation in Kansas. The answers to the Court's questions were, in our view, clear and did not require extensive argument. First, we urged that the Court need not order immediate desegregation, but it had power to permit a gradual adjustment. The scope of equity is broad. The function of the decree would be to reconcile the personal and present interest of the Negro citizens whose constitutional rights had been violated with the public interest in safeguarding the integrity of the public school system. We found abundant precedent to justify the delay required to strike a proper balance between the needs of the plaintiffs and the consequences of giving the desired relief. Furthermore, we did not believe that it was legally or practically feasible for the Supreme Court to tell the Topeka Board of Education what nonsegregated school system should be substituted for the one theretofore maintained, nor should it prescribe the course to be followed in effecting the substitution. These decisions were to be made with reference to local conditions that had not been germane to the question of whether segregation per se was unconstitutional and were not reflected in the record from which the appeal was taken. They were determinations to be made by local officials, familiar with local conditions and responsible for local educational policy and for the general administration of the school system. Those officials, in our view, should be granted maximum latitude, consistent with the rights of other parties. Finally, we suggested that the Supreme Court's order simply reverse the judgment of the district court and remand the case with directions to enter a decree consistent with the May 17 opinion. We suggested further that the district court be directed to retain jurisdiction until the final termination of Topeka's segregated schools. The separate brief of the Topeka Board of Education took generally the same positions as we.

The plaintiffs in all of the four state cases asked that the Supreme Court's decree declare in the clearest possible language that segregation in public education is a denial of equal protection of the laws. They argued further that desegregation should be immediate—that any postponement or delay in complying with the Court's judgment was neither legally nor morally justifiable. They cited empirical studies and respected opinion to support their argument that the forthright way is more effective than gradualism. Pointing out that whereas Topeka's plan to desegregate "as rapidly as practicable" had been adopted more than a year earlier, 85 percent of the Negro children in Topeka's public schools remained segregated; the brief asserted that "there is little excuse for the school board's not having already completed desegregation."[23] Delay, they argued, is tantamount to denial.

While arguing that gradual adjustments were constitutionally impermissible, the appellants conceded that various and necessary administrative factors made immediate relief "as of tomorrow" physically impossible. These included such factors as the need for redistricting and redistribution of teachers and pupils. The appellants urged that the Supreme Court's opinion and mandate specifically instruct the district courts that any decree entered by a district court should specify (1) that the process of desegregation be commenced immediately, (2) that the school officials be required to report their progress periodically to the trial courts, and (3) that an outer time limit be set by which desegregation must be completed, in no case later than September 1, 1956.

MORE DELAY AND MORE PROGRESS

By mid-November 1954 Kansas was ready to appear in court when called. I had been in touch with the other states, the District of Columbia, and the numerous friends of the court and found that they, too, were ready. All felt that an early decision was desirable to assist school boards and administrators in planning for the school term commencing in September 1955. None foresaw delay.

On October 9, Justice Robert H. Jackson suffered a fatal heart attack. Justice Jackson was appointed to the Supreme Court by President Roosevelt in 1941, and except for an extended absence while serving as war crimes prosecutor, he served on the Court until his death. On May 17, while recuperating from an earlier heart attack, he had left a convalescent bed to be present at the reading of the Court's unanimous opinion on the merits in *Brown I*. Notwithstanding his joining in that opinion, the southern lawyers regarded him as friendly—one who might be sensitive to the problems that they foresaw in the desegregation process. They were particularly dismayed at his passing.

On November 8 the president nominated Circuit Judge John Marshall Harlan, of New York, to fill the vacancy. The nominee was the grandson of the earlier John Marshall Harlan who had served on the Supreme Court for thirty-four years and was the author of the often-cited dissent in *Plessy* ("our constitution is color blind"). The younger Harlan was a former Rhodes scholar and Wall Street lawyer with a notable record of public service. His personal and professional credentials were impeccable, but since the Senate was in special session to consider the censure of Senator Joseph McCarthy, hearings on the Harlan nomination were delayed until mid-February 1955. More than four months after his nomination, Justice Harlan was confirmed and finally seated on the supreme bench on March 28, 1955.

On November 24, 1954, I received notice from the clerk of the Supreme Court that "in view of the absence of a full court" *Brown* and its companion cases were continued.[24] A date to which the cases were continued was not indicated. Four months later a telegram addressed to the attorney general advised that the school segregation cases had been assigned for hearing on Monday, April 11.[25] With the confirmation of Justice Harlan it was assured that a full complement of justices could be present for the arguments on that date.

On February 23, 1955, the Topeka Board of Education announced the third step in its desegregation program, which was to become effective at the opening of the 1955–56 school term.[26] One of the all-Negro schools would be closed, and new boundaries were to be drawn along geographic lines for the district's elementary school attendance areas.

The implementation of the announced plan meant that commencing in September 1955, no student in the Topeka system would be assigned to an elementary school on the basis of race. Geography and the location of the student's home determined the school he or she would attend. In a few exceptional situations students were permitted to choose between alternatives. The exceptions applied to blacks and whites alike and were intended as temporary expedients pending the formulation and implementation of the final plan. The result was not necessarily a racial mix in each of the schools in the system. Schools in which black students were formerly segregated were located in black neighborhoods and continued to be all or predominately black, whereas those in white neighborhoods remained all or mostly white. We did not then regard these demographic facts as legally significant. The 1954 decision, as we understood it, only prohibited segregation in public schools when required or permitted by state law. It had no impact on racial separation resulting from patterns of population distribution.

The third step in Topeka's desegregation plan was announced after the briefs on reargument had been filed. A copy of the plan and the board's resolution of approval were forwarded to the clerk of the Supreme Court and made part of the files in the case. It was also discussed during the later oral argument.

THE LAST GO-AROUND

My third trip to Washington was as aide to General Fatzer. We flew, arriving on Friday evening, April 8. Again, we were put up at the Sheraton-Carlton. Sunday afternoon we enjoyed a visit with our adversaries, Messrs. Marshall, Carter, Greenberg, and the others, at their suite in the Sheraton-Park Hotel. They were cordial and expressed their satisfaction at the progress of desegregation in Topeka and other Kansas communities. I could see no significant conflict between their objectives and ours. Yet on the next day we would be in the Supreme Court cast as adversaries.

Sunday evening had been reserved for a session with the other attorneys who would sit on our side of the table. Again, we met in the Sheraton-Carlton suite occupied by the Virginia group. The sixteen months that had elapsed since the last arguments had wrought changes in the group. The most notable absence was that of John W. Davis, who had withdrawn from the South Carolina case after the 1954 decision and had died two weeks before the third round of arguments. This time the South Carolina argument would be shared by S. E. Rogers and Robert McC. Figg, the South Carolina lawyers who had handled the case on the trial level. Mr. Moore, of Virginia, had suffered a heart attack late in 1954 and had begun an extended vacation in Europe. His part in the Virginia case had fallen upon Archibald G. Robertson, a senior partner in Mr. Moore's firm. Mr. Robertson was a native Virginian and a graduate of the law school at the University of Virginia who had practiced law in Richmond for more than forty years. I saw him as an only partially reconstructed rebel, an able and forceful advocate, but lacking the urbanity of Mr. Moore. Delaware would be represented by its new attorney general, J. Donald Craven. For Dick Fatzer, who was to speak for Kansas, this was the first opportunity to meet with the attorneys from the other states. Also invited to the Sunday evening preargument meeting were the attorneys representing the six states who would appear amici curiae.

The meeting was agreeable but not significantly productive. There was some speculation about the position that might be taken by Justice Harlan, whom the southern lawyers appeared to regard as unfriendly. I did not feel the consistent and coordinated focus that had been present in the strategy sessions preceding the earlier arguments. Absent was the unassertive but strong leadership of Mr. Davis, whose enormous prestige had drawn the other lawyers to his views and modes of expression. More important perhaps, there was no longer a single overriding issue common to all cases—whether segregation per se was unconstitutional. *Brown II* was different. Each of the five cases had resumed its separate identity. Although the attorneys in all of the cases expected to ask for time for gradual adjustment, each was preoccupied with the unique facts of his own case and would fashion his argument accordingly. Ultimately, each case would be disposed of with a separate decree. In this milieu the opportunity for consensus was limited.

When the Court convened at noon on April 11, 1955, twenty-two lawyers waited to be heard; six for the NAACP-related plaintiffs; seven for the states and the District of Columbia; and eight for the states appearing as amici curiae. The United States, also a friend of the court, was represented by Simon E. Sobeloff, solicitor general.

As the justices moved to their places at the bench, I was conscious that the seating chart that I had memorized earlier was no longer accurate. Justice Harlan, who was commencing his third week on the Court, was seated at the extreme left end of the panel. Justices Minton, Clark, and Burton had each moved a step higher on the seniority ladder and was appropriately reseated. Also, the docket showed that the cases had been rearranged for the purpose of argument. Kansas would go first, followed in order by Delaware, the District of Columbia, and the consolidated South Carolina-Virginia case. Then the Court would hear the amici arguments.

When we had discussed his speech before going to court, General Fatzer had suggested that he might commence his presentation by congratulating the Court on the 1954 decision. I had demurred, instinctively feeling that such exuberance by a vanquished litigant was hardly consistent with proper courtroom decorum. To me it seemed to impinge on the good faith of the arguments I had made in the earlier appearances. I was pleased when he began his speech in a more restrained vein, announcing at the outset, "Today we appear not as an adversary. We appear here to be of assistance if we can to the court in helping it see that proper decrees are imposed and made."[27]

It was the general's plan to follow closely the line of argument that we had developed in our brief, but in the Supreme Court as elsewhere, the best laid plans often go awry. Questions from the bench began immediately and continued during most of the allotted time. The justices seemed particularly concerned about the possibility of gerrymandering in fixing the new boundaries of attendance areas. Many of their questions sought information that was in the peculiar knowledge of the board and should more properly have been addressed to a representative of the board. The attorney general was in the extraordinary position of being asked by the Court to respond for a party that had implicitly but clearly declined to be represented by him.[28] The board was the beneficiary of a free ride.

With respect to the content of the Supreme Court's decree, the general urged that the judgment be reversed and that the case be remanded to the district court and that the board of education be permitted "without the interference of any decree" to carry out its plan of desegregation; that the district court retain jurisdiction to hear, upon notice, objections to the implementation of the plan.

Mr. Carter's responsive argument was brief. Generally, he was in accord with Mr. Fatzer, although he asked for greater particularity in the terms of the decree. First, he wanted an express declaration that the Kansas statute was unconstitutional and void. Second, he asked for a specific decree that segregation be ended by September 15, 1955. He did not believe that the board's third step was adequate. Further action would be required.

As the week progressed the attention of the Court shifted from Kansas to Delaware and the District of Columbia, to South Carolina and Virginia, and to the six amici states and the United States Department of Justice. During more than three days of argument the justices heard and exchanged views with twenty-two lawyers, all of whom enjoyed a considerable amount of professional distinction and each of whom had his unique style and perspective. Their arguments affirmed a few basic propositions that had been assumed: (1) Each case was unique; (2) local conditions were of the highest significance in developing desegregation plans; and (3) implementation of the 1954 decision was the ultimate responsibility of the district courts and state and local officials. Generally, the states contended for a mandate couched in the most general terms and a minimum amount of federal judicial supervision. The plaintiffs argued for a decree containing specific directions to the district courts and judicial supervision continuing until the termination of segregation in the defendant school districts.

Toward the end of the third day, Mr. Simon E. Sobeloff, solicitor general of the United States, arose to speak on behalf of the government—the seventh and last friend of the court to be heard. At the outset he provided smiles by observing that the proceedings had reached a stage where the Court might wish to invoke for its own protection the Eighth Amendment, which guarantees against cruel and unusual punishment. Taking a position on middle ground, the

solicitor general urged that the Supreme Court instruct the courts below to direct the segregated districts to make a prompt beginning of
the integration process and that the process be completed as speedily
as feasible.[29]

I did not return to court on the fourth day to hear the conclusion
of the arguments. For me, oral discourse, oratory, and bombast had
reached the point of diminishing returns. I became a tourist, bent on
visiting my country's shrines. It was a bright and beautiful day. The
cherry trees edging the Tidal Basin, the lawns, the gardens, and the
sky were ablaze with color. With hundreds of school children, both
black and white, I stood in line to glimpse the interior of the White
House. At the Lincoln Memorial I stood before the Daniel Chester
French image of the Great Emancipator. Later in the day I went
aboard a river boat for a trip down the Potomac to Mount Vernon. A
half-hour on the wide, tree-lined river brought us to the landing
where, with a hundred or so other tourists, I debarked and trudged
up the hill to pay homage to the first president and the mansion
where he had lived and died. As I now recall, there were no blacks in
the group, although Mount Vernon and its gracious gardens had
been built and maintained largely by the hands of black slaves. History records that George and Martha Washington were the uneasy
owners of 300 Negroes whose emancipation was directed in the president's will.

Returning to the city, I checked out of the hotel and boarded a
plane for Kansas. I traveled alone. It had been twenty-eight months
since I first went to Washington to tell the Supreme Court what I believed to be the Kansas view of Topeka's segregated schools. That sor-
tie and the events that followed had been incomparable personal experiences. Although I was emerging as a loser, I had no regrets. I was
satisfied that I had looked and talked and behaved like a lawyer. It
was a long time before I knew that I had seen and heard and even
had a part in the making of history.

THE LAST WORD—ALMOST

The decision on the mandate came promptly.[30] It was announced
on May 31, six weeks after the marathon arguments of mid-April.
The opinion was again written by the chief justice, who spoke for a

unanimous court. It was short and contained no surprises. After reaffirming the 1954 finding that segregation in public education is unconstitutional, the Court declared that "all provisions of federal, state or local law requiring or permitting such discrimination must yield to this principle." The impact of this language was patently intended for all segregated school systems, whether parties, friends of the court, or strangers to the pending cases. Wishful thinkers could no longer hope that in another case, another segregation law might be upheld.

The balance of the opinion was less definite. The Court recognized that full implementation might require the solution of varied local school problems that could best be solved by the courts in which the cases were originally heard. Each case was remanded to the court of origin without detailed instructions. No deadline dates were prescribed. The trial courts were admonished to use their traditional equity powers in balancing the personal interests of the plaintiffs in their admission to nondiscriminating schools with the public interest in the orderly conduct of the districts' programs of public education, and to retain jurisdiction until desegregation was accomplished. Finally, the district courts were directed to undertake such proceedings and enter such orders and decrees "as are necessary and proper to admit to public schools on a racially non-discriminatory basis *with all deliberate speed* the parties to these cases" (emphasis added).[31]

The order was expected to have little impact in Kansas, where the desegregation process was well under way and would be completed as rapidly as practicable. Speaking for the attorney general, I told the press representatives that the Court had followed the Kansas recommendation and had, in my view, made a reasonable disposition of the matter. Mr. Dickinson, president of the board of education, was pleased, feeling that the Supreme Court had agreed with the Topeka plan. Superintendent Godwin thought the decision a fair one. Mr. Burnett, president of the Topeka NAACP branch, expressed no dissatisfaction, but reserved comment until the national leaders of his organization had spoken.[32] Except for those particularly concerned, few Kansans expressed interest in the decree. Most were preoccupied with the mundane problems of their own lives and were indifferent to or unaware of the affairs of the Topeka Board of Education.

Outside of Kansas the reaction to the *Brown II* decision was generally temperate. The NAACP, after some reflection, was gratified. From a few recalcitrant states there were protests, but most affected states appeared to accept the decision with varying degrees of cheerfulness and to commence the process of desegregation.[33] The position taken by the Supreme Court permitted each side to claim a measure of victory. The proponents of segregation rejoiced at the absence of deadlines and the Supreme Court's deference to local district courts and diverse local conditions. The NAACP drew satisfaction from the unqualified reaffirmation of the principle that all segregation in public education is unconstitutional and the assurance that such segregation would be terminated with reasonable promptness under federal judicial supervision.

Although time for compliance had been the paramount concern of the 1955 arguments, a schedule for desegregation remained in uncertainty after the decision. In lieu of a timetable the Court ordered that desegregation proceed with "all deliberate speed." Predictably, the phrase was interpreted differently by those affected, each side adopting the understanding that was most favorable to its interests. Southern leaders foresaw the need for many years of deliberation before desegregation could be finally accomplished and that such delay was within the limits set by the Supreme Court. The NAACP saw it differently. What is "deliberate speed"—on its face an oxymoron—but a scholar's delight? Although the chief justice used the phrase in his opinion without reference to its source, Richard Kluger finds the phrase much too subtle to have been the creation of Earl Warren.[34] Research discloses that it appears elsewhere in judicial writing. Justice Frankfurter had used the phrase in earlier opinions and is said to have suggested its appropriateness for the *Brown II* mandate. In 1911 Justice Holmes had written that state action was sufficient "if it proceeds, in the language of the English Chancery, with all deliberate speed."[35] Notwithstanding its prior use, its judicial history was hardly sufficient to give precise content and meaning to "deliberate speed." So the quest for its origin and possible meaning began. Justice Frankfurter and former Harvard associates searched the literature of English Chancery for clues to the origin of the phrase. Philip Elman, one-time clerk to Justice Frankfurter who was on the solicitor general's staff during the *Brown* years, recalls that the NAACP retained legal historians in England to find out where Holmes had found it.[36] Without success in finding the genesis of "with all deliberate speed" in the language of the English Chancery practice, the researchers turned their attention to English literature. There, the inquiry was more fruitful. The mystic British poet Francis Thompson, in his work entitled "The Hound of Heaven," had portrayed Divinity's pursuit of man as with "deliberate speed," which he equated with "unhurrying chase," "unperturbed pace," and "majestic instancy." Poetry rather than precedent may have been the source of the words that became the guideline of the desegregation process. My own conclusion is that, however eloquent, the phrase "with all deliberate speed" adds little to the self-imposed limitation adopted by the Topeka Board of Education three years earlier—"as rapidly as practicable." The post–*Brown II* search for origin and meaning confirms the judgment that I formed years ago—lawyers have ways of making simple things complex.

On August 24, 1955, Judges Huxman, Mellott, and Hill sat in Topeka for the purpose of formulating a judgment and decree in *Brown*. At issue was whether the Topeka Board of Education had fully complied with the Supreme Court's decision. The evidence submitted included the board's four-step plan for desegregation then in progress. The attorney general's office did not participate in this proceeding. The decision of the court, rendered on October 28, 1955, concluded as follows:

It is the conclusion of the court that while complete desegregation has not been accomplished in the Topeka School System, a good faith effort toward that end has been made and that, therefore, the plan adopted by the Board of Education of the city of Topeka be approved as a good faith beginning to bring about complete desegregation. Jurisdiction of the cause for the purpose of entering the final decree is retained until the court finds that there has been full compliance with the mandate of the Supreme Court.[37]

Although the board's plan was fully implemented by September 1, 1961, no further orders were then issued by the district court.

My final *Brown*-related service to posterity occurred on June 29, 1955, when I received notice from the clerk that the Supreme Court had awarded the appellants judgment against the appellees for the appellant's taxable costs in the amount of $1,300.84. On the same day I forwarded the statement to Peter Caldwell for the attention of his board. What followed after that date is another story. I leave its telling to someone who was there.

Afterword

The Court, the case number, and the title (with some modification) are the same, but in 1994 *Brown v. Board of Education* is a different lawsuit from the one filed by Oliver Brown in 1951. The parties are different, the lawyers are different, the Court is differently constituted, and the issues raised were not then thought of.

Oliver Brown died in 1961, but his spirit and his case go marching on. The daughter, on whose behalf he sued, remains in the case in a changed role. She is now one of several parents who have intervened on behalf of their minor children seeking to enforce the mandate of *Brown II*. By reason of a general reorganization of Kansas public schools in 1966, the Board of Education of Topeka no longer exists as a corporate entity. Its successor is United School District No. 501, Shawnee County, Kansas, governed by a board of seven members elected from districts.

Time and the grim reaper have ended the careers of most of the actors in the original cast. Judges Huxman, Mellott, and Hill are deceased, as are the attorneys who appeared before them, with three exceptions. Robert Carter and Jack Greenberg, the NAACP lawyers who assisted at the trial, now live in New York City. Willis McQueary, the state's representative at the 1951 trial, survives after years of law practice in Osawatomie, the place where John Brown began his ascent to martyrdom and glory. In 1994 *Brown* is pending before a single-judge bench where the parties are represented by attorneys who were either unborn or babes in their mothers' arms when Oliver Brown first went to court.

Of the lawyers who participated in *Brown I* on appeal, Robert Carter, my adversary, and I survive. None of the counsel from other states who addressed the Court from my side of the table are living. In 1957 I left the office of the Kansas Attorney General to join the faculty of the University of Kansas School of Law, where I taught until I received emeritus status in 1982. No longer a participant in the case, my perspective of later proceedings has been the limited one of a less than fully informed observer; my interest has continued. Three of my former students are among current counsel of record.

The great issue raised in *Brown I* has long been settled. No question remains as to the constitutionality of laws that require, permit, or result in racial segregation. Firmly established by *Brown II* is the duty of public officials responsible for the operation of public school systems that formerly were segregated to desegregate and to remove all vestiges of such segregation with reasonable promptness. The repeal of segregation laws, removal of barriers to desegregation, and a neutral stance is not enough. Under post-*Brown* cases and legislation, school boards must act affirmatively to achieve the greatest possible degree of desegregation within the limits of practicality. The questions that now arise concern the nature and dimensions of the duty to desegregate. What must the board do to comply with the *Brown* mandate? Has it done enough?

After the October 1955 approval of the board's plan as a good-faith beginning to bring about desegregation of Topeka's schools, twenty-four years elapsed before further action in the case. Although the board's four-step plan was fully implemented by September 1, 1961, no order was sought or obtained from the court finally approving the plan or terminating the court's jurisdiction. Twelve years followed without protest or formal complaint, and the board and most Topekans assumed that the matter was at rest.

Between September 10, 1973, and September 7, 1979, four separate cases were filed in the federal court raising questions as to whether the Topeka Board of Education and its successor, Unified School District No. 501, had complied with the mandates of *Brown I* and *Brown II*.[1] Although none of the cases resulted in noteworthy judgments, a by-product of the litigation was an investigation by the Office of Civil Rights of the Department of Health, Education, and Welfare (HEW). Finding that Topeka was not in compliance, HEW commenced administrative proceedings to withhold federal financial assistance to the school district under the terms of Section 601 of Title VI of the Civil Rights Act of 1964.[2] In 1976 the board submitted a new plan acceptable to HEW, and the proceedings were abandoned.

In November 1979 an order was made reactivating *Brown* and permitting Linda Brown and other black parents and their children to intervene and seek their remedy for the board's alleged failure to desegregate within the framework of that case.[3]

After seven years of pretrial motions, discovery, and other time-consuming and expensive preliminary proceedings, the resurrected *Brown* was tried over a period of three weeks in October 1986. The issue was whether the *Brown* mandates had been complied with. Six months later the court entered judgment for the district. It found that Unified District 501 maintained an integrated, unitary school system and that there was no evidence of the purposeful discrimination found in *Brown* to be unlawful.[4] The relief sought was denied. The plaintiffs appealed, not to the Supreme Court, but to the Court of Appeals for the Tenth Circuit. On December 11, 1989, a panel of three appellate judges, by a vote of two to one, reversed the findings of the district court and remanded the case for appropriate disposition.[5] The next step was an appeal by the school district to the Supreme Court, which sent the case back to the court of appeals for further consideration.[6] The appellate court reaffirmed its earlier decision,[7] and the Supreme Court declined to consider the matter further.[8] The court of appeals' decision stood.

With the encouragement of the district court, the parties resumed negotiations, and on July 25, 1994, the court approved the school district's third desegregation proposal. When the proposal is implemented, it is expected that Unified School District No. 501 will be in compliance with the Supreme Court's mandates. Implementation, which will require the closing of some existing schools, construction of new buildings, reassignment of students, and curriculum restructuring, may take three years. Thus, forty-three years after Oliver Brown filed his lawsuit, forty-two years after the Topeka Board of Education resolved to desegregate its elementary schools "as rapidly as practicable," forty-one years after Justice Frankfurter thought the *Brown* case was moot, and forty years after the Supreme Court declared segregation in public schools unconstitutional, vestiges of unlawful segregation remain in Topeka, and the school officials continue to be subject to the court's jurisdiction.

REFLECTIONS

Among the personalities that I encountered during the *Brown* episode there was none that I admired more than John W. Davis. In him I saw not only a scholar, a gentleman, and a superb advocate, but a venerable and wise man. He had been around a long time and had seen much of life. In his white hair I saw an assurance of sagacity and judgment and wisdom. I have now reached an age equal to that of John W. Davis when he spoke for South Carolina in the Supreme Court of the United States. I have become increasingly conscious of the words of another twentieth-century American, H. L. Mencken, who wrote, "The older I grow the more I distrust the familiar doctrine that age brings wisdom." Questions for which I had ready answers half a lifetime ago now perplex me. Distinctions between good and bad, right and wrong, virtue and fault have become less distinct. I am seldom able to respond to the inquirer who asks "why?" I have no answer when asked why full compliance with the *Brown* mandates has been so delayed, why the fruits of Oliver Brown's victory continue to elude his children and grandchildren.

One impression stands out—law and litigation do not supply all the answers to human problems. Law provides minimum standards of conduct and defines basic human rights and responsibilities. Litigation provides the means to determine and enforce what the law requires. The resolution of human conflict requires more—understanding, compassion, and mutual respect. These can best be achieved by talking together, by good-faith efforts to work things out. Friendships seldom emerge from adversary proceedings. There is no judicial remedy that can require one person to agree with or like or respect another.

In the *Brown* context, the constitutionality of segregated schools and the nature and extent of the board's duty to desegregate could only be determined by courts in an adversarial setting. Those determinations were made early in the case's history. The remaining questions related to the time and manner of compliance. I wonder, without deciding, if at that stage the conference room might have provided a more appropriate forum than the courtroom. The tentative resolution of the controversy reflected in the court's order of July 25, 1994, was largely the result of negotiation. If settlement through compromise and agreement was possible in 1994, was it less so twenty years and $2 million earlier?

Few deny that racial equality in America is still a goal to be accomplished and that reality falls short of the goal. The nearness of the goal and the pace of our approach are matters about which thoughtful people may disagree. As a white man, well educated, well fed, a beneficiary of America's bounty, I reflect on the experiences of a lifetime that has continued through most of the twentieth century and am optimistic. If I were black, young, and facing an uncertain future, I might see things differently.

Interviewers who seek my comments on *Brown* always ask me three questions: Why were you assigned to argue such an important case? How did you feel about the case? and Do you regret your role in the case?

My answer to the first question is simple: I was the person beckoned by the fickle finger of fate. I cannot answer the second question in the form in which it is cast. As a lawyer familiar with judicial precedents as well as with the history, traditions, and experience of Kansans and other Americans, I then felt and still feel that my arguments were sound at the time and in the forum in which they were heard. As a human being applying personal standards of conscience and rationality, I felt that the position of the state of Kansas was indefensible. At the same time I did not regard my personal view and bias as relevant. The issue was one of law. To the third question, do I regret my role, I answer, no. *Brown* afforded me an opportunity that few lawyers of my generation have enjoyed—the privilege of supplying information to the Supreme Court of the United States to be considered in deciding one of the most important cases in American judicial history. That the Court found the arguments of my adversaries more persuasive than mine does not, in my view, reflect unfavorably on my character or the quality of my advocacy. The lawyer takes his cases as they come to him. He creates neither the facts nor the law. His job is to see that the forum is right, that the issues are properly drawn, and that the court is fully and fairly informed as to his client's view of the facts and his understanding of the law. I did these things as well as I could.

I have always believed and I now concede that the decision reached in *Brown* was inevitable. I do not diminish the vision of Oliver Brown and the other Topeka parents nor the advocacy skills of Thurgood Marshall and his associates when I express the feeling that the doctrine of separate but equal would have fallen had there been no *Brown* case. It might have happened at another season and in a different forum, but the time had come for the rule in *Plessy*'s case to go. It had outlived its reason for being. It no longer squared with the American conscience and understanding. After eight decades of living, I cling to the naive belief that, in the long run, history is just.

As a child, I knew my paternal grandfather. It was he who first kindled my ambition to become a lawyer. He was born in the state of Indiana, five years before Kansas became a territory and Topeka a town. At the time of his birth all black people were excluded from the public schools of his state. Other states made it a crime to teach a Negro slave to read without the consent of his master. In Missouri, which supplied many of the first Kansas immigrants, schools for the teaching of black and mulatto children were forbidden by law. My father was born in Kansas seven years before the Supreme Court ruled in *Plessy v. Ferguson*. Although the law provided otherwise, many Negro children were then either unschooled or segregated in schools that were patently inferior. By the time of my birth twenty-four years later, the black child's right to an equal though separate educational opportunity had acquired constitutional stature but was still often dishonored in practice.

Then came 1954 and *Brown*. From the perspective of human history the law's progress from total denial to total acceptance during the course of three lifetimes has the quality of drama. To the victim of discrimination it is not fast enough. To counsel patience in the face of delayed justice is to ask the wronged to tolerate the intolerable. In a truly just world relief would be immediate. But the real world is still striving toward justice, and the tempo of history is slow. Though my mind is still open, I wonder if confrontation and coercion can hasten its deliberate pace.

As I write these paragraphs *Brown v. Board of Education* has been pending for more than forty years, and some of its issues are still undetermined. The decades since *Brown* was first docketed have vastly enlarged the opportunities for blacks to share in the bounty of America. At the same time, Americans sense a resurgent racism, an increasing lack of interracial respect, and a growing estrangement of blacks and whites. The question that I raise is whether without *Brown* and its progeny history might have achieved the goals that society seeks and have avoided the stresses of conflict. Few would deny that confrontation in the courtroom is better than confrontation in the streets, but any adversary encounter breeds division and resentment. In a better world there would be a better way.

In my youth I lived near towns where a black person found on the streets after sundown risked an arrest for vagrancy. At harvest time I saw the lone black member of the threshing crew taking his meals in the kitchen while other workers were served in the dining room. Among the good people who were my childhood neighbors, the highest compliment that could be paid to a person of African descent was that "he is as decent as a white man."

As a student at the University of Kansas in the mid–1930s, I attended classes taught by members of an all-white faculty who answered to all-white administrators. Black students were excluded from or not invited to participate in most student activities. Denied the opportunity to compete in intercollegiate sports, restricted to special seating areas at university events, occupying specially designated tables in the university dining facility, living apart from the white student community, blacks saw their white counterparts only in the classroom, the laboratory, and the library. They were Jayhawkers but, perhaps, Jayhawkers, second class.

As a pre–World War II law student and employee of the state of Kansas, I lived in Topeka. There I knew few blacks. Their homes were on streets that I seldom traveled, but I knew they were part of Topeka's population. I saw black men cleaning the Statehouse corridors; I read newspaper reports of activities at Topeka's all-black schools. I heard, but cannot vouch for, the story that periodically blacks were admitted to the Gage Park swimming pool for one day only, after which the pool was drained and refilled for the exclusive use of whites during the ensuing period. In restaurants ostensibly serving the public I saw signs announcing that colored people would be served in sacks only. As a moviegoer, I saw blacks seated in a section of the balcony reserved for them and usually called "nigger heaven."

During World War II, I served in the Army of the United States along with millions of other men and women of my generation. Many of them were black, but I did not often see them. Most were housed separately, fed separately, trained separately, and assigned to all-black companies and battalions commanded by white officers. They handled cargo and military supplies, drove trucks, operated mess halls, laundries, and sterilization and bath facilities. They were seldom assigned to positions where medals were won.

Fifty years later our across-the-street neighbors are black. Black teachers and administrators serve the University of Kansas. Black students enjoy the opportunities and benefits that the university provides to other students. Black athletes participate fully and often dominate intercollegiate sports. Topeka, in spite of lingering doubts, has made a good-faith and substantially effective effort to integrate its schools. Black members sit on the board of education, and a black educator has occupied the chair once held by Kenneth McFarland. Elsewhere in the community, blacks and whites enjoy equal access to public places and equal opportunity in the marketplace. These things within my personal experience, augmented by knowledge of black achievements elsewhere, persuade me that Americans are nearing the goal of equality before the law. The more elusive but more important goal is the time and place where people stand equal before one another.

Notes

The following abbreviations are used to identify frequently cited references.

KCC   *Kansas Constitutional Convention.* A reprint of the proceedings and debates of the convention that framed the Constitution of Kansas at Wyandotte in July 1859. Edited by J. S. King and Winfield Freeman. Topeka: Kansas State Printer, 1920.

KSHS Kansas State Historical Society, Center for Historical Research, State Archives Offices, Attorney General Archive, *Brown v. Board of Educ.* File.

SCA   Supreme Court Arguments as reproduced in Leon Friedman, ed., *Argument: The Oral Argument before the Supreme Court in Brown v. Board of Education of Topeka, 1952–1955,* with an introduction by Kenneth Clark and Yale Kamisar. New York: Chelsea House, 1969.

Scott Transcript of an interview with Charles S. Scott, one of the attorneys for the plaintiffs, by Dr. James C. Duram and Mr. Robert Bunting on June 25, 1970. On file in the archives of the Dwight D. Eisenhower Library, Abilene, Kansas.

TDC   *Topeka Daily Capital.* A newspaper published in Topeka, Kansas. Now called the *Topeka Capital-Journal.*

TR   Transcript of Record, *Brown v. Board of Educ. of Topeka, Shawnee County, Kansas,* Case No. T–316 Civil, United States District Court, District of Kansas.

UKLL   The University of Kansas Law Library. Rice Room Collection. *Brown v. Board of Educ.* File.

INTRODUCTION

1. 347 U.S. 483 (1954).
2. *Brown v. Board of Educ.,* 98 F. Supp. 797 (Kan. 1951).
3. *Briggs v. Elliott,* 98 F. Supp 529 (E.D.S.C. 1951); 103 F. Supp. 920 (E.D.S.C. 1952).
4. *Davis v. County School Board of Prince Edward County, Virginia,* 103 F. Supp. 337 (ED Va. 1952).
5. *Gebhart v. Belton* (S.C. Del.), 91 A 2d 137 (1952).
6. *Bolling v. Sharpe* (Cert. to U.S.C.A., D.C. Cir.), 347 U.S. 497 (1954).
7. Richard Kluger, *Simple Justice* (New York: Alfred A. Knopf, 1976).
8. 163 U.S. 537 (1896). *Plessy* was not a school case. It involved segregation in public transportation.
9. 275 U.S. 78 (1927). In *Gong Lum* a Chinese student was classified as colored and excluded from the white school in her district. The classification was held to be within the lawful powers of the public school officials of Mississippi.
10. William H. Harbaugh, *Lawyer's Lawyer: The Life of John W. Davis* (New York: Oxford University Press, 1973), 531–35.

CHAPTER ONE. 1951

1. TR, 146. The witness had, however, expressed reservations about the Monroe neighborhood.
2. Ibid.
3. *Missouri ex rel Gaines v. Canada,* 305 U.S. 337 (1938).
4. 305 U.S. at 349.
5. Minnie Finch, *The NAACP: Its Fight for Justice* (Metuchen, N.J. and London: Scarecrow Press, 1981), 122–23.
6. *Sipuel v. Oklahoma State Board of Regents,* 332 U.S. 631 (1948).
7. *Fisher v. Hurst,* 333 U.S. 147 (1948).
8. *Sweatt v. Painter,* 339 U.S. 629 (1950).
9. *McLaurin v. Oklahoma State Regents,* 339 U.S. 637 (1950).
10. Finch, *The NAACP,* 136–38.

11. Loren Miller, *The Petitioners: The Story of the Supreme Court of the United States and the Negro* (New York: Pantheon Books, 1966), 344–46.

12. Finding of Fact No. 3, TR, 245.

13. Finding of Fact No. 7, TR, 245.

14. Daniel Fitzgerald, ed., *Gone but Not Forgotten: The Lost Schools of Topeka*, Shawnee County Historical Society Bulletin No. 67 (Topeka, November 1990), 1.

15. Kan. Gen. Stat. 1949, sec. 72–1601.

16. Ibid., secs. 72–1601 and 72–1724.

17. *TDC*, April 5, 1951, 1.

18. 167 Kan. 395 (1949).

19. Scott, 6–7. A copy of the transcript of the Duram and Bender interview with Charles Scott on June 25, 1970, is in the archives of the Dwight D. Eisenhower Library at Abilene, Kansas. The portion quoted is on pages 6 and 7.

20. 347 U.S. 483 (1954).

21. TR, 1.

22. Kluger, *Simple Justice*, 395.

23. Discussion, author and Constance Baker Motley, senior judge, U.S. District Court, Southern District of New York, September 24, 1990, Lawrence, Kansas.

CHAPTER TWO. THE HISTORICAL CONTEXT

1. Connecticut, Massachusetts, New Hampshire, New Jersey, New York, Pennsylvania, Rhode Island, Vermont, Ohio, Indiana, Illinois, Maine, Michigan, Iowa, and Wisconsin.

2. Delaware, Georgia, Maryland, North Carolina, South Carolina, Virginia, Kentucky, Tennessee, Louisiana, Mississippi, Alabama, Missouri, Arkansas, Florida, and Texas.

3. Ch. 50, act of September 9, 1850, 31st Cong., 1st sess., 9 Stat. 452.

4. Minnesota Territory included parts of the Northwest Territory and the Louisiana Purchase. Slavery was prohibited in the Northwest Territory by the Ordinance of 1787, which was adopted by Congress after formation of the Union (ch.8, act of August 7, 1789, 1st Cong., sess. 1, 1 Stat. 50, 51), and in the north part of the Louisiana Purchase (ch. 22, sec. 8, act of March 6, 1820, 16th Cong., sess. 1, 3 Stat. 545, 548). The act creating the Oregon Territory (ch. 177, sec. 14, act of August 14, 1848, 30th Cong., sess. 1, 9 Stat. 323, 329) provided that the territory and its residents should be subject to the constraints of the Ordinance of 1787.

5. Ch. 49, sec. 2, act of September 9, 1850, 31st Cong., sess. 1, 9 Stat. 447.

6. Ch. 51, sec. 1, act of September 9, 1850, 31st Cong., sess. 1, 9 Stat. 453.

7. Ch. 22, sec. 8, act of March 6, 1820, 16th Cong., sess. 1, 3 Stat. 545, 548.

8. Ch. 59, secs. 1, 19, act of May 30, 1854, 33rd Cong., sess. 1, 10 Stat. 277–78, 283–84.

9. Carroll D. Clark and Roy S. Roberts, *People of Kansas* (Topeka: State Planning Board, 1936), App. Table 1, 208–9.

10. D. W. Wilder, *Annals of Kansas, 1541–1885,* new ed. (Topeka: Kansas Publishing House, 1886), 75–77.

11. T. D. Thacher, "The Rejected Constitutions," *KCC,* App. E., 702–13.

12. *KCC,* 56, 121.

13. *KCC,* 269–70, 548.

14. A proposal to strike the word "white" failed in the general election of 1867. Yet in the following year the Kansas legislature ratified the Fifteenth Amendment to the United States Constitution, which prohibited the states from using race as a criterion of suffrage.

15. *KCC,* 147.

16. *KCC,* 175–83, 192–93.

17. *KCC,* 583.

18. Ch. 20, sec. 3, act of January 29, 1861, 36th Cong., sess. 1, 12 Stat. 126.

19. In 1856 and 1857 a rump legislature of free-state sympathizers was elected and convened under the proposed Topeka constitution. Although it was probably more representative of the bona fide residents of the territory than the officially recognized body, its existence was without lawful authority and its acts had no legal effect.

20. 1855 Kan. Terr. Stat., ch. 144, sec. 1.

21. 1858 Kan. Terr. Sess. Laws, ch. 8, sec. 71.

22. *Board of Educ. of Ottawa v. Tinnon,* 26 Kan. (2d ed.), 1 (1881).

23. 1861 Kan. Sess. Laws, ch. 76.

24. 1861 Kan. Sess. Laws, ch. 76, Art. 3, sec. 2 (Tenth).

25. Kan. Gen. Stat. 1868, ch. 18, Art. 5, sec. 75; ch. 19, Art. 5, sec. 57.

26. 1867 Kan. H.J. 79; 1867 Kan. S.J. 76.

27. 1867 Kan. Sess. Laws, ch. 69, sec. 7.

28. Ibid., ch. 125, sec. 1.

29. H.B. 219 (1870).

30. *Proc. of Legis. Assembly of the St. of Kan.* (1870), 661.

31. 1874 Kan. Sess. Laws, ch. 49.

32. 1876 Kan. Sess. Laws, ch. 122.

33. Annual Report State Supt. of Pub. Inst. (1876), 72.

34. N. I. Painter, *Exodusters: Black Migration to Kansas* (New York, 1977; paperback, Lawrence: University Press of Kansas, 1986).

35. 1874 Kan. Sess. Laws, ch. 123, sec. 1.

36. 1879 Kan. Sess. Laws, ch. 81, sec. 1, Kan. Gen. Stat. 1949, 72–1724. Held unconstitutional by *Brown v. Board of Educ.,* 347 U.S. 483 (1954).

37. Leavenworth, Atchison, and Topeka.

38. Hutchinson.

39. In Lawrence, schools in the part of the city lying north of the Kansas River were segregated. In other parts of the district all the schools were racially mixed.

40. Pittsburg and Wichita.

41. Atchison and Topeka.

42. Coffeyville, Fort Scott, Kansas City, Leavenworth, Parsons, Salina.

43. *Board of Education of Ottawa v. Tinnon*, 26 Kan. (2d ed.) 1 (1881); *Knox v. Board of Education of Independence*, 45 Kan. 152 (1891); *Cartwright v. Board of Education of Coffeyville*, 73 Kan. 32 (1906); *Rowles v. Board of Education of Wichita*, 76 Kan. 361 (1907); *Woolridge v. Board of Education of Galina*, 98 Kan. 397 (1916); and *Webb et al. v. School District No. 90 in Johnson County*, 167 Kan. 395 (1949).

44. *Williams v. Board of Education of Parsons*, 79 Kan. 202 (1908), 81 Kan. 593 (1910); and *Wright v. Board of Education of Topeka*, 129 Kan. 852 (1930).

45. *Thurman-Watts v. Board of Education of Coffeyville*, 115 Kan. 328 (1908), and *Graham v. Board of Education of Topeka*, 153 Kan. 840 (1941).

46. *Richardson v. Board of Education of Kansas City, Kansas*, 72 Kan. 629 (1906).

47. *Reynolds v. Board of Education of Topeka*, 66 Kan. 672 (1903).

48. 66 Kan. at 678–79.

49. 26 Kan. at 19.

50. *Kansas Educational Journal*, Aug. 1866, 69.

51. P. McVicar, *Seventh Ann. Rept. St. Supt. of Pub. Instr.* (Topeka, 1861–1867), 49–50.

52. 1867 Kan. Sess. Laws, ch. 125, sec. 1.

53. P. McVicar, *Eighth Ann. Rept. St. Supt. of Pub. Instr.* (Topeka, 1868), 344.

54. See minority report on H.B. 219, 1870 in *Proc. of Legis. Assembly of the St. of Kan.* (1870), 662.

55. *Kansas Educational Journal*, Emporia (September 1870).

56. Quoted in J. C. Carper, "The Popular Ideology of Segregated Schooling: Attitudes toward the Education of Blacks in Kansas, 1854–1900," *Kansas History: A Journal of the Central Plains* 1: 4 (Winter 1978): 260.

57. McVicar, *Seventh Ann. Rpt.*, 50.

58. Carper, "The Popular Ideology of Segregated Schooling," 260–61.

59. Ibid., 261–62.

60. Statement dated March 1, 1880, quoted in Edna Tutt Frederickson, "John P. St. John: The Father of Constitutional Prohibition," (Ph.D. dissertation, University of Kansas, n.d.), 89.

61. Frederickson, "John P. St. John," 85.

62. Ibid., 88.

63. Painter, *Exodusters*, 259.

64. 1905 Kan. Sess. Laws, ch. 414, sec. 1.

65. Kan. H. R. Jour. 723 (1905).

CHAPTER THREE. WHY ME?

1. Richard Kluger, *Simple Justice* (New York: Alfred A. Knopf, 1976), 548.

2. Clifford Griffin, *The University of Kansas, A History* (Lawrence: University Press of Kansas, 1974), 209–10; Larry Peace, "Colored Students and Graduates of the University of Kansas," *Graduate Magazine* 8 (May 1909): 293–303; *University Courier*, February 12, 1886.

3. Griffin, *The University of Kansas*, 626–32; Marcet Haldeman-Julius, "What the Negro Students Endure in Kansas," *Haldeman-Julius Monthly* 7: 2 (January 1928): 5–16.

4. Griffin, *The University of Kansas*, 626.

5. Haldeman-Julius, "What the Negro Students Endure."

6. Earl Tipton, untitled article in *The Dove: A Liberal Journal of Discussion*, April 20, 1925.

7. Kluger, *Simple Justice*, 374.

8. Executive Order No. 9981, July 26, 1948.

9. Kan. Gen. Stat. 1949, secs. 75–702 to 75–709.

CHAPTER FOUR. IN THE TRIAL COURT

1. 28 U.S.C. 2281 (since repealed).

2. TR, 139.

3. Scott, 6.

4. Mellott to Huxman and Hill, dated March 5, 1951. Copy in UKLL.

5. 28 U.S.C. 2284(5) (now repealed).

6. Mellott to Huxman, March 6, 1951. Copy in UKLL.

7. Huxman to Mellott and Hill, June 1, 1951. Copy in UKLL.

8. Kan. Gen. Stat. 1949, sec. 75–108.

9. Ibid., sec. 75–702.

10. Huxman to Mellott and Hill, June 1, 1951. Copy in UKLL.

11. Mellott to Hill, June 4, 1951. Copy in UKLL.

12. Hill to Mellott, June 5, 1951. Copy in UKLL.

13. Mellott to Huxman, June 6, 1951. Copy in UKLL.

14. Mellott to Huxman and Hill, June 12, 1951. The transcript of the proceedings at the attorney general's appearance before Judge Mellott is in the court file, Case No. T–316. Copy in UKLL.

15. TR, 14–15.

16. Huxman to Mellott, March 6, 1951. Copy in UKLL.

17. TR, 19–61.

18. TR, 59.

19. TR, 68–81.

20. TR, 88–94.

21. TR, 94–96.

22. TR, 98.

23. TR, 102.

24. TR, 109–10.

25. TR, 136.

26. TR, 118.

27. TR, 169–70.

28. TR, 191–96.

29. TR, 196–205.

30. TR, 206–11.

31. TR, 233.

32. See Brief of Defendants in court file, Case No. T–316.

33. *Briggs et al. v. Elliott et al.,* 98 F. Supp. 529 (1951).

34. Letters were exchanged between Judge Mellott and Chief Judge Parker of the South Carolina court (see file in Case No. T–316). Robert L. Carter and Thurgood Marshall were among counsel for the plaintiffs in both cases.

35. *Briggs v. Elliott.*

36. Harold R. Fatzer to J. Lindsay Almond, July 13, 1951. General Fatzer explained further in the same letter: "I might say that the main basis of the plaintiffs' contention in the Topeka case was that segregation violated the Fourteenth Amendment. Evidence was introduced on this point by college professors and instructors, both colored and white, to which we objected to at every stage. However, Judge Huxman of the Circuit Court, and a member of the three-judge federal court overruled our objection and permitted opinion testimony as to the undesirableness of segregation, and that in the opinion of the witness it was unconstitutional. This was the first time that I ever knew of a court permitting a witness to testify as to whether a particular statute was unconstitutional, as I was always taught this was a question for the judges themselves to determine. Nevertheless, we are living in a new age and apparently the rules and evidence of procedure should be different" (copy in KSHS).

37. Scott, 12.

38. Huxman to Mellott and Hill, July 13, 1951. Copy in UKLL.

39. Ibid.

40. TR, 245–46.

41. *TDC,* August 4, 1951, 1.

CHAPTER FIVE. 1952—YEAR OF INDECISION

1. TR, 248–49.

2. 28 U.S.C. sec. 1253.

3. TR, 250.

4. *TDC,* November 9, 1951, 11.

5. Edward J. Bander, comp., *Justice Holmes ex Cathedra* 229. (Charlottesville, Va.: Michie Company, 1966).

6. Chester James Antieau, "The Ghost of Gong," *Journal of the Bar Association of the State of Kansas* 20 (November 1951): 211.

7. Schuyler W. Jackson, "More To Do about Master Brown and Missie Gong," *Journal of the Bar Association of the State of Kansas* 20 (February 1952): 288.

8. Melvin C. Poland, "Grievous Error," *Journal of the Bar Association of the State of Kansas* 20 (February 1952): 294.

9. Kan. Gen. Stat. 1949, secs. 21–915 to 21–936.

10. Ibid., secs. 41–701 to 41–726.

11. Ibid., secs. 21–918 to 21–929 and sec. 41–1107.

12. 98 F. Supp. 529 (1951).

13. *Briggs et al. v. Elliott et al.*, 342 U.S. 350 (1952).

14. *Briggs et al. v. Elliott et al.*, 103 F. Supp. 920 (1952).

15. T. C. Callison, attorney general of South Carolina, to Fatzer, September 17, 1952, KSHS.

16. William H. Harbaugh, *Lawyer's Lawyer: The Life of John W. Davis* (New York: Oxford University Press, 1973), 482–83.

17. Almond to Fatzer, March 11, 1952, KSHS.

18. *Davis et al. v. County School Board of Prince Edward County, Va., et al.*, 103 F. Supp. 337 (1952).

19. Copies of the amicus briefs are on file in UKLL.

20. See Richard Kluger, *Simple Justice* (New York: Alfred A. Knopf, 1976), 315–21.

21. *Appendix to Appellant's Brief.* Copy in UKLL.

22. Fatzer to Almond, August 1, 1952. Copy in KSHS.

23. Byrnes to Fatzer, September 8, 1952, KSHS.

24. Fatzer to Byrnes, September 10, 1952. Copy in KSHS.

25. Almond to Fatzer, September 9, 1952, KSHS.

26. Lyle Schwilling, "Board Will Not Defend Racial Stand," *TDC*, October 7, 1952, 1.

27. Ibid., 8.

28. Ibid.

29. *Brown et al. v. Board of Educ. et al.*, 344 U.S. 1 (1952).

30. Moore to Wilson, October 29, 1952, KSHS.

31. "Board Kills Plan to Argue Segregation," *TDC*, November 4, 1952, 1.

32. *Bolling et al. v. Sharpe et al.*, 344 U.S. 873 (1952).

33. *Gebhart et al. v. Belton et al.*, 91 A. 2d 137 (1952).

34. *Gebhart et al. v. Belton et al.*, 344 U.S. 891 (1952).

35. *Brown et al v. Board of Education et al.*, 344 U.S. 141 (1952).

36. *TDC*, November 25, 1952, 1.

37. *TDC*, November 26, 1952, 1.

38. Telegram, Fatzer to Harold E. Willey, clerk, Supreme Court of the United States, November 28, 1952. Copy in KSHS.

39. Fatzer to Oberhelman, November 28, 1952. Copy in KSHS.

40. *TDC*, December 2, 1952, 1.

41. Anna Mary Murphy, "Segregation Suit to Make History," *TDC*, November 30, 1952, Sunday Magazine, 1.

42. *Brown et al. v. Board of Education et al.*, Brief of Appellees 5.

43. Kluger, *Simple Justice*, 694.

44. *TDC*, December 5, 1952, 1.

45. 344 U.S. at 142.

46. *TDC*, December 5, 1952, 1.

47. Telegram, Fatzer to Willey, December 5, 1952. Copy in KSHS.

CHAPTER SIX. IN THE SUPREME COURT

1. Paul M. Angle, *Created Equal? The Complete Lincoln-Douglas Debates of 1858* (Chicago: University of Chicago Press, 1958), 299–300.

2. Chalmers M. Roberts, "Legal Giants to Vie in the Segregation Case," *Washington Post*, December 7, 1952, 1.

3. Ibid.

4. Mary Ann Harrell, *Equal Justice under Law. The Supreme Court in American Life*, rev. ed. (Washington, D.C.: Foundation of the Federal Bar Association, 1975), 115–16.

5. Chalmers M. Roberts, "Court Arguments Begin Today in 5 School Segregation Cases," *Washington Post*, December 9, 1952, 1.

6. The transcript of the arguments was edited by Leon Friedman and published in 1969 by Chelsea House Publishers of New York under the title *Argument: The Complete Oral Argument before the Supreme Court in Brown v. Board of Education of Topeka, 1952–1955*. I have used this copy of the transcript to refresh and confirm my recollection of things that I said, heard, and observed during the arguments. All references to and quotations from the arguments are based on the transcript edited by Friedman and are cited as SCA.

7. SCA, 13.

8. SCA, 17.

9. *Roberts v. City of Boston*, 59 Mass. 198 (1850). School segregation was upheld in *Roberts* despite a Massachusetts constitutional provision that all persons were equal before the law.

10. SCA, 20.

11. SCA, 21.

12. SCA, 24.

13. SCA, 27.

14. Richard Kluger, *Simple Justice* (New York: Alfred A. Knopf, 1976), 719.

15. SCA, 29.

16. SCA, 30–31.

17. *Reynolds v. Board of Educ.*, 66 Kan. 672 (1903).

18. SCA, 31–32.
19. SCA, 55.
20. SCA, 33.
21. SCA, 35.
22. "Advocacy before the Supreme Court: Suggestions for Effective Case Presentations," *American Bar Association Journal* 37 (November 1951): 803.
23. Almond to Wilson, December 23, 1952, KSHS.
24. Ruth Snyder to Fatzer, July 24, 1954, KSHS; emphasis added.

CHAPTER SEVEN. 1953—SECOND TIME AROUND

1. Stephen E. Ambrose, *Eisenhower: The President*, vol. 2 (New York: Simon & Schuster, 1984), 125–27. The president had moved quickly to integrate completely the armed services and to desegregate public facilities in the District of Columbia.
2. Anna Mary Murphy, "Negro Teacher Purge to Begin in Kansas," *TDC*, April 6, 1953, 1.
3. Ibid.
4. Anna Mary Murphy, "Firing Negro Teachers to Be Contested," *TDC*, April 7, 1953, 1.
5. Board member Dickinson had refused to waive written notice of the special meeting the board had attempted to call on December 1, 1952, to consider the attorney general's request that the board authorize its attorney to assist in briefing prior to the December 9 argument.
6. See Richard Kluger, "At Loggerheads," in *Simple Justice* (New York: Alfred A. Knopf, 1976), chap. 23.
7. Ibid.
8. 345 U.S. 1114 (1953). The text of the order follows.
"Each of these cases is ordered restored to the docket and is assigned for reargument on Monday, October 12, next. In their briefs and on oral argument counsel are requested to discuss particularly the following questions insofar as they are relevant to the respective cases:
(1) What evidence is there that the Congress which submitted and the State legislatures and conventions which ratified the Fourteenth Amendment contemplated or did not contemplate, understood or did not understand, that it would abolish segregation in public schools?
(2) If neither the Congress in submitting nor the States in ratifying the Fourteenth Amendment understood that compliance with it would require the immediate abolition of segregation in public schools, was it nevertheless the understanding of the framers of the Amendment (a) that future Congresses might, in the exercise of their power under section 5 of the Amendment, abolish such segregation, or (b) that it would be within the judicial

power, in light of future conditions, to construe the Amendment as abolishing such segregation in public school?

(3) On the assumption that the answers to questions 2 (a) and (b) do not dispose of the issue, is it within the judicial power, in construing the Amendment, to abolish segregation in public school?

(4) Assuming it is decided that segregation in public school violates the Fourteenth Amendment (a) would a decree necessarily follow providing that, within the limits set by normal geographic school districting, Negro children should forthwith be admitted to schools of their choice, or (b) may this Court, in the exercise of its equity powers, permit an effective gradual adjustment to be brought about from existing segregated systems to a system not based on color distinctions?

(5) On the assumption on which questions 4 (a) and (b) are based, and assuming further that this Court will exercise its equity powers to the end described in question 4 (b): (a) should this Court formulate detailed decrees in these cases; (b) if so, what specific issues should the decrees reach; (c) should this Court appoint a special master to hear evidence with a view to recommending specific terms for such decrees; (d) should this Court remand to the courts of first instance with directions to frame decrees in these cases, and if so what general directions would the decrees of this Court include and what procedures should the courts of first instance follow in arriving at the specific terms of more detailed decrees?

The Attorney General of the United States is invited to take part in the oral argument and to file an additional brief if he so desires."

9. *TDC,* June 9, 1953, 1, 2.

10. 346 U.S. 100 (1953).

11. Wilson to Moore, June 10, 1953. Copy in KSHS.

12. Moore to Wilson, June 12, 1953, KSHS.

13. Wilson to Moore, June 22, 1953. Copy in KSHS.

14. Moore to Wilson, June 22, 1953, KSHS.

15. Almond to Fatzer, June 22, 1953, KSHS.

16. Byrnes to Arn, June 15, 1953, KSHS.

17. Memorandum for File re: *Brown et al.,* June 17, 1953, KSHS.

18. The compiled reports were later edited and published. See Bernard D. Reams, Jr., and Paul E. Wilson, *Segregation and the Fourteenth Amendment in the States* (Buffalo, N.Y.: Williams S. Hein, 1975).

19. See, e.g., Kluger, *Simple Justice,* 650–51; Ambrose, *Eisenhower,* 124–26, 142–43, 189–90.

20. Brownell to Fatzer, July 24, 1953, KSHS.

21. Moore to Brownell, July 28, 1953. Copy in KSHS.

22. *TDC,* September 6, 1953, 1.

23. Ibid.

24. *TDC,* September 5, 1953, 1.

25. *TDC,* September 9, 1953, 1.

26. J. Lee Rankin, U.S. assistant attorney general to Fatzer, September 11, 1953, KSHS.

27. Wilson to Carter, September 19, 1953. Copy in KSHS.

28. Oliver Wendell Holmes, Jr., *The Common Law* (Boston, 1881, 1923), 1.

29. SCA, 206.

30. Ch. 77, sec. 35, act of May 20, 1862, 37th Cong., sess. 2, 12 Stat. 394; ch. 156, sec. 17, act of June 25, 1864, 38th Cong., sess. 1, 13 Stat. 187.

31. Ch. 217, sec. 1, act of July 23, 1866, 39th Cong., sess. 1, 14 Stat. 216; ch. 308, act of July 28, 1866, 39th Cong., sess. 1, 14 Stat. 343.

32. *Cong. Globe,* 41st Cong., sess. 2, 3273; sess. 3, 1053–1061; 42nd Cong., sess. 2, 68, 2484, 2539–42, 3057–8, 3099–3100, 3122–3125.

33. SCA, 209.

34. See Reams and Wilson, *Segregation and the Fourteenth Amendment* for a state by state examination.

35. Kan. Sen. J. (1867), 43.

36. Kan. Sen. J. (1867), 76; Kan. House J. (1867), 79.

37. 1861 Kan. Sess. Laws, ch. 76, art. 3, sec. 1; 1865 Kan. Sess. Laws, ch. 46, sec. 1.

38. 1867 Kan. Sess. Laws, ch. 49, sec. 7.

39. Harry McMullan, attorney general of North Carolina, to Fatzer, December 8, 1953, KSHS.

40. Luther A. Huston to Fatzer, December 1, 1953.

CHAPTER EIGHT. JUDGMENT DAY

1. Frank R. Kent, Jr., "Supreme Court to Hear Cases on School Segregation Today," *Washington Post,* December 7, 1953, 1.

2. SCA, 180–93.

3. SCA, 195.

4. SCA, 206.

5. Richard Kluger, *Simple Justice* (New York: Alfred A. Knopf, 1976), 671.

6. Yale Kamisar, "The School Desegregation Cases in Retrospect: Some Reflections on Causes and Effects," in SCA, xviii.

7. Ibid.

8. SCA, 207.

9. SCA, 215.

10. Thaddeus Stevens, a representative from Pennsylvania, was a Radical Republican leader during the drafting of the Reconstruction Amendments. An ardent proponent of Negro rights, some historians have argued that he was motivated by a desire to humiliate the aristocrats of the South.

11. SCA, 216–17.

12. SCA, 239.

13. Ibid.

14. SCA, 250.

15. SCA, 259.

16. SCA, 265–66.

17. SCA, 266–68.

18. *Kansas City Times,* December 9, 1953, 2.

19. SCA, 284–90.

20. SCA, 320–21.

21. Kluger, *Simple Justice,* 857–83. Also Public Broadcasting System program with same title, 1992.

22. *Topeka State Journal,* May 17, 1954, 1.

23. *TDC,* May 18, 1954, 1.

24. Ibid.

25. *New York Times,* May 18, 1954, 20.

26. *TDC,* May 18, 1954, 2.

27. 347 U.S., 492–93.

28. Ibid., 493.

29. *New York Times,* May 18, 1954, 1.

30. James Reston, "A Sociological Decision," *New York Times,* May 18, 1954, 20.

31. Benjamin M. Cardozo, *The Nature of the Judicial Process* (New Haven: Yale University Press, 1921), 65–66. Quoted in Reston, "A Sociological Decision," 20.

32. *Bolling v. Sharpe,* 347 U.S. 497 (1954).

33. *Dred Scott v. Sanford,* 60 U.S. (19 How.) 393 (1857).

34. Fatzer to Chief Justice Earl Warren, May 20, 1954. Copy in KSHS.

35. Carter to Wilson, June 1, 1954, KSHS.

CHAPTER NINE. BROWN II

1. Richard Kluger, *Simple Justice* (New York: Alfred A. Knopf, 1976), 623.

2. Harold R. Fatzer, "Repercussions of the School Segregation Cases" (address to Southern Regional Conference of Attorneys General, San Antonio, Texas, April 9, 1954). Copy in KSHS.

3. Harry McMullan, attorney general of North Carolina, to Fatzer, May 11, 1955, KSHS.

4. Eugene Cook, president, National Association of Attorneys General, to Nathaniel L. Goldstein, attorney general of New York, July 21, 1954. Copies to all state attorneys general, KSHS.

5. General Cook overlooks the fact that the initial intervention had been by Brownell's predecessor, James P. McGranery, and that the Supreme Court had expressly invited the attorney general to participate in the 1953 arguments.

6. "Memorandum to All Attorneys General from Eugene Cook." Copy in KSHS.

7. Don Eastvold, attorney general of Washington, to Cook, July 26, 1954. Copy in KSHS.

8. F. J. Cloud to Fatzer, *Leader—Courier* (Kingman, Kansas), July 8, 1954. KSHS.

9. Wilson to Carter, May 19, 1954. Copy in KSHS.

10. Carter to Wilson, June 1, 1954, KSHS.

11. Wilson to Carter, June 18, 1954. Copy in KSHS.

12. *Supplemental Brief for the Board of Education on Questions 4 and 5 Propounded by the Court*, Case No. 1, October 1954 Term, Supreme Court of the United States.

13. Kansas cities were eligible to become cities of the first class upon reaching a population of 15,000. When a city had achieved first-class status it remained so classified even if the population later declined to less than 15,000.

14. Hutchinson.

15. Pittsburg and Wichita.

16. Lawrence (partially segregated) and Salina.

17. Coffeyville.

18. Atchison, Kansas City, Leavenworth, and Parsons.

19. Fort Scott.

20. Carter to Wilson, September 1, 1954, KSHS.

21. Fatzer to Caldwell, October 14, 1954. Copy in KSHS.

22. Caldwell to Fatzer, October 25, 1954, KSHS.

23. *Brief for Appellants in Case No. 1 et al., on Further Reargument*, 20, 21.

24. Willey to Wilson, November 22, 1954, KSHS.

25. Willey to Fatzer, March 22, 1954, KSHS.

26. The plan was presented to the board and discussed at the regular meeting on February 7. *TDC*, February 8, 1955, 1. It was approved on February 23.

27. SCA, 339.

28. SCA, 338–50.

29. SCA, 503.

30. *Brown et al. v. Board of Education of Topeka et al.*, 349 U.S. 294 (1955).

31. Ibid., 301.

32. "Court Ruling on Schools Praised Here," *TDC*, June 1, 1955, 1.

33. Luther A. Huston, "High Court Tells States to End Pupil Segregation Within Reasonable Time," *New York Times*, June 1, 1955, 1.

34. Kluger, *Simple Justice*, 742–43.

35. *Virginia v. West Virginia*, 222 U.S. 17, 20 (1911).

36. Philip Elman, interviewed by Norman Silber, "The Solicitor General's Office, Justice Frankfurter and Civil Rights Litigation, 1946–1960, An Oral History," *Harv. L. Rev* 100 (February 1987): 817, 842–43.

37. *Brown et al. v. Board of Education of Topeka et al.*, (D.C. Kan.), 139 F. Supp. 468, 470 (1955).

AFTERWORD

1. *Johnson v. Whittier*, T–5430, September 10, 1973; *U.S.D. no. 501 v. Weinberger*, 74–160-CS, August 7, 1974; *Miller v. Board of Educ.* 79–1408, August 8, 1979; and *Chapman v. Board of Educ.* 79–1473, September 7, 1979.

2. Section 601 provides: "No person in the United States shall, on the ground of race, color or national origin be excluded from participation in, be denied the benefits of, or be subjected to discrimination under any program or activity receiving Federal financial assistance."

3. *Brown v. Board of Educ. of Topeka*, 84 FRD 383 (D.C. Kan. 1979).

4. *Brown v. Board of Educ. of Topeka*, 671 F. Supp. 1290 (D.C. Kan. 1987).

5. *Brown v. Board of Educ. of Topeka*, 892 F. 2d 851 (10th Cir. 1989).

6. *Board of Educ. v. Brown*, 112 S. Ct. 1657, 118 L. Ed. 2d 381 (1992).

7. *Brown v. Board of Educ. of Topeka*, 978 F. 2d 585 (10th Cir. 1992).

8. *Unified School District of Shawnee County, Kansas v. Smith*, 113 SC 2994, 125 L. Ed. 688 (1993). See also Kristin L. Hays, "Topeka Must Correct '54 Case," *TDC*, June 22, 1993, 1.

Index